I0147867

Underwater Archaeology and Cultural Resources

Underwater Archaeology and Cultural Resources:

Methodology, Preservation and Communication – A Dialogue between Denmark and Greece

Edited by Sanne Hoffmann, Athena Trakadas
and Panagiotis Athanasopoulos

Monographs of the Danish Institute at Athens, vol. 27

Underwater Archaeology and Cultural Resources:
Methodology, Preservation and Communication – A Dialogue between Denmark and Greece
© The Danish Institute at Athens and Aarhus University Press 2025

Monographs of the Danish Institute at Athens, vol. 27

Series editor: Sanne Hoffmann
Type setting: Ryevad Grafisk
This book is typeset in KP Sans, Avenir LT Pro and Minion Pro and printed on G-print 130g
Cover: Alex Tourtas
Cover illustration: Alex Tourtas
Printed at Narayana Press
1st edition, 1st imprint
Printed in Denmark 2025

ISBN 978 87 7597 835 9 (printed book)
ISBN 978 87 7645 015 9 (e-pdf)
ISBN 978 87 7645 052 6 (epub)
ISSN 1397 1433

AARHUS UNIVERSITY PRESS
Helsingforsgade 25
8200 Aarhus N
unipress@unipress.au.dk
aarhusuniversitypress.dk

The publication of this book was financed by: The Augustinus Foundation

PEER
REVIEWED

/ In accordance with requirements of the Danish Ministry of Higher Education and Science, the certification
means that a PhD level peer has made a written assessment justifying this book's scientific quality.

FSC
www.fsc.org
MIX
Paper | Supporting
responsible forestry
FSC® C010651

Contents

Introduction

Introduction

Sanne Hoffmann

One of the most important purposes and privileges of the Danish Institute in Athens is promoting and facilitating scientific research, cultural exchange, and communication between Denmark and Greece. This volume is a manifestation of one such exchange, having grown out of a series of paired lectures on underwater archaeology and cultural resources held at the Institute in the Fall of 2023 and Spring of 2024, given by leading Danish and Greek scholars.

The lecture series was organized as a collaboration between the Danish Institute at Athens and the Greek Ephorate of Underwater Antiquities, with generous support from the Danish Agency for Culture and Palaces fund for International Cultural Exchange. The lectures and discussions were recorded and are available on The Danish Institute at Athens YouTube channel: https://www.youtube.com/@thedanishinstituteatathens747.

The first spark of inspiration for this lecture series was a single PowerPoint slide, presented many years ago during a lecture I attended by Dr. Jens Auer at the University of Southern Denmark in Esbjerg, when the Master's degree programme in Maritime Archaeology was still active. The slide showed a map of known shipwrecks located around the coasts of Europe. Two countries stood out, swarming with red spots: Denmark and Greece. The similarities between the two were both striking and inspiring to a Danish classical archaeologist with underwater interests, and the thought of bringing the regions together in dialogue was born. Now, some dozen years later, the Danish Institute at Athens provided the perfect setting to bring researchers together to present – and explore – what was hinted at in the map in terms of shared attributes, as well as differing approaches between the two regions.

Denmark and Greece both boast long diverse coastlines with wide-ranging waters and irreplaceable cultural heritage tied to the sea, such as shipwrecks and submerged settlements. Consequently, both countries have been at the forefront of developing the discipline of underwater archaeology, which served as the overarching theme of the lecture series. Archaeology, however, is not an isolated field, but intertwined with conservation and dissemination, and so for me it was necessary to include these fields in the topic and title of the series: "Underwater Archaeology and Cultural Resources: Methodology, Preservation and Communication – A Dialogue between Denmark and Greece".

The project, however, could not have manifested without the invaluable help of my co-organizers Dr. Athena Trakadas, Dr. Panagiotis Athanasopoulos, and Dr. Dimitris Kourkoumelis. It was their expertise in underwater and maritime archaeology that allowed the series and subsequent publication to be successful, and I am most grateful for all their efforts and support.

This volume captures vital cross-cultural and scientific exchanges that took place at the Institute, highlighting best practices and innovations in the exploration, preservation and communication of underwater cultural heritage. It contains 12 articles that were originally presented in pairs. Each of these pairs was followed by discussions led by invited expert discussants. These exchanges are available only in the recordings online, but for this introduction I will add a few of the essential comments or questions raised for each set of presentations.

In the first chapter, Athena Trakadas presents and cross-references the Danish and Greek evolution and theoretical and methodological approaches to underwater cultural heritage ("Archaeology and Underwater Cultural Resources: Reviewing a Sea-change in Theory and Practice"). This chapter highlights cutting-edge projects in Denmark and Greece, while tracking the historiography and trajectory of the field more broadly. Throughout this chapter, Trakadas introduces and contextualizes the broader themes and topics found throughout the rest of the volume, offering an important comment on the state of the field of underwater archaeology and setting the stage for continued reading and discussion on future directions within these scientific areas.

The presentation by Trakadas is followed by Klara Fiedler, who addresses the circumstances and potential consequences of development-led archaeology ("Development-led Maritime Archaeology in Denmark: Legislation, Management Practices and Research Output"). Fiedler presents the background for the current situation in Denmark and discusses what the prerequisites for such archaeological work mean for the quality of the documentation, the potential research possibilities, as well as the long-term preservation and management of the sites.

The subsequent discussion was led by co-organizer Dimitris Kourkoumelis, Director of the Greek Ephorate of Underwater Antiquities. By presenting the Greek legislation and circumstances for underwater archaeological work, he addressed the many difficulties with proper protection and funding. Discussion also focused on how Greek rescue excavations, similar to Danish development-led work, are

undertaken by state institutions, but funding can be both private and from the state.

In the third article, Peter Moe Astrup continues the discussion on focusing development-led projects toward specific research questions ("Towards a New Understanding of the Early Mesolithic: The Role of Underwater Archaeology, Strategies, and Problem-oriented Focus Areas"). Astrup presents a series of case studies of Early Mesolithic submerged landscapes, exploring the implications of working within limited areas when trying to decipher a larger site. He argues that a conscious theoretical and methodological problem-oriented approach is essential. Along with interdisciplinary collaborations these focuses can enable and qualify the knowledge extracted and facilitate research.

Following Astrup, Maria Geraga, together with George Papatheodorou, present a series of case studies for the use of remote sensing techniques underwater ("Marine Remote Sensing Techniques for the Study of Underwater Cultural Heritage Sites: Case Studies from the Eastern Mediterranean Sea"). The authors base their discussion on the results of a series of projects undertaken in Greece, highlighting how remote sensing has fundamentally reshaped our ability to engage with underwater archaeology and the material record of the Aegean more broadly.

Afterwards, the discussant, George Papatheodorou, Professor of Environmental and Geological Oceanography in the Geology Department and Dean of School of Natural Sciences of the University of Patras, stressed the positive correlation between the two presentations and the methods discussed. He noted, however, the interesting differences in the kind of finds that might be made in the Nordic vs. the Southern waters, with more organic material from the North (e.g. tree-trunks, leaves, shoes). This may be due to the variations in the levels of oxygen in the seabed, with sand grain sizes being a factor.

Methodological questions remain the focus of Aoife Daly's contribution, focalised through a detailed review of the analytical potential of wooden finds in underwater archaeology ("Tree-ring Science for Maritime Archaeology: What Timber in Ships Can Tell Us"). Through extensive and well-mapped case studies, Daly demonstrates how dendrochronological analysis has revolutionized our ability to explore topics like vessel origin, ship-building practices and trade networks.

With the plethora of methodological options from the previous articles presented, George Koutsouflakis then turns the focus to one of the most prominent questions in the field: the matter of the budget ("Methodology Against Budget: A Compromised Business"). He discusses the challenges of the often-limited budgets of archaeological projects in terms of fixed costs, typically logistics such as transport and accommodation, and flexible cost, often tied to the desired outcome of the project, such as project-length and scientific equipment. Koutsouflakis stresses how a strong focus on suitable methodology before beginning field work not only maximizes the scientific outcome but also minimizes the flexible costs.

Discussant Christos Agouridis, archaeologist at the Hellenic Institute of Marine Archaeology and the Ephorate of Paleoanthropology and Speleology, addressed the amounts of resources it requires to build maps of references, such as presented by Daly and necessary for the use of (dendro-)chronology. She noted that could only be done by the pillars in scientific works: collaboration and academic networks, as well as generous foundations. As remarked also in the previous discussion with Geraga and Astrup, the panel agreed there is notable differences between the find groups, as Northern Europe has relatively generous amount of wood preserved versus very few samples found in Southern Europe, where other find groups such as amphorae, provide rich information in terms of function, chronology, and exchange. A last important point was the need to prioritize students on sites, despite the resources required to facilitate them and educate on archaeological sites.

With the article by Angeliki Zisi, we are brought into the topic of preservation ("Underwater Perspectives: Dialogue with Heritage Conservators"). Based on a case study of the Lechaion Harbour near Corinth – one of the rare Greek sites where wooden structures have been found – Zisi discusses the variety of conservation questions and issues that may arise on underwater cultural heritage, during excavation and preservation *in situ*. Zisi notes the benefit, if not necessity, of having conservators on site during excavations. She argues that this allows not only for the best possible preservation practice but also contributes to the analysis of archaeological material and site interpretation more broadly.

Following Zisi, Kristiane Strætkvern presents the intricate processes of preserving archaeological material retrieved from underwater sites, primarily focusing on shipwrecks ("Out of the Water Perspectives: Dialogue with Heritage Conservators"). While describing the conditions for preservation of wood, in particular waterlogged wood, Strætkvern discusses the challenges of the procedure, as it is both time- and space-consuming, especially when entire wrecks are lifted. She highlights the benefits and often necessities of salvaging wrecks, while addressing the need for goodwill and resources for such projects to be able to be executed.

Following the presentations, discussant Georgianna Moraitou, Head of Conservation, Physical-Chemical Research and Archaeometry Department at the Hellenic National Archaeological Museum, addressed the questions of how to preserve and protect underwater structures *in situ*. It was agreed that this is a work in progress, trying to use organic materials, such as hessian bags as has been used in Lechaion, while studying their longevity still. Strætkvern added to the discussion that when the circumstances of the find context allows it, in terms of preservation, it is often preferable to rebury the finds – not least due to the aforementioned storage needs. There was in the end a broad agreement that – when budget allows – as pointed out by Zisi, conservators should be present during excavations for both preservation and research purposes.

For the lecture series the preservation theme included another event with lectures by Anne Marie Høier Eriksen and Yiannis Issaris. Eriksen, on behalf of and in collaboration with David Gregory, gave the first presentation on Gregory's preservation research project at the National Museum of Denmark ("ENDURE: Sustainable Preservation of Underwater Archaeological Sites: A Novel Approach to Cultural Heritage Management"). Eriksen discussed *in situ* preservation, a main focus of the Endure project (www.endureerc.com), with examples of degradation in the marine environment and potential solutions. The following lecture by Issaris ("Submerged Legacies: Connecting the Cultural with the Natural in a Common Narrative of Maritime Heritage Preservation") discussed the underwater heritage sites as frail ecosystems, and the importance of holistic approaches to optimize preservation efforts. Afterwards, Athena Trakadas led the discussion where the topics of understanding sites as ecosystems and *in situ* preservation continued, especially on how to protect both the environment and the material cultural heritage – including the influence and urgency of climate change impacts and rising sea levels. Unfortunately, it was not possible to include the written contributions of Eriksen and Issaris, but their presentations and discussion can be viewed online at: https://www.youtube.com/watch?v=j6eIt2-F4pI.

The article by Andreas Kallmeyer Bloch shifts our attention to the final theme of this volume: communication ("Unlocking the Depths: Engaging Audiences through Artistic Perspectives in Maritime Archaeology"). Bloch focuses on a specific site off the coast of Costa Rica, where two Danish slave shipwrecks have been recovered, and how collaborations with professional communicators and artists have allowed for both traditional and innovative methods of bringing the story of the site to life. He highlights the benefits of communicating both the story of the site and the archaeological project, as it allows for

documentation and multi-faceted storytelling at the same time. It allowed for Bloch to be an active part in how the project was presented, while reaching and engaging a broad audience.

Alexandros Tourtas continues the discussion on scientific dissemination in his presentation centred around his publication *The Antikythera Mechanism in Comix*. ("The Antikythera Mechanism in Comix: Communicating Maritime Archaeology through a Multimodal Narrative Medium"). Tourtas addresses the general problem for academics aiming to reach wider readership and the general public, arguing for the production of distinct narratives created for specific target groups, all based in robust scientific study. To support this claim, Tourtas presents his own work with graphic novels, in which his conscious use of several narrative axes manages to address a specific young adult target group, as well as create an educational work for a mature audience. As such it proves an effective medium for the above-mentioned argument.

Discussant Theodokis Theodoulou, marine archaeologist at the Greek Ephorate of Underwater Antiquities, began the discussion by stressing the importance of communicating scientific archaeological work to a broad public in a time when misinformation otherwise flows very easily. Tourtas added that it is an additional problem when archaeologists themselves might subscribe to unsubstantiated and even farfetched theories, in an attempt to attract attention to their work and to sell a story. To this Bloch mentioned the issue of archaeologists not being actively educated in non-academic communication. Finally, there was a lively discussion on how one might communicate the somewhat less exciting processes of dating, interpreting, and understanding material culture – along with the various uncertainties it entails – in an interesting and yet truthful narrative.

In the next article, Anders Jensen turns the focus to communication of maritime cultural heritage in museum exhibitions ("The New Strandingsmuseum

St George: Concepts Behind the New Museum in Thorsminde"). Jensen presents the case of a museum centred around the wreck of HMS *St George* on the Danish west coast. He details how general narratives are presented around the specific story of *St George*, such as strandings, rescue operations and salvages in Denmark. Jensen discusses the philosophy and methods of communication used within the exhibition aimed at a broad target audience, with the specific objective of stimulation and inspiration.

In the next and final article, Eleni Stefanou continues the topic and role of museum exhibitions through a case study of the Museum of Aegean Boatbuilding and Maritime Crafts ("Contemporary Approaches to Traditional Wooden Boatbuilding: The Case of the Museum of Aegean Boatbuilding and Maritime Crafts (MNNTA) in Samos, Greece"). Stefanou argues that the museum represents a new visitor-orientated approach dedicated to all aspects of wooden shipbuilding and maritime crafts of the Aegean, and moves beyond object-oriented museological schemes. She details the multimodal aspects and topics presented, while discussing the importance of preserving and communicating these lesser-known parts of maritime history.

Discussant Ioanna Berbili, Curator at the Hellenic Maritime Museum in Greece, started the discussion by noting that the presented examples were both very new exhibitions following current practices of being educational hubs, while also striving to be entertaining. It was discussed how the two presented site-specific museums worked actively to engage the local community, while also functioning as local workplaces and attractions for poten-

tial tourists. This range of diverse and sometimes contradictory aims consequently necessitates the development of careful strategic plans that blend scientific rigor with societal and economic responsibilities. The panel agreed that these museums must strive also to document and preserve local history and maritime traditions, which are not always to be found in material culture.

Thus concludes the very short introduction to the presentations – and discussions – in which we are brought through several interconnected themes and aspects of Danish and Greek maritime and underwater cultural heritage, in terms of methodologies, preservation efforts, and dissemination possibilities, all of which are working on budgets and especially carried by scholarly passions.

I wish to thank my co-editors Athena Trakadas and Panagiotis Athanasopoulos, on behalf of whom I also extend our deepest gratitude to all the authors and discussants. Without their gracious and highly qualified efforts, the lectures and this volume would not have been possible. Many thanks are due also to Alexandros Tourtas, whose artwork for the cover of this volume beautifully captures the theme and our ambition of tying together Danish and Greek maritime archaeology and underwater cultural heritage.

This publication is most generously funded by the Augustinus Foundation, for which we are very grateful.

Sanne Hoffmann
Director
The Danish Institute at Athens

Archaeology and Underwater Cultural Resources:

Reviewing a Sea-change in Theory and Practice

Athena Trakadas

Abstract

Denmark and Greece both possess vast territorial waters that hold irreplaceable tangible cultural heritage including shipwrecks and submerged settlements. With the wide variety of archaeological material recovered – beginning with the Antikythera wreck in Greece over a hundred years ago and the Viking-Age ships at Skuldelev in Denmark over fifty years ago – datasets have increased vastly in number and type. Initially, the traditional approaches to studying datasets of these two countries focused on associating archaeological material with specific historical periods, cultural groups or historical narratives.

Touching upon select examples from Greece and Denmark, this chapter traces the general evolution of approaches to underwater cultural resources through the practice of archaeology and offers a view of possible future directions. As the talks given during the 2023-24 lecture series at the Danish Institute at Athens demonstrate, an intellectual momentum exists to pose more probing and interdisciplinary questions of underwater cultural assemblages. I pose that today the practice of underwater archaeology has reached a stage of reflection: knowledge generated from underwater cultural resources can inform and drive the broader methodological and theoretical basis in the field of archaeology, as well as natural marine science disciplines, and vice-versa.

Introduction

It is estimated that c. 70% of the globe is covered by water.[1] Within such a vast expanse, the tangible remains of evidence of human activities – cultural resources – are numerous. Lost ships alone are estimated to number around 3 million globally, and the number of other finds such as airplanes and submerged settlements are unknown.[2] About 50 years ago, when these resources first started to be investigated more scientifically, the approaches in traditional seafaring nations like Greece and Denmark focused on associating archaeological remains with specific chronologies, cultural groups or historical narratives. This is no longer a tenable or sustainable practice. A wide variety of archaeological material is now available for study and resulting datasets and their types are abundant. Resultantly, the practice of underwater archaeology has, I believe, reached a stage where knowledge generated from underwater excavations can inform and drive the broader theoretical and methodological basis in the discipline, in natural marine sciences, as well as the way data are disseminated. The chapters that are collected in this volume highlight research undertaken in these two countries that illustrate the discipline's sea-change.

In order to provide some background, I first want to give a decidedly limited overview of the develop-

---

1   NASA, n.d.
2   UNESCO 2007, 4.

ment of studying underwater cultural resources in Greece and Denmark – my perspective from having dipped my toes in the waters of both. In doing so, I point to a few representative projects that I believe illustrate key developments not only in these countries but the field at large. Second, I discuss what I believe are the possible future directions of the practice: the theoretical and methodological turn, including interdisciplinary engagement with natural sciences.

Some terminology

Before we set sail, however, I would like to clarify some terminology. In the last century, "ship archaeology", "underwater archaeology", and "nautical archaeology", have been commonly applied terms used in English to describe our particular field of study. In the last two decades, "maritime archaeology" and "marine archaeology" are now more common; all sometimes applied interchangeably by practitioners, a majority of the time without providing definitions.

For example, George Bass writes:

…the study of maritime cultures by means of archaeology is not the same as underwater archaeology. … maritime archaeology is still defining itself… Nautical archaeology is the archaeology of the ship, whether the ship is on land, under water, partly on land or under water, or in some cases still afloat. …. the study of ports and harbors and those who peopled them is usually considered a part of nautical archaeology, just as it is in the broader field of maritime archaeology.[3]

Over 30 years earlier, Keith Muckleroy gave an even broader definition, one that I personally prefer:

…the scientific study of the material remains of man and his activities at sea…maritime archaeology is con-

cerned with all aspects of maritime culture; not just technical matters, but also social economic, political, religious, and a host of other aspects…[4]

Even within Greek and Danish, the commonly-used terms to describe our practice focus on the environment: *Η Εφορεία Εναλίων Αρχαιοτήτων* (translated as The Ephorate of Underwater Antiquities), although *εναλίων* usually is also translated as "marine" in English. The Danish *marinarkæologi* is translated as "marine archaeology".

These various terms reflect the development of the theoretical approaches to the field: some focus specifically on ships, no matter where they are found, and others focus on the environment and yet others on human activity at and by the sea. Regardless of the adjectives set before 'archaeology', the primary source is material culture. Initially, analyses of these tangible remains, and supportive data, were primarily rooted in the humanities, but as with the wider discipline of archaeology, this has expanded considerably to include natural- and social science analyses.

The terminology of the UNESCO 2001 Convention on the Protection of the Underwater Cultural Heritage defines its subject matter for the purpose of the Convention as:

1. (a) 'Underwater cultural heritage' means all traces of human existence having a cultural, historical or archaeological character which have been partially or totally under water, periodically or continuously, for at least 100 years such as:

(i) sites, structures, buildings, artefacts and human remains, together with their archaeological and natural context;

3   Bass 2011, 3-4.

4   Muckelroy 1978, 4.

(ii) vessels, aircraft, other vehicles or any part thereof, their cargo or other contents, together with their archaeological and natural context; and

(iii) objects of prehistoric character.[5]

Although Greece and Denmark have not yet ratified the Convention, my co-organisers Sanne Hoffmann, Panagiotis Athanasopoulos, Dimitris Kourkoumelis, and I chose the UNESCO definition of "underwater archaeology" for the lecture series as a way to highlight the environment in which a variety of tangible cultural resources are found.

Fig. 1. General view of the *Mentor* shipwreck underwater excavation (Kythera, 1802) (Hellenic Ministry of Culture/Ephorate of Underwater Antiquities/MeSEP. Photo: Yiannis Issaris).

Earlier approaches

Sponge divers have played an important role in locating some of the earliest underwater sites in Greece. When Lord Elgin's brig *Mentor*, which was carrying off to England part of the antiquities removed from the Acropolis when it sank off the port of Avlemonas on the island of Kythera, in September 1802, sponge divers were called upon to recover the ancient cargo. The divers, using surface-supplied air, worked at depths just over 20 m to salvage material in 1802-03.[6] Since 2009, archaeological excavation of the site has been directed by Dimitris Kourkoumelis with not just an eye to documenting the remaining material culture, but also the ship's structure and the marine biological environment of the wrecking site (Fig. 1).[7]

The now well-known shipwreck off Antikythera was discovered at 55+ m depth by sponge divers in 1900, who, with the assistance of the Greek Royal Navy, recovered material culture from the site in

1900-01.[8] This mid-1st century BC wreck carried a cargo largely comprised of bronzes, marble sculptures and the Antikythera mechanism (alluded to in the most recent Indiana Jones film!), the last of which Alexandros Tourtas approaches as a graphic novel in his chapter in this volume.

The invention of the commercial self-contained, demand regulator Aqua Lung in 1943 by French naval officer Jacques-Yves Cousteau and engineer Emile Gagnan meant that the sponge divers and fishermen, who had previously been the ones finding shipwrecks, could be joined under water by explorers and eventually, archaeologists. Cousteau re-visited the Antikythera site in 1953, and subsequent investigation was carried out in 1976 by the Ephorate of Underwater Antiquities and Cousteau's diving team on board *Calypso*.[9] This campaign was engrained in popular memory to English-speaking audiences in the TV programme *The Cousteau Odyssey* as the 1978 episode "Diving for Roman Plunder".[10] Since

---

5   UNESCO 2001, Article 1.
6   Leontsinis 2023.
7   Kourkoumelis & Tourtas 2014; Hellenic Ministry of
    Culture 2021.

8   Kaltsas et al. 2012.
9   Marchant 2015.
10 Cousteau et al. 1978; the episode can be accessed on You Tube at: https://www.youtube.com/watch?v=rph2sJqsFyI, Accessed February, 2025.

Fig. 2. The excavation of the Skuldelev ships in 1962 (©Viking Ship Museum in Roskilde, Photo: Viking Ship Museum's archive).

2012, several teams have been recovering material from the deep site with the Return to Antikythera Project, using re-breathers and testing 1-atmosphere pressure suits.[11]

The invention of the Aqua Lung – or Self-contained Underwater Breathing Apparatus (SCUBA) – and the freedom it presented for discovering material culture under water also was put to use soon after its introduction in Denmark. In 1956 some worked wood – identified as belonging to a Viking ship – was discovered at a site called Skuldelev, near Roskilde, off the island of Zealand. Diving campaigns were undertaken between 1957 and 1959, led by Curator of the Medieval Department at the National Museum of Denmark, Olaf Olsen and soon-to-be Curator of Maritime Archaeology and Ships at the National Museum, Ole Crumlin-Pedersen. Although only several metres deep, the site was difficult to excavate in unclear waters. Complicating matters, the site appeared to be comprised of several ships,

pilings, and large stones. In 1962, a cofferdam was built around the site and five ships, purposely sunk in the 11th century to block a navigable channel, were documented and excavated (Fig. 2).[12]

In these examples, access to the sites, although limited, was first or only gained by diving – a costly, potentially dangerous, and time-consuming way to be able to approach submerged cultural remains compared to terrestrial projects. These are still important factors in investigating underwater sites. With implementing the still-costly cofferdam solution to excavate at Skuldelev, in order to make it a relatively 'dry' site, more people could work at one time, and more work hours could be spent excavating, making it possible to complete investigations in a campaign of months instead of years.

After the 1976 season at Antikythera, investigations in Greece continued to focus on surveying and excavating shipwrecks using SCUBA. This can be

---

11   Return to Antikythera 2025.

12   Crumlin-Pedersen & Olsen 2002; Trakadas 2002; 2011, 41.

due to a variety of factors of some of the shipwreck sites: generally good visibility, warm waters and shallowness – that is, under 30 m, the generally safe maximum operating depth of SCUBA. Since the late 1980s, the Early Helladic wreck at Dokos (dated to 2200 BC), the Bronze Age wreck at Point Iria (dated to 1200 BC), a Classical shipwreck off the Island of Kythera (dated to the end of the 4th century BC), the Classical-period shipwreck off Alonnisos/Peristera (late 5th century BC) were partially excavated.[13] These were found due to, and subsequently investigated because of, their large ceramic cargoes (the ship at Alonnisos having carried c. 4000 amphora), which are visible and tend to survive under water as opposed to the comparatively poor preservation of the wooden hulls in the Mediterranean marine environment.[14]

Shipwrecks, however, were not just the main attraction in Greece. Remote-sensing methods were adopted early on as a proven methodology to locate and document sites, instead of simply SCUBA diving or relying solely on reports from sponge divers and fishermen. In the 1950s and 1960s, investigations of now-submerged settlements began to take place using photography, stereoscopy and geophysical (acoustic) methods – the Hellenic Federation of Underwater Activities (EOYDA), along with partners from abroad, investigated submerged settlements off the Peloponnese – Classical-period Helike and Halieis, Roman Kenchreai, Bronze-Age Pavlopetri and Roman Asopos/Plytra – and Neolithic Agios Petros in the Northern Sporades, to name a few.[15] Geophysical investigations were carried out to investigate the harbour of Gythion, the Bay of Sami on Kephallonia, and the harbour of the island of Poros.[16] Similarly, recent international interdisciplinary research projects have involved geophysical surveys of ancient port infrastructure at Kyllene and Aegina.[17] The Classical and Hellenistic slipways and ship-sheds in Piraeus were re-surveyed beginning in 2002 by the Danish-Greek Zea Harbour Project based at the Danish Institute at Athens.[18]

In Denmark, perhaps due to the situation of relative sea level change creating shifting coastlines, some of the major excavations of shipwrecks have been taken place on land. Since the 1990s, this comprises the nine Roskilde ships – including the longest Viking longship at c. 35 m, the medieval Gedesby ship, and the eight well-preserved Renaissance shipwrecks at Christianshavn in Copenhagen.[19] Underwater investigations do continue: more recent projects include the surveys of the 17th-century shipwrecks in Femeren Belt and the excavation of the Kolding cog.[20] These were all projects undertaken by museums, conducting developer-paid archaeology prior to building works; the last was a research project conducted by the National Museum's Centre for Maritime Archaeology (1993-2003). The challenges faced in conducting research when carrying out developer-paid archaeology is addressed by Klara Feidler in her chapter in this volume.

A notable project, however, that involved private citizens conducting investigations offshore includes the 19th-century English ship-of-the-line HMS *St George,* which ran aground near Thorsminde on the western coast of Jutland in 1811.[21] It was repeatedly salvaged since it sank, but in the 1980s more regular campaigns took place, which now form the col-

---

13   e.g., Vichou & Kyriakopoulou 1989; Phelps et al. 1999; Hadjidaki 1992; 1996; Kalamara 2022.

14   Kalamara 2022.

15   Shaw 1967; Jameson 1972, 195; Harding et al. 1969; Efstratiou 1985.

16   Scoufopoulos & McKernan 1975; Stavrolakes 1975; Stavrolakes & Edgerton 1974.

17   Pakkanen et al. 2010; Georgiou et al. 2021.

18   Lovén 2011; 2021; Lovén & Schaldemose 2011; Lovén & Sapountzis 2019.

19   Gøthche 2006; Bill 1998; Lemée 2006.

20   Johansen 2019; Hyttel et al. 2015; Thomsen 2011; 2012; Hocker & Daly 2006.

21   Jepsen 2019.

lection of the Strandingsmuseum St George, which Anders Jensen discusses in detail in this volume.

These projects focused on well-preserved wooden shipwrecks sometimes fully excavated and conserved, like the original Skuldelev ships were, at the National Museum of Denmark. The methods applied are time consuming, and costly – which Kristiane Strætkvern and Angeliki Zisi discuss in this volume. However, because of the excellent environmental conditions that can create optimal circumstances for the preservation of organics, there are also present in Denmark the extensive remains of submerged prehistoric sites in shallow waters. Particular mention should be given to the Tybrind Vig site (Erte-bølle Culture site, c. 5300–3950 BC) excavated between 1978-87 in just 3 m of water. Several more key Stone-Age sites have been since investigated, including Tudse Hage.[22] The research of these types of prehistoric sites is touched upon in this volume by Klara Feidler and Peter Moe Astrup.

Although a very brief list, the projects that I've referenced above illustrate some overall points:

1. *Expanding site-types*: The practice of underwater archaeology doesn't concentrate solely on shipwrecks but includes port infrastructure, submerged settlements, and even airplanes. The level of preservation, due to the cold, and less saline waters of the Baltic and North Seas are quite different than what is experienced in the Aegean and larger Mediterranean basin. Given the level of preservation of wooden shipwrecks in Danish waters, there initially has been a focus on their constructional classification and place within technological developments of shipbuilding. Indeed, dendrochronology has a robust history withing Denmark and Scandinavia as a whole, as illustrated by Aoife Daly in this volume. Similarly, the early shipwreck investigations in Greece followed perhaps a Mediterranean-wide

preoccupation with focusing on the cargoes of these vessels – understandably, as it is usually the more durable remains of ceramics or worked stone and not the wooden hull that is well preserved in warmer waters populated by destructive marine borers. This has impacted material cultural studies, centring on assigning specific cultural groups or historical narratives, or assisting in establishing ceramic typologies.[23]

A transition of looking at the land-sea interface began in the early 1990s, with a theoretical approach of the "Maritime Cultural Landscape", developed first by Christer Westerdahl in Scandinavia.[24] Although not a methodology *per se,* it is a theoretical framework that, when investigating the past, considers the environmental parameters of the sea, winds, currents, and seabed. This has not only been significant when investigating shipwrecks and site formation processes under water, but it has been key for establishing paleoenvironments for a considerable number of now-submerged prehistoric settlements both around the coasts of Denmark and Greece, inhabited by populations that lived along the coastline and exploited marine resources.

2. *Developing methodologies*: Although SCUBA diving is still a technique used to access archaeological sites under water, there remain challenges, as George Koutsouflakis discusses in this volume: remote-sensing techniques like geophysical surveys are now more commonly applied for documenting archaeological sites – contributing to a reduction of people-power, sometimes cost, and providing the benefit of efficient large-scale and deep-water coverage. This is demonstrated by new documentation of submerged settlements such as Bronze-Age Pavlopetri,[25] and in this vol-

---

23   Harpster 2023, 18-22.
24   Westerdahl 1992; 2007.
25   Henderson et al. 2011.

   22   Andersen 2013; Gregory & Matthiesen 2023.

ume, Maria Geraga and George Papatheodorou illustrate these advantages with the Classical-Hellenistic harbour at Kyllene, Greece.

3. *To excavate (or not):* Given the numerous challenges of excavating underwater cultural resources, and the following process (and costs) of conservation, *in-situ* preservation is less and less the exception. It is also the first of the "Rules concerning activities directed at underwater cultural heritage" of the Annex to the UNESCO 2001 Convention on the Preservation of the Underwater Cultural Heritage and now commonplace:

Rule 1. The protection of underwater cultural heritage through *in situ* preservation shall be considered as the first option. Accordingly, activities directed at underwater cultural heritage shall be authorized in a manner consistent with the protection of that heritage, and subject to that requirement may be authorized for the purpose of making a significant contribution to protection or knowledge or enhancement of underwater cultural heritage.[26]

This has previously been demonstrated through the SASMAP Project (the EU-funded Development of Tools and Techniques to Survey, Assess, Stabilise, Monitor and Preserve Underwater Archaeological Sites),[27] which included case-studies in Greece and Denmark. It was used as an example to build upon for newer research, particularly with the preservation of sites that include a variety of organics, as discussed by Anne Marie Høier Eriksen, during the lecture series in Athens.[28]

Directions

I earlier posed that the practice of underwater archaeology has presently reached a stage of reflection: knowledge generated from underwater survey and excavations can drive and be informed by the broader theoretical and methodological basis of the field of archaeology – but it also must seriously look beyond the humanities. Additionally, tangible material culture has – and continues to face – a number of natural and anthropogenic threats globally, not the least, impacts of the effects of climate change and alternate prioritisations that result in the de-funding of protection of heritage cultural schemes. Some of the theoretical and methodological directions that I believe will become more and more relevant include, but are not limited to:

1. *Identities of 'maritime cultures':* Within research of shipwrecks, the culture-historical interpretive approach of the material culture is giving way to methods of enquiry that consider these movable objects as occupying liminal spaces, moving between a myriad of cultural dynamics in the course of a single voyage. This is not to assign one or two cultural groups to a ship during its period of use but recognising the fluidity of contact and interwovenness of maritime communities. Engaging with network analyses has demonstrated new ways to examine these movements; developing cultural landscape approaches are also removing the perceived boundaries of the marine environment.[29] This is where the inclusion of intangible cultural heritage – the lifeways, oral histories, customs and orientation of coastal settlements and peoples – can supplement and complement the analyses of material culture and the maritime environment. Scholars are using new terminology for this as well – such as "Mari-

---

26 UNESCO 2001, Annex.
27 Manders & Gregory 2015; Gregory & Manders 2015.
28 Not included in this volume, but the ENDURE underwater heritage project material can be found at: https://www.endureerc.com/, Accessed February, 2025.

29 e.g., Harpster 2023; El Safadi et al. 2020; Leidwanger & Knappett 2018.

time and Underwater Cultural Heritage", or more broadly, "Ocean Heritage".[30] Such encompassing definitions of heritage and how to communicate these are discussed by Eleni Stefanou in this volume.

2. *Capacities and access:* One of the early practitioners in the field, George Bass, said "it is easier to teach an archaeologist to dive than a diver to be an archaeologist".[31] I don't think that this necessary holds true. The legacy of the field's development can be seen quite clearly in the Mediterranean: the located shipwreck sites, the majority of which lie near the coasts of northern Mediterranean shores do not reflect a historical accuracy, but a modern history of capacity and access.[32] There were not more ships sailing along the southern coast of present-day France in Antiquity and just one ship off the coast of Tunisia. This imbalance of discovery/data points is due to a myriad of factors: the advent of SCUBA technology, access to it, politics, economics, and not the least, a legacy of colonisation.[33]

The democratisation of the practice of underwater archaeology and sustainability of managing maritime cultural resources is just beginning to take effect through targeted capacity-building and more appropriately, capacity-sharing programmes;[34] this also includes acknowledging the debt owed to avocational practitioners. Early on, I think it is fair to say that some of the major shipwreck excavations never would have been successful without the role of avocational as well

as professional archaeologists. For example, since 1973 in Greece, the Hellenic Institute of Marine Archaeology – HIMA / *Το Ινστιτούτο Εναλίων Αρχαιολογικών Ερευνών* (I.EN.A.E.)[35] has been involved in a variety of shipwreck surveys and excavations (as George Koutsouflakis' chapter in this volume attests). (This type of cooperation is well established in the UK through the *Adopt a Wreck* scheme and Citizen Science endeavours in Australia.)[36] It is about the equity of stakeholders and opening the doors for wider engagement and shared storytelling and encouraging other ways of telling a story. This is revisited in this volume by Andreas Kallmeyer Bloch and Alexandros Tourtas in their chapters.

3. *A broader marine science:* The practice of underwater archaeology can no longer be solely considered within the confines of the humanities and should extend to the natural marine sciences. The early advent of geophysical surveys within the field has demonstrated the interdisciplinary nature of methodological approaches. Yet, marine science largely tends to be seen as encompassing the physical oceanographic sciences (hydrography, biological, chemical and geological oceanography) whilst underwater archaeology is usually perceived as a minor partner to or on the receiving end of datasets from these disciplines, simply due to the environment in which the resources we study are present.

However, data from underwater cultural resources can help us understand how near-shore and marine ecosystems achieved their present form through establishing environmental baselines, and resultantly to identify the pressures upon them. This can be seen from the recent scientific results derived from studying the marble

30   Henderson et al. 2025; Trakadas 2024; 2022; Holly et al. 2025.

31   G. Bass, personal communication, 1997, but often repeated, see Green 2008, 1599.

32   See for example, Parker's map and the updated Oxford Roman Economy Project versions; Parker 1992; Strauss 2013.

33   Trakadas & Corbin 2021.

34   Lezak 2024.

35   HIMA 2022-25.

36   Nautical Archaeology Society n.d.; GIRT n.d.

sculptures of the Antikythera shipwreck.[37] Shipwrecks are reef environments; they can provide historical datasets to help us gauge future patterns regarding pollution, impacts of climate change, and other short and long-term hazards like ocean acidification. This paradigm shift in how to consider marine sciences is part of a movement supported by the UN Decade of Ocean Science for Sustainable Development 2021-30 initiative,[38] a multi-disciplinary approach to natural-cultural heritage discussed by Yiannis Issaris during the lecture series in Athens.

Summary

The theoretical and methodological approaches and future directions I have chosen to highlight here are the result of a combination of contextual factors: national legislation, institutional structuring and jurisdiction, political situations, finances, and will power, etc., all of which can't be addressed here – nor would I be the person to speak for their roles in Denmark and Greece. But these factors are each addressed in major and minor ways by the authors in the chapters collected in this volume. Individually and collectively, they possess a depth of knowledge of different aspects of underwater cultural resources.

Greece and Denmark are two countries that have long histories in investigating material cultural remains under water, within the different environments of the Mediterranean and Baltic and North Seas. It is the similarities and the differences of these histories – and future pathways – that were shared, discussed and debated in the presentations and responses of this lecture series in Athens, reflected throughout the chapters collected in this volume. We hope the result not only opens new paths of enquiry and engagement amongst our Danish and Greek colleagues but can be but a spark in enacting some sea-change in the field.

Athena Trakadas
Saxo Institute, University of Copenhagen, Denmark
trakadas@hum.ku.dk

Bibliography

ANDERSEN, S. H. (ED.) 2013
Tybrind Vig. Submerged Mesolithic Settlements in Denmark, Aarhus.

BASS, G. 2011
'The development of maritime archaeology', in *The Oxford Handbook of Maritime Archaeology*, A. Catsambis, B. Ford & D. Hamilton (eds), Oxford, 3-16.

BILL, J. 1998
'Shallow-water craft from medieval Denmark. The identification of a specialized regional ship type', *Archaeonautica* 14, 87-102.

COUSTEAU, J., M. MERCOURI & L. KOLONAS 1978
'Diving for Roman Plunder', *The Cousteau Odyssey*, KCET, Cousteau Society.

CRUMLIN-PEDERSEN, O., & O. OLSEN 2002
The Skuldelev Ships I: Topography, Archaeology, History, Conservation and Display, Roskilde.

EFSTRATIOU, N. 1985
Agios Petros. A Neolithic Site in the Northern Sporades: Aegean Relationships during the Neolithic of the 5th Millennium, Oxford.

---

37 Ricci 2019.
38 https://oceandecade.org/, Accessed February, 2025; Trakadas et al. 2019; Henderson et al. 2025; Holly et al. 2025.

GEORGIOU, N., X. DIMAS, E. FAKIRIS, D. CHRIS-
TODOULOU, M. GERAGA, D. KOUTSOUMPA, K.
BAIKA, P. KALAMARA, G. FERENTINOS & G. A.
PAPATHEODOROU 2021
'Multidisciplinary Approach for the Mapping, Automatic Detection and Morphometric Analysis of Ancient Submerged Coastal Installations: The Case Study
of the Ancient Aegina Harbour Complex', *Remote Sensing* 13, 4462.

GIRT N.D.
*Gathering Information via Recreational and Technical
(GIRT) Scientific Divers.*
Available at: https://www.girtsd.org/, Accessed Febru-
ary, 2025.

GREEN, J. 2008
'Maritime archaeology', in *Encyclopedia of Archaeology*,
D.M. Pearsall (ed.), Cambridge, MA, 1599-605.

GREGORY, D. & M. MANDERS (EDS) 2015
*Best practices for locating, surveying, assessing, monitor-
ing and preserving underwater archaeological sites, SAS-
MAP Guideline Manual 2.* Amersfoort.

GREGORY, D. & H. MATTHIESEN 2023
'Defining the Burial Environment', in *Handbook of Ar-
chaeological Sciences*, A.M. Pollard, R.A. Armitage &
C.A. Makarewicz (eds), Hoboken, 1075-88.

GØTHCHE, M. 2006
'The Roskilde ships', in *Connected by the Sea: Proceed-
ings of the Tenth International Symposium on Boat and
Ship Archaeology, Denmark 2003*, L. Blue, A. Englert &
F. Hocker (eds), Oxford, 252-8.

HADJIDAKI, E. 1992
'Η ανασκαφή του Κλασικού Ναυαγίου της Αλοννήσου',
ΕΝΑΛΙΑ IV:½, 16-25.

HADJIDAKI, E. 1996
'Underwater Excavations of a Late Fifth Century
Merchant Ship at Alonnesos, Greece: the 1991-1993
Seasons', *Bulletin de Correspondance Hellénique* 120-2,
561-93.

HARDING, A., G. CADOGAN & R. HOWELL 1969
'Pavlopetri: An Underwater Bronze Age Town in Laco-
nia', *Annual of the British School at Athens* 64, 113-42.

HARPSTER, M. 2023
Reconstructing a Maritime Past, New York.

HELLENIC MINISTRY OF CULTURE 2021
*Αποτελέσματα της υποβρύχιας αρχαιολογικής έρευνας
2020 στο ιστορικό ναυάγιο ΜΕΝΤΩΡ.*
Available at: https://www.culture.gov.gr/el/Information/
SitePages/view.aspx?nID=3646, Accessed February,
2025.

HENDERSON, J. C., C. GALLOU, N. C. FLEMMING
& E. SPONDYLIS 2011
'The Pavlopetri Underwater Archaeology Project: investigating an ancient submerged town', in *Submerged Pre-
history*, J. Benjamin, C. Bonsall, C. Pickard & A. Fischer
(eds), Oxford, 207-18.

HENDERSON, J., G. HOLLY, A. REY DA SILVA & A.
TRAKADAS 2025
'The Cultural Heritage Framework Programme: High-
lighting the Contribution of Marine Cultural Heritage
to the UN Decade of Ocean Science for Sustainable
Development (2021-2030)', *Oceans* 6:1, 1.

HIMA 2022-25
*Το Ινστιτούτο Εναλίων Αρχαιολογικών Ερευνών / Hel-
lenic Institute of Marine Archaeology.*
Available at: https://ienae.gr/, Accessed February, 2025.

HOCKER, F. & A. DALY 2006
'Early cogs, Jutland boatbuilders, and the connection
between East and West before AD 1250', in *Connected*

by the Sea: Proceedings of the Tenth International Symposium on Boat and Ship Archaeology, Denmark 2003, L. Blue, A. Englert & F. Hocker (eds), Oxford, 187-94.

HOLLY, G., J. HENDERSON, A. REY DA SILVA, A. EDWARDS, H. COCKS & A. TRAKADAS 2025
Heritage in the UN Decade of Ocean Science for Sustainable Development (2021-2030) and Beyond, Cultural Heritage Framework Programme Blue Paper 1, Edinburgh. doi.org/10.2218/ED.9781836451358

HYTTEL, F., B. S. MAJCHCZACK, J. DENCKER & M. SEGSCHNEIDER 2015
The Excavations on the wreck of Lindormen, Roskilde.

JAMESON, M. H. 1972
'Halieis, at Porto Cheli in the Argolid', The International Journal of Nautical Archaeology 1, 195-6.

JEPSEN, P. U. 2019
The Last Voyage, Holstebro.

JOHANSEN, M. 2019
Undersøgelserne af "kanonvraget" SWARTE ARENT, Roskilde.

KALAMARA, P. 2022
'Different approaches to the protection and enhancement of underwater archaeological sites: Acquirements and Aspirations', Annals of Marine Science 6:1, 21-33.

KALTSAS, N., E. VLACHOGIANNI & P. BOUYIA (EDS) 2012
The Antikythera Shipwreck. The ship, the treasures, the mechanism, Athens.

KOURKOUMELIS, D. & A. TOURTAS 2014
'Excavations on the Mentor Shipwreck', Nautical Archaeology. The publication of the Nautical Archaeology Society, Summer 2014, 6-7.

LEIDWANGER, J. & C. KNAPPETT (EDS) 2018
Maritime Networks in the Ancient Mediterranean World, Cambridge.

LEMÉE, C. P. P. 2006
Renaissance Shipwrecks from Christianshavn, Roskilde.

LEONTSINIS, G. 2023
Το ναυάγιο του Μέντορος στις ακτές των Κυθήρων και η διάσωση των γλυπτών του Παρθενώνα, Athens.

LEZAK, S. 2024
'From capacity building to capacity sharing', Nature Sustainability 7, 1-3.

LOVÉN, B. 2011
The Ancient Harbours of the Piraeus, Volume I.1. The Zea Shipsheds and Slipways: Architecture and Topography, Aarhus.

LOVÉN, B. 2021
The Ancient Harbours of the Piraeus, Volume III.1. The Harbour Fortifications of the Mounichia and Kantharos Harbours – Architecture and Topography, Aarhus.

LOVÉN, B. & I. SAPOUNTZIS 2019
The Ancient Harbours of the Piraeus, Volume II. Zea Harbour: The Group 1 and 2 Shipsheds and Slipways – Architecture, Topography and Finds. Aarhus.

LOVÉN, B. & M. SCHALDEMOSE 2011
The Ancient Harbours of the Piraeus, Volume I.2. The Zea Shipsheds and Slipways: Finds, Area 1 Shipshed Roof Reconstructions and Feature Catalogue, Aarhus.

MANDERS, M. & D. GREGORY (EDS) 2015
Guidelines to the process of underwater archaeological research, SASMAP Guideline Manual 1, Amersfoort.

MARCHANT, J. 2015
'Exploring the Titanic of the Ancient World', Smithsonian Magazine, February 2015.

Available at: https://www.smithsonianmag.com/history/exploring-titanic-ancient-world-180953977/, Accessed February, 2025.

MUCKELROY, K. 1978
Maritime Archaeology, Cambridge.

NASA N.D.
Earth Observatory Water Cycle Overview.
Available at: http://earthobservatory.nasa.gov/Features/Water/, Accessed February, 2025.

NAUTICAL ARCHAEOLOGY SOCIETY N.D.
Adopt a Wreck.
Available at: https://www.nauticalarchaeologysociety.org/pages/category/adopt-a-wreck, Accessed February, 2025.

PAKKANEN, J., K. BAIKA, M. GERAGA, D. EVANGELISTIS, E. FAKIRIS, S. HEALTH, D. CHRISTODOULOU, M. IATROU & G. PAPATHEODOROU 2010
'Archaeological topographical survey and marine geophysical investigation at ancient and medieval harbour of Kyllini/Glarentza (NW Peloponnese, Greece)', in *XIX Congress of the Carpathian Balkan Geological Association Thessaloniki, Greece (Geologica Balcanica Abstracts)*, A. Chatzipetros, V. Melfos, P. Marchev & I. Lakova (eds), Thessaloniki, 283-4.

PARKER, A. J. 1992
Ancient Shipwrecks of the Mediterranean and the Roman Provinces, Oxford.

PHELPS, W., Y. LOLOS & Y. VICHOS (EDS) 1999
The Point Iria Wreck: Interconnections in the Mediterranean ca. 1200 B.C., Athens.

RETURN TO ANTIKYTHERA 2025
The Project.
Available at: https://antikythera.org.gr/, Accessed February, 2025.

RICCI, S. 2019
'Benthic Community Formation Processes of the Antikythera Shipwreck Statues Preserved in the National Archaeological Museum of Athens (Greece)', *Journal of Maritime Archaeology* 14, 81-106.

EL SAFADI, C., F. STURT & L. BLUE 2020
'Exploring maritime engagement in the Early Bronze Age Levant: a space/time approach', *Journal of Eastern Mediterranean Archaeology and Heritage Studies* 8:3-4, 250-72.

SCOUFOPOULOS, N. C. & J. G. MCKERNAN 1975
'Underwater Survey of Ancient Gythion, 1972, *The International Journal of Nautical Archaeology* 4:1, 103-16.

SHAW, J. W. 1967
'Shallow-water Excavation at Kenchreai', *American Journal of Archaeology* 71:3, 223-31.

STAVROLAKES, N. P. 1975
'Greece. Poros: survey of a site at the harbour entrance', *The International Journal of Nautical Archaeology* 4:2, 377-8.

STAVROLAKES, N. P. & H. E. EDGERTON, 1974
'Greece. Sami Bay, Cephallonia', *The International Journal of Nautical Archaeology* 3:2, 330.

STRAUSS, J. 2013
Shipwrecks Database. Version 1.0.
Available at: oxrep.classics.ox.ac.uk/databases/shipwrecks_database/, Accessed February, 2025.

THOMSEN, M. H. 2011
Femern Bælt-forbindelsen Marinarkæologisk rapport: Dykkerbesigtigelse af kystnære side scan sonar-, magnetometer- og luftfotoanomalier i dansk farvand, Roskilde.

THOMSEN, M. H. 2012
Femern Bælt-forbindelsen Marinarkæologisk rapport: Marinarkæologisk forundersøgelse af produktionsområde til tunnelelementer samt geofysiske anomalier omkring tunneltracé, Roskilde.

TRAKADAS, A. 2002
'Maritime archaeology: Perspectives from Denmark', *ΕΝΑΛΙΑ* 6, 130-5.

TRAKADAS, A. 2011
'The Skuldelev reconstruction project: progress and perspectives', in *ACUA Underwater Archaeology Proceedings 2011*, F. Castro & L. Thomas (eds), Washington, DC, 41-8.

TRAKADAS, A. 2022
'The Cultural Heritage Framework Programme: Ensuring a Place for Cultural Heritage's Contribution to the UN Decade of Ocean Science', *Marine Technology Society Journal* 56:3, 110-1.

TRAKADAS, A. 2024
'The importance of integrating cultural heritage into the UN Ocean Decade', in *Threats to Our Ocean Heritage: Bottom Trawling*, C. Jarvis (ed.), Cham, v-viii.

TRAKADAS, A. & A. CORBIN 2021
'Maritime Archaeology and Covid-19', *Journal of Maritime Archaeology* 16:1, 1-2.

TRAKADAS, A., A. FIRTH, D. GREGORY, D. ELKIN, U. GUERIN, J. HENDERSON, J. KIMURA, D. SCOTT-IRETON, Y. SHASHOUA, C. UNDERWOOD & A. VIDUKA 2019
'The Ocean Decade Heritage Network: integrating cultural heritage within the UN Decade of Ocean Science 2021-2030', *Journal of Maritime Archaeology* 14:2, 153-65.

UNESCO 2001
2001 Convention on the Protection of Underwater Cultural Heritage, Paris.
Available at: https://www.unesco.org/en/legal-affairs/convention-protection-underwater-cultural-heritage?hub=412, Accessed February, 2025.

UNESCO 2007
The UNESCO Convention on the Protection of Underwater Cultural Heritage, CLT/CIH/MCO/2007/PI/38, Paris.
Available at: https://unesdoc.unesco.org/ark:/48223/pf0000152883, Accessed February, 2025.

VICHOU, G. & V. KYRIAKOPOULOU 1989
'Αυτοψία στον Υποβρύχιο Αρχαιολογικό Χώρο του Δοκού (Μάιος 1989)', *ΕΝΑΛΙΑ* 1.β, 12-3.

WESTERDAHL, C. 1992
'The maritime cultural landscape', *The International Journal of Nautical Archaeology* 21, 5-14.

WESTERDAHL, C. 2007
'Fish and ships. Towards a theory of maritime culture', *Deutsches Schiffahrtsarchiv* 30, 191-236.

Development-led Maritime Archaeology in Denmark:

Legislation, Management Practices and Research Outcome

Klara Fiedler

Abstract

The field of archaeology in Denmark, in both terrestrial and maritime disciplines, is primarily funded by developers. Robust legislation and management practices ensure that archaeological screening is carried out as part of the government's application system for development projects. In recent years, an upsurge in marine development projects, coupled with improved quality and accessibility of geophysical data for archaeological screening, has significantly increased the number of development-led investigations in Danish maritime archaeology. It is a requirement in Danish heritage management that archaeological development-led investigations should produce new knowledge about the past. A requirement that, with the resources available, has been difficult to meet in practice. The funding provided by developers does not cover the scientific post-processing of survey and excavation results. Consequently, the research outcome from these archaeological investigations is relatively modest, which creates a disparity between the resources allocated to maritime archaeology and the impact of research and relevance to the broader community. This raises the question as to whether each archaeological excavation should be a scientific investigation in its own right or if it is sometimes acceptable to settle for safeguarding the archaeological data for the future. How can heritage legislation and research practices evolve in the future to better incorporate research questions into development-led maritime archaeology – and where do we find the resources to pursue these questions?

A brief history of development-led maritime archaeology in Denmark

Maritime archaeology in Denmark originated in the 1950s, initially focusing on shipwrecks. However, by the 1970s, the field expanded to include the survey, excavation, and research of submerged Stone Age settlements and paleo-terrains.[1] A long coastline and shallow protected natural environments in the nearshore Danish waters provide ideal conditions for the preservation of paleo-terrains and their legally protected submerged Stone Age sites. Today, as a result of favourable preservation conditions due to sheltered waters with low erosion rates and the presence of anaerobic sediment layers, easy access from the coast, and a tradition of an active survey approach from both professionals and engaged members of the public, Denmark has the highest number of known submerged prehistoric sites in Europe (Fig. 1).[2] Due to Denmark's geographical

---

1   Uldum 2017.

2   Bailey et al. 2020; Fischer & Petersen 2018.

Fig. 1. Known Stone Age sites and artefacts on the Danish seafloor (Illustration: Klara Fiedler, © The Viking Ship Museum). Contains data from EMODnet: *EMODnet Digital Bathymetry (DTM 2022)* and from *Fund- og Fortidsminder*.

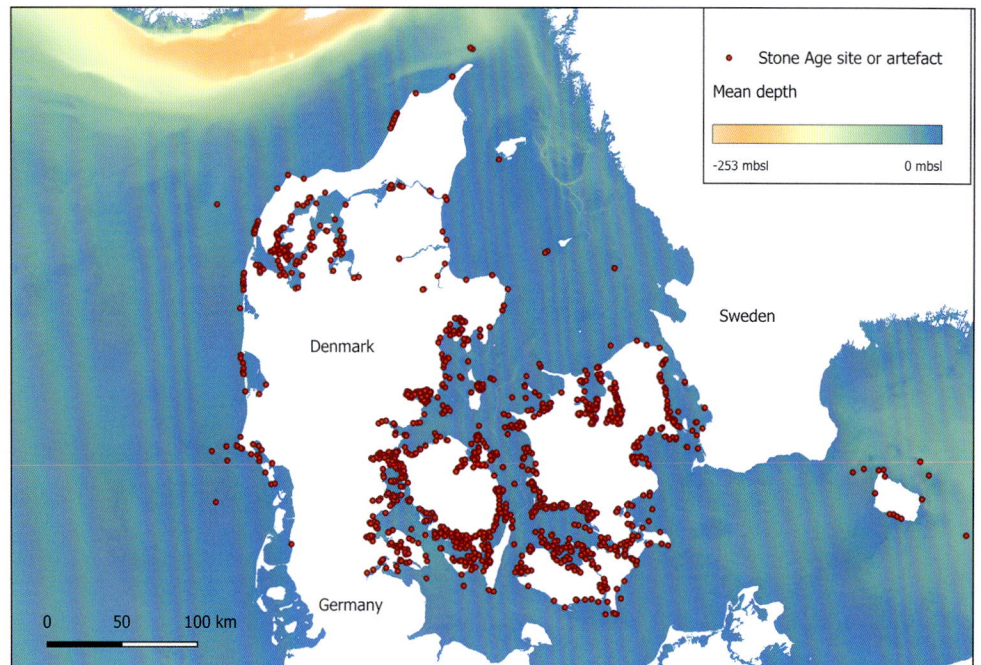

location and preservation conditions, shipwrecks are also abundant in Danish waters (Fig. 2).

In the early days of maritime archaeology in Denmark, as in many other European countries, excavations were mostly research driven. The discovery and following excavation between 1957 and 1962 of the five Skuldelev ships from the Late Viking Age initiated the establishment of the field of maritime archaeology in Denmark.[3] In 1963, the discipline secured its own research department within the National Museum of Denmark, *Skibshistorisk Laboratorium*, located in Roskilde. On the initiative of local museums, archaeological investigations of Stone Age sites began in the 1970s and this has resulted in excavations of some of the best preserved known nearshore Mesolithic settlements in Denmark such as Tybind Vig and Rønæs Skov.[4] These sites have yielded large amounts of preserved organic artefacts including dugout canoes, remains of fish weirs, and various wooden artefacts and fibres.

The administration of maritime cultural heritage was placed in a government agency in the 1970s, at that time known as the Danish Conservation Agency *(Fredningsstyrelsen)*. The organisation and location of the agency has changed several times and it is now called the Agency for Culture and Palaces (*Slots- og Kulturstyrelsen*) and positioned within the Ministry of Culture.[5] In 1984, all cultural heritage on the seabed which is older than 100 years was protected under the Danish Cultural Heritage Act.[6] As a result of the Valletta Convention of 1992,[7] many European countries legislated that the developer is responsible for the costs of archaeological investigations caused by the developer's work – the "polluter pays" principal.[8] In Denmark, the legal foundation for developer funding for both terrestrial and maritime archae-

---

[3] Crumlin-Pedersen 2002.
[4] Andersen 2013; 2009.

[5] Uldum 2017.
[6] Naturfredningsloven 1984.
[7] Council of Europe 1992.
[8] Andersson et al. 2010, 14; Linden & Webley 2011, 2.

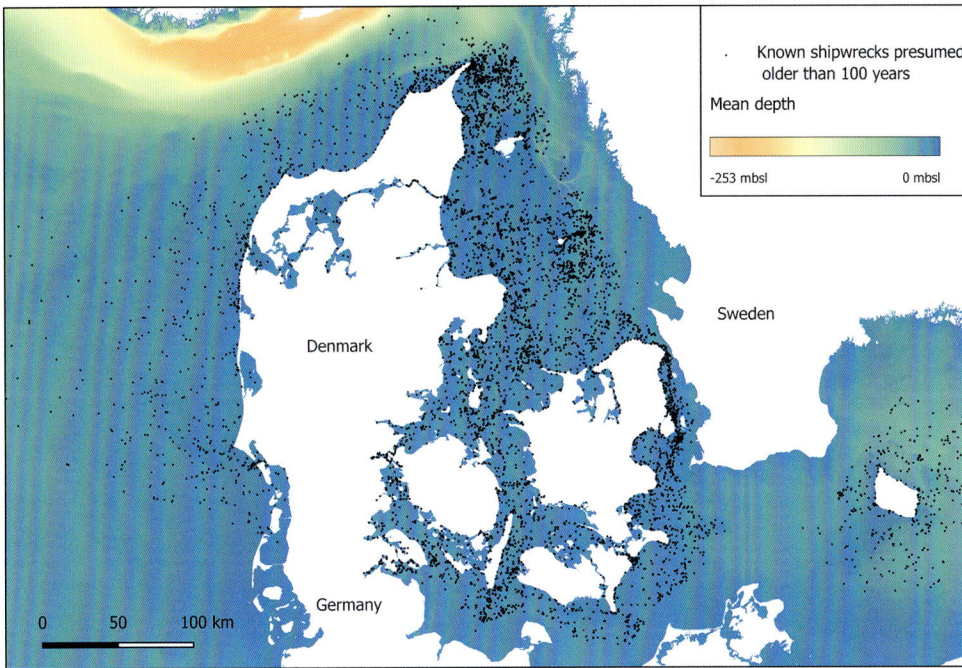

Fig. 2. Known shipwrecks (presumed older than 100 years) on the Danish seafloor (Illustration: Klara Fiedler, © The Viking Ship Museum). Contains data from EMODnet: *EMODnet Digital Bathymetry (DTM 2022)* and from *Fund- og Fortidsminder.*

ology has been in place since 2002.[9] Although, in practice, developer funding for maritime archaeology has been a part of heritage management since the mid-80s as result of the legal protection of all cultural heritage on the seabed in 1984.[10]

The system for archaeological responsibility for development-led archaeology shifted between 1997 and 2004 from a national to a decentralized system.[11] Today, local museums have responsibility for the archaeology within their region. There are currently five museums with maritime archaeological responsibilities in Denmark.[12]

In Denmark, the development-led system is not built on competitive tendering, as is the case in other European countries such as Sweden or Britain.[13] Development-led archaeology in Denmark is conducted only by appointed local museums. Budgets and project designs for developer-funded excavations are determined by local museums that also conduct the work, but this must be approved by the Agency for Culture and Palaces to ensure that budgets are reasonable, and project designs meet the standards set by the agency.[14]

The Agency for Culture and Palaces and the local museums are involved early in the planning process of development-led projects. As part of the consultation process, the museum undertakes an archival study of the area for planned development to assess whether there is a reasonable presumption that there is important cultural heritage preserved within the area and whether the development in question is a threat to such heritage. The cost of this initial evaluation is not developer funded, instead,

---

9   The Danish Museum Act 2001 (Museumsloven 2001). Denmark has not ratified the UNESCO 2001 Convention on the Protection of the Underwater Cultural Heritage.

10 Naturfredningsloven 1984; Bemærkninger til Museumslov 2001, Til § 43.

11 Uldum 2008.

12 The five Danish museums with maritime archaeological responsibility are currently (2025): Langelands Museum, Moesgaard Museum, Nordjyllands Kystmuseum, Strandingsmuseum St George and the Viking Ship Museum.

13 Andersson et al. 2010; Linden & Webley 2011.

14 Linden & Webley 2011; Slots- og Kulturstyrelsen 2025a.

Fig. 3. Test excavation with mechanical excavator and wet sieving of sediments in a development area in Denmark (Photo: © The Viking Ship Museum).

it is covered by the local museum. The Agency for Culture and Palaces then decides on the basis of the evaluation whether an archaeological survey within the areas is required. If a survey is required, this usually begins with a geoarchaeological analysis in the form of a desk-based assessment of geophysical and geotechnical data supplied by the developer. The purpose of the geoarchaeological analysis is to identify anomalies that may represent archaeological artefacts/sites and to identify "hotspots" for Stone Age sites in the submerged paleo-terrain. As a result of the desk-based assessment, development can either be rerouted around potential heritage, i.e. leave sites to be preserved *in situ* (as in line with Danish heritage legislation and the first Rule of the Annex to the UNESCO 2001 Convention on the Protection of the Underwater Cultural Heritage)[15] or the areas that will need to be investigated in a more intrusive manner can be limited. The desk-based assessment is, if necessary, followed up by an archaeological field survey or test excavation. The aim of the survey or test excavation is to evaluate the extent and state of preservation of a site (Fig. 3). On the basis hereof, the museum assesses the significance of the site and prepares a recommendation for the Agency for Culture and Palaces. It is again the decision of the agency whether the site in question should be excavated. Excavation and an excavation report, presenting the documentation of the investigation, is prepared by the local museum and funded by the developer.

Over ten years ago, in 2013, an international evaluation of maritime archaeology in Denmark was

15   Museumsloven 2001; UNESCO 2001.

published.[16] The evaluation concluded, among other things, that the development-led system in Denmark was focused on risk removal and data collection rather than research agendas. The development-led projects did not, in the eyes of the evaluation board, produce new knowledge about the past in a sufficient way. This was a major criticism of the Danish development-led system. The critique has been acknowledged across a broad spectrum of the Danish heritage sector and, since 2013, several initiatives have been launched in response. Nevertheless, over ten years since the intentional evaluation, the research outcome and public outreach of development-led investigations has remained modest.

In summary, the bar in Danish management of development-led maritime archaeology is set high: all heritage over 100 years of age is protected by law, all development-led work on the seabed undergoes archaeological screening and all archaeological sites and artefacts that can arguably produce new knowledge of the past are either preserved *in situ* or excavated at the cost of the developer. Still, the output of most developer-led maritime excavations does not go beyond an excavation report which merely presents data from the individual site. Publication, broader synthesis and public outreach are often lacking.

In the following, I will highlight some of the strengths and challenges in the management of Danish development-led maritime archaeology and present some of the inbuilt dilemmas in management practice. Finally, I would like to bring forth renewed discussion about how production of new knowledge can be increased from the large number of archaeological excavations currently being conducted on the Danish seabed.

Strengths of the development-led system

It is important to highlight that the Danish development-led system, which builds on the Danish Museum Act from 2001, has some clear strengths for the management and protection of underwater cultural heritage:

–   No archaeological site can be destroyed or disturbed by development without prior archaeological assessment.
–   A much higher number of archaeological sites are excavated than in purely research-based archaeology – AND THE FUNDS ARE PROVIDED.
–   The management system for development-led maritime archaeology enables a high degree of *in situ* preservation, as the museums and the Agency for Culture and Palaces are involved in the early stages of development planning.
–   Many marine development projects extend over large areas from which geophysical and geotechnical data are collected. These data are then made available for archaeological analyses and enables an analysis of the landscapes surrounding archaeological sites on a large scale.

... And some challenges

–   Under the current management practice of Danish legal framework, the developer's economic obligations are limited to "mitigating" the damage to a specific site which includes excavation and a report. Funds for research and dissemination to the public are lacking. The development-led system contains no mechanism to support synthetic research that would realise the full potential of the data from individual excavations.

---

16   Olivier et al. 2013.

This leads to a lot of fragmented knowledge and a lack of larger synthesis.[17]

– Legal obligation to carry out excavation projects on limited time schedules (to avoid delaying development work) is prioritised at the local museums. This often leads to a backlog in unfinished reports as well as in other tasks such as research and public outreach.

– Archaeologists dealing with development-led archaeology must address whichever archaeological material is present in any given development area and must, within restricted timeframes, be able to develop good research questions for the sites at hand.[18] Hence, many excavations, despite of their potential for creating new knowledge about the past, end up as "preservation by record".

– Developer funded tasks make up the vast majority of the museums' archaeological work. As a consequence, most maritime archaeologists at the Danish local museums are primarily "field archaeologists". Their primary tasks are to prepare, conduct, and report rescue excavations. Hence, not only the funding for research is lacking at the museums, but to some degree the research qualifications and experience are also lacking.

– Finally, insufficient funding for post-processing can result in the excavated material being exaggerated as extraordinary, because it must bear the weight of the result of the investigation "on its own".[19]

Dilemmas

There is a discrepancy between the function of development-led archaeology in the Danish management system and what many academic archaeologists expect from it. This discrepancy has been a point of discussion in serval Northern European countries, e.g. by Fitzpatrick for the UK planning system,[20] and by Andersson et al.[21] for the Swedish system. The management system is accused of focussing on risk removal – that is, moving cultural heritage out of the way so development can proceed. This has been a recurring point of critique in evaluations of both terrestrial and maritime development-led archaeological investigations in Denmark.[22] The Danish system has been described as "…a self-contained rescue sector".[23]

The critique of the management system has led to several initiatives, at different levels, to strengthen research in development-led projects. A change in the Danish Cultural Heritage Act in 2012[24] introduced a series of quality requirements for museums, including a requirement that a museum must publish approximately 18 peer-reviewed scientific article over a 5-year period and that publications must primarily be based on developer-funded archaeology.[25] A step in the opposite direction has been taken with the bill for the new Museum Reform 2024,[26] where the publication requirement for museums has been set significantly lower, with a requirement to publish one peer reviewed scientific article over a 3-year period.[27] Another initiative to strengthen research in development-led projects is national research strategies.[28] The strategies were formulated as a response to the international evaluation of terrestrial archaeology from 2009.[29] The strategies have been prepared,

17   Linden & Webley 2011.
18   Andersson et al. 2010, 22.
19   Beck 2021.

20   Fitzpatrick 2011.
21   Andersson et al. 2010.
22   Kulturarvsstyrelsen 2009; Statsrevisorerne 2018; Oliver et al. 2013.
23   Kristiansen 2009, 646.
24   Lov om ændring af Museumsloven, LOV nr. 1391 af 23/12/2012.
25   Slots- og Kulturstyrelsen 2021, 16.
26   Lov om ændring af Museumsloven, LOV nr. 1680 af 30/12/2024.
27   Arbejdsgruppen om museumsreform 2023, 55-7.
28   Slots- og Kulturstyrelsen 2024b.
29   Kulturarvsstyrelsen 2009; Roland 2018.

and are recurrently being updated, on behalf of the Agency for Culture and Palaces, by specialists from Danish museums and universities, focussing on different archaeological periods and site types for both terrestrial and maritime archaeology. The strategies are guidelines for the local museums and are intended to be used by them when they assess the significance of a site.[30] It is a requirement that the local museums, in the assessment of a site for potential excavation, refer to the national strategies and to the research strategies of the museum.[31]

As a response to the criticism, it has also been stressed in the guidelines from the Agency for Culture and Palaces that it is a requirement for a developer funded excavation, that the assessment of the site demonstrates how the site in question will produce significant new knowledge about the past.[32] The output of a developer funded excavation is a report that, in the guidelines from the Agency for Culture and Palaces, is described as "…the detailed, professional documentation of an investigation that forms the basis for future archaeological research".[33]

As a consequence, the museums are, in practice, obligated to produce an evaluation of a site that highlight the research potential – elaborating on the "significant new knowledge" that it would contribute to the archaeological record. If the Agency for Culture and Palaces, on the basis of the evaluation, decides that the site should be excavated, the museum is subsequently obliged to conduct an excavation funded by the developer. However, the conduct of research is not technically permitted under this funding.[34] This results in a disparity between the research potentials drawn up in the initial assessment of the site and the research outcomes in the excavation report.

It also raises the question of how, when, where, and under which resources should this "future archaeological research"[35] be conducted on the foundation of the developer-funded report?

Ways forward for research in maritime development-led archaeology in Denmark?

There is today no doubt that archaeological investigations should create new knowledge about the past. This is also cemented in the guidelines by the Agency for Culture and Palaces. A site's potential to produce significant new knowledge about the past is within the evaluation criteria used for deciding whether a site should be excavated.[36] It is also a requirement of the Agency for Culture and Palaces that the museums with archaeological responsibility conduct research based on developer funded excavations.[37]

But what is the criteria for a successful research-guided development-led project? Each individual project or excavation cannot be published as a peer reviewed article or form the basis for a large dissemination outreach for the public in its own right, nor does every excavation warrant it.

If an excavation has an investigative, rather than a documentary approach, with a clearly defined research agenda that falls in line with the research strategies of the museum and/or the national research strategies, then we have a data creation approach that forms the basis for larger synthesis. Rather than focussing narrowly on how many of the development-led archaeological excavations lead directly to a publication of the particular site, the local museums could, to a much higher degree than what is practiced today, let the museums research strate-

---

30   Roland 2018.
31   Slots- og Kulturstyrelsen 2024b.
32   Beck 2021; Slots- og Kulturstyrelsen 2024a.
33   Slots- og Kulturstyrelsen 2025b; 2020, 1, own translation.
34   Beck 2019, 209.

35   Slots- og Kulturstyrelsen 2025b; 2020, 1, own translation.
36   Slots- og Kulturstyrelsen 2024a.
37   Slots- og Kulturstyrelsen 2021, 16.

gies guide the research question in developer funded investigations. This would be a step away from the public management approach were all development projects, regardless of their geographical location, are treated equal, i.e. equal evaluation criteria for the research potential of archaeological sites by all local museums. It would, admittedly, be a challenge on an administrative level, to secure transparency for developers on evaluation criteria, if these, based on different research agendas, differ between the individual museums, but it would also allow the museums to be more focussed in their data creation: moving away from an approach of attempting to document "everything" towards selectively targeting which sites to excavate and which data to collect.

Furthermore, I would argue that there is a need for greater academic specialisation at the museums to improve the research outcome of the development-led projects. More project managers within development-led archaeology need to have academic credibility and research experience, e.g. a PhD. Despite the obvious benefits of academic specialisation at the museums, archaeologists working with development-led archaeology must, to some degree, remain generalists, as they must be able to assess all cultural heritage within a given development area. A stronger academic foundation could further be achieved, with closer cooperation with universities. This would mean that niche specialist knowledge regarding specific sites, artefacts or analyses, could be included as early as the archaeological evaluation of a site in order to ensure that the research questions serve as a guideline throughout the process of planning, excavation, and post-processing. One could argue that in Denmark, where the responsibility for developer-funded archaeology lies with local museums – thus with institutions conducting research – the basic framework for moving towards a more research-oriented approach to developer-funded archaeology is already in place.

Regarding the funding for research within development-led maritime archaeology, it might not be entirely unthinkable to introduce some kind of developer funding. This was actually suggested by the evaluation board in the international evaluation of maritime archaeology in 2013.[38] It is argued in the evaluation report that there is, in fact, no legal barrier to conduct research as part of a developer-funded project, but rather administrative practices hinder it.[39] One option might be that a percentage of each development-led project goes to a fund reserved for research projects – administered either decentralized through the museums or nationally by the Agency for Culture and Palaces. To increase the research outcome of Danish maritime archaeology – and go beyond data presentation of individual sites – better funding, creating the foundations for this work, has to be in place. As long as such funding is not imposed on the developer, or financed as part of the museums' grants, the only option for the museums is to actively seek funding for research. This is a time-consuming and costly task, which is challenging for the museums to conduct, and is often second priority to the legally mandatory rescue excavations. Nevertheless, it is, within the present structure of Danish cultural heritage management system for development-led maritime archaeology, the only option for conducting research.

In order to fulfil the potential of the large number of excavations currently conducted in Danish waters – and in order to continue justifying the large amount of resources being put into maritime archaeology by developers – renewed discussion is needed on how these surveys and excavations are translated into new knowledge about the past, and how we make this knowledge accessible for academia and the public.

Klara Fiedler
The Viking Ship Museum, Roskilde, Denmark
kf@vikingeskibsmuseet.dk

---

38   Oliver et al. 2013, 10-5.
39   Oliver et al. 2013, 12.

Bibliography

ANDERSEN, S. H. 2009
Ronæs Skov. Marinarkæologiske undersøgelser af en kystboplads fra Ertebølletid (Jysk Arkæologisk Selskabs skrifter 64), Højbjerg.

ANDERSEN, S. H. 2013
Tybrind Vig. Submerged Mesolithic settlements in Denmark (Jysk Arkæologisk Selskabs Skrifter 77), Højbjerg.

ANDERSSON C., A. LAGERLÖF & E. SKYLLBERG 2010
'Assessing and Measuring. On quality in development-led archaeology', *Current Swedish Archaeology* 18, 11-28.

ARBEJDSGRUPPEN OM MUSEUMSREFORM 2023
Anbefalinger til en reform af statsanerkendte museers opgaver og tilskud, Copenhagen. Available at: https://kum.dk/fileadmin/_kum/1_Nyheder_og_presse/2023/Museumsreform-rapport-2023.pdf, Accessed May, 2025.

BAILY, G., S. H. ANDERSEN & T. J. MAARLEVELD 2020
'Denmark: Mesolithic Coastal Landscapes Submerged', in *The Archaeology of Europe's Drowned Landscapes*, G. Baily, N. Galanidou, H. Peeters, H. Jöns & M. Mennenga (eds), Cham, 39-76.

BEMÆRKNINGER TIL MUSEUMSLOV 2001
Forslag til Museumslov. Lovforslag 152 af d. 31. januar 2001.

BECK, A. S. 2019
'Arkæologisk viden på spil', *Gefjon: arkæologi og nyere tid* 4, 201-15.

BECK, A. S. 2021
'De lovpligtige udgravninger og begrebet "ny viden"', *Arkæologisk Forum* 44, 18-25.

COUNCIL OF EUROPE 1992
European Convention on the Protection of the Archaeological Heritage (Revised) (European Treaty Series – No. 143), Valetta.

CRUMLIN-PEDERSEN, O. 2002
The Skuldelev Ships. Topography, Archaeology, History, Conservation and Display (Ships and Boats of the North, Volume 4.1.), Roskilde.

FISCHER, A. & P. V. PETERSEN 2018
'Denmark – a sea of archaeological plenty', in *Oceans of Archaeology* (Jysk Arkæologisk Selskabs skrifter 101), A. Fischer & L. Pedersen (eds), Aarhus, 68-83.

FITZPATRICK, A. 2011
'Development-led archaeology in the United Kingdom: a view from AD 2010', in *Development-led Archaeology in Northwest Europe. Proceedings of a Round Table at the University of Leicester 19th–21st November 2009,* L. Webley, M. V. Linden, C. Haselgrove & R. Bradley (eds), Oxford, 139-56.

KRISTIANSEN, K. 2009
'Contract archaeology in Europe: an experiment in diversity', *World Archaeology* 41, 641-8.

KULTURARVSSTYRELSEN 2009
International evaluering af vidensudviklingen i forbindelse med den arkæologiske undersøgelsesvirksomhed efter den nye Museumslov fra 2002, Copenhagen.

LINDEN, M. V. & L. WEBLEY 2011
'Introduction: development-led archaeology in northwest Europe. Frameworks, practices and outcomes', in *Development-led Archaeology in Northwest Europe. Proceedings of a Round Table at the University of Leicester 19th–21st November 2009,* L. Webley, M. V. Linden, C. Haselgrove & R. Bradley (eds), Oxford, 1-8.

LOV OM ÆNDRING AF MUSEUMSLOVEN, LOV NR. 1391 AF 23/12/2012.
Available at: https://www.retsinformation.dk/eli/lta/2012/1391, Accessed May, 2025.

MUSEUMSLOVEN 2001, LOV NR. 473 AF 07/06/2001.
Available at: https://www.retsinformation.dk/eli/lta/2001/473, Accessed May, 2025.

NATURFREDNINGSLOVEN 1984, LBK NR. 530 AF 10/10/1984.
Available at: https://www.retsinformation.dk/eli/lta/1984/530, Accessed May, 2025.

OLIVER, A., B. VARENIUS, M. PIETERS, M. SEG-SCHNEIDER, F. LÜTH & L. HØST-MADSEN 2013
International Evaluation of Marine Archaeology in Denmark. Report of the Working Group 2013, Copenhagen.
Available at: https://slks.dk/fileadmin/user_upload/dokumenter/KS/kulturarv/fortidsminder/Arkaeologi_under_vand_doc/FINAL_6__Kulturstyrelsen_International_Evaluation_of_Marine_Archaeology_in_Denmark__22._april_2013.pdf, Accessed May, 2024.

ROLAND, T. 2018
'Making Choices — Making Strategies: National Strategies for Archaeology in Denmark', *Internet Archaeology* 49. https://doi.org/10.11141/ia.49.5

SLOTS- OG KULTURSTYRELSEN 2025A
Introduktion for bygherre.
Available at: https://slks.dk/omraader/kulturarv/arkaeologi-og-havbundens-fortidsminder/introduktion-til-bygherre/introduktion-for-bygherre, Accessed May, 2025.

SLOTS- OG KULTURSTYRELSEN 2024A
Væsentlige fortidsminder.
Available at:https://slks.dk/arkaeologisk-vejledning/introduktion-for-bygherre/vaesentlige-fortidsminder, Accessed May, 2025.

SLOTS- OG KULTURSTYRELSEN 2025B
Beretning og kulturhistorisk rapport.
Available at: https://slks.dk/omraader/kulturarv/arkaeologi-og-havbundens-fortidsminder/vejledning-til-museer/beretning, Accessed May, 2025.

SLOTS- OG KULTURSTYRELSEN 2020
Notat. Retningslinjer for udformning af beretning for arkæologiske undersøgelser udført i henhold til museumsloven. Den 1. juli 2020, Fortidsminder, Center for Kulturarv, Copenhagen.

SLOTS- OG KULTURSTYRELSEN 2021
Krav og anbefalinger til Statsanerkendte museer. Juli 2021, Copenhagen. Slots- og Kulturstyrelsen, Copenhagen.

SLOTS- OG KULTURSTYRELSEN 2024B
Arkæologiske strategier for udgravninger.
Available at: https://slks.dk/arkaeologisk-strategier/om-strategierne, Accessed May, 2025.

STATSREVISORERNE 2018
Rigsrevisionens beretning om arkæologiske undersøgelser afgivet til Folketinget med Statsrevisorernes bemærkninger (No. 14/2017), Copenhagen.
Available at: https://www.rigsrevisionen.dk/revisionssager-arkiv/2018/mar/beretning-om-arkaeologiske-undersoegelser, Accessed May, 2025.

ULDUM, O. 2008
'Marinarkæologisk fortidsmindeforvaltning og den decentrale museumsstruktur', *Arkæologisk Forum* 19, 20-3.

ULDUM, O. C. 2017
'Hvor har vi været? Dansk marinarkæologi i det nye årtusinde', in *Nordisk marinarkæologi fast forankret*, O. Uldum & M. Sylvester (eds), Rudkøbing, 11-5.

UNESCO 2001

2001 Convention on the Protection of Underwater Cultural Heritage, Paris.
Available at: https://www.unesco.org/en/legal-affairs/convention-protection-underwater-cultural-heritage?hub=412, Accessed February, 2025.

Methodology

Towards a New Understanding of the Early Mesolithic:

The Role of Underwater Archaeology, Strategies, and Problem-Oriented Focus Areas

Peter Moe Astrup

Abstract

The submerged landscapes and the archaeological remains found in them can fill many gaps in our knowledge that cannot be done solely with the materials found on land. This chapter shows how developer-led underwater projects and archaeological research projects can be designed to address and answer specific questions/knowledge lacunae. Experiences from Moesgaard Museum's efforts in determining the role of the coast in southern Scandinavia are used to show why a strategic and problem-oriented approach is required in underwater archaeology.

Introduction[1]

The seabed in southern Scandinavia contains numerous traces of a submerged landscape that is thought to be the remnant of a once important habitat for Mesolithic hunter-gatherers. Large parts of this landscape were gradually flooded by rising seas between 9500 and 4000 BC and perceptions of the Early Mesolithic cultures (9500-6400 BC) have, consequently, been based almost exclusively on former inland settlements far from the contemporary coastlines. This is in sharp contrast with the situation in the Late Mesolithic (6400-4000 BC), when most of the known settlements were in coastal areas, and there is a rich record of the specialized coastal culture (including hunting and fishing gear) and more sedentary occupations. As a result, the Early and Late Mesolithic societies are understood as almost diametrically opposed with regard to their reliance upon marine resources and their degree of sedentism. Many researchers describe a shift in subsistence economy around 6400 BC, when societies first began to seriously orient themselves to the sea and the exploitation of its resources.[2] This shift has important implications for the way many archaeologists have interpreted cultural developments and has therefore also been debated in recent years.[3]

It should be apparent that submarine landscapes and the archaeological remains found in them have the potential to answer a range of questions and fill many gaps in our knowledge that cannot be done solely with the materials found on land. This is especially true with regards to the role of coasts in the Early Mesolithic. It is not yet known what role they played for people and whether coastal settlements were more widespread than they appear in the record so far. These questions have been raised since the Maglemose Culture was first recognized in the

1   Acknowledgements: This work was supported by the Augustinus Foundation (project number 21-1637) and by an ERC synergy grant (project number 101119164).

2   Larsson 1990; Andersen 1995; 2001; Jensen 2001.
3   Astrup 2018; Boethius 2018.

beginning of the 20th century, and many archaeologists have suggested that the coast played a major role.[4] However, the archaeological evidence for this remains scarce, and we do not know significantly more today than we did 100 years ago. In large part this is because most of the Early Mesolithic coastlines are submerged at depths where they have not been explored by divers – neither marine archaeologists nor recreational divers. In short, a targeted research effort is needed if we will understand Early Mesolithic societies' connection to the coast.

Aims and methods

The main objective of this chapter is to demonstrate how developer-led underwater projects and archaeological research projects can be designed to address and answer specific questions/knowledge lacunae. This chapter is primarily based on the author's work to discover the origins of the earliest coastal cultures in southern Scandinavia (and address the problems discussed in the introduction). Experience from both developer-led and research projects has shown why it is important to have a strategic and problem-oriented approach.

Strategies and problem-oriented approaches

In Denmark it is the party initiating a development project that is responsible for the expenses of archaeological work done prior to construction. This means that in general, Danish marine archaeology is financed by construction firms and most of the large underwater investigations have been done in connection with large infrastructure projects such as harbour extensions and wind farms. Accordingly, projects have dictated where the archaeological work

was done and what was investigated – and therefore typically what questions have been addressed.

The Agency for Culture and Palaces (abbreviated as SLKS from the Danish *Slots- og Kulturstyrelsen*) has overall responsibility for managing marine archaeology in Denmark. It does this in collaboration with five museums that each has their own geographic area of responsibility. In addition to evaluating the museums' professional assessments of the necessity for archaeological investigations preceding projects, SLKS authorizes the project descriptions, budgets, and accounting. SLKS also develops strategies that provide museums with a basis for planning and prioritizing archaeological investigations. It is intended that the museums will use SLKS' national strategies to justify their methods of investigation and budget priorities. In short, the intention of the strategies is to make explicit the actual research questions facing Danish marine archaeology that typically will require a focused and coordinated national effort to address. For example, the 2022 SLKS strategy concerning the Early Stone Age is based on how to plan, prioritize, and conduct underwater investigations to locate sites from this period. The strategies are usually developed by a team of researchers who are specialized in the period or themes that are key to the strategy.

SLKS has also instructed the individual museums to prepare a research and investigation strategy that reflects the museum's own focus areas. The museums can, for example, have a strategy that is tailored to an important locality in their area of responsibility or a methodology that the museum's employees are specialists in using. The most important thing is that the strategy is based on the various themes which the museum has chosen to prioritize. The goals for both the national and individual strategies are the same – to bring the archaeological data into play and make explicit how priorities are set. The strategies also work to ensure that archaeologists reflect over their approaches. The choice of a specific excavation method will always result from an evaluation of the

4   Sarauw et al. 1903; Fischer 2001; Astrup 2018.

objective, research question(s), the actual archaeological situation, preservation conditions, and the budget.[5] A problem-oriented approach is essential because of the almost inevitable destruction of the archaeological record that occurs during investigations. Therefore, it is important that the responsible archaeologists consider which possibilities exist with the various available methods to address concrete, predefined research questions that can create new knowledge. This can, for example, be part of the process of ensuring the proper samples are taken during survey/excavation. It is also critical that archaeologists constantly take stock of the situation and be prepared to modify strategies based on the actual situation encountered (for example, if unexpected features or finds are encountered). It is also necessary for excavation methodology to change over time as innovative technologies give new possibilities.

Many investigations at Stone Age sites are done by excavating square metre units (typically, one square at a time). However, it is often difficult to recognize and document larger features, cultural layers, and activity areas that encompass large areas and multiple excavation units. For example, recognizing habitations or other substantial, permanent constructions structures from the earlier periods of the Stone Age is difficult if only one square metre is opened at a time. Locating these features usually requires noticing faint differences in colour and texture that can only be done by comparing the fill in them with the surrounding surfaces. With a single excavation unit that measures at most 1 x 1 m open, and especially with the conditions accompanying marine archaeology (e.g. poor visibility), this is extremely difficult. Therefore, it would be immensely helpful to open larger areas when possible, in order to find potential structures and other large coIstructions. The point is that during underwater excavation it is much harder to find these features than on land. It is crucial that marine archaeologists recognize this limitation, as

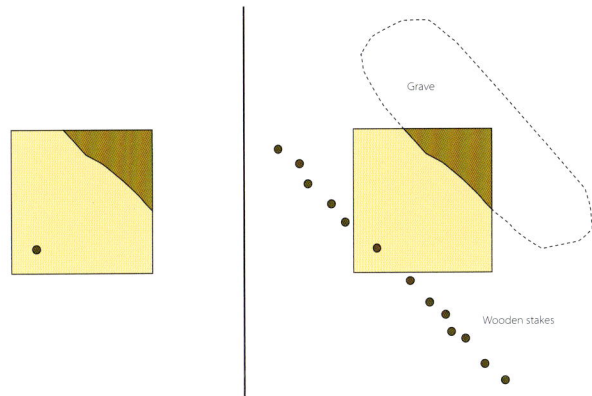

Fig. 1. A hypothetical illustration of why it can be difficult to recognize structures using square metre excavation units (illustration by the author).

otherwise these features will escape detection. This also places extreme demands on documentation methods, so that when only small units are sequentially opened the divers' observations can later be combined to form a more complete picture of the site (see, for example, Fig. 1).

Current challenges and initiatives

One of the tools that has been developed and employed in collaboration between the Danish museums, SLKS and industry is "geoarchaeological analysis". Its goal is to develop a detailed picture of the archaeological potential in a given area prior to the initial survey work. The museums typically rely on a wide range of data including geological borings, geophysical data, sediment mapping, etc. The developer is obligated to provide the data required to evaluate the archaeological potential of the area affected by the project. Usually, new sea-level curves and landscape models are created based on these data, and expected archaeological hotspots are identified. Thus, it is the geoarchaeological analysis that

---

5   Lass Jensen 2019, 24.

is used to prioritize where marine archaeological survey work is to be done.

There is almost always an expectation that geoarchaeological analyses will be done in connection with the larger development projects at sea (offshore windmill parks, raw material extraction, etc.) The models used to plot prehistoric landscapes and coastlines during the analysis are constantly improving due to better geophysical and dating methods. There is, likewise, a growing body of data that can be incorporated into analyses. The challenge now is largely becoming how to deal with the enormous areas covered by the landscape reconstructions and narrow down the location of potential archaeological hotspots. Three challenges that make it difficult to get the maximum utility from developer-led investigations are:

1. It is not known how important the coast was to people in the Early Mesolithic Period in southern Scandinavia and therefore how extensive coastal settlements were. Because of this, it is difficult to identify hotspots when it is unclear how much emphasis should be placed on archaic coastlines as opposed to areas that were inland at the time. Likewise, it is difficult to know where potential Maglemose coastal settlements would be located relative to the numerous coastal sites from the subsequent Kongemose and Ertebølle Periods – as well as their placement in relation to contemporary inland settlements.

2. Another challenge is that many of the hotspots identified during the geoarchaeological analysis are at depths or under sediment deposits that make it almost impossible to investigate or take samples systematically. At present, when investigating areas that lay deep underwater it is only possible to use a suction pipe to bring up materials from the seabed to be sorted in the ship's hold or on land. From shallower waters (down to about 20 m depth), it is possible to bring up materials with a long-armed machine excavator

for sorting. Another (expensive) alternative is to use divers – although only if the archaeological layers are not buried by thick sediments. All three methods can cause extensive destruction of the archaeological record (diving perhaps less so) and the finds lose much of their contextual information when they reach the surface. Despite this, there frequently are no real alternatives. New methods must be developed to preserve the vital contextual information that now is usually lost. Archaeologists will have to grapple with the pros and cons of the different methods. Could one possibility be to take whole blocks of sediment up from the seabed that can be investigated and documented under controlled conditions on land?

3. A third challenge is that the likelihood of detecting an Early Mesolithic site during an initial survey is generally quite small. This is not necessarily because the choice of where to investigate was faulty but could also be the result of thinly-spread settlements on the Early Mesolithic landscape, which means that even likely hotspots have a low probability of actually having been occupied. Often this means that it is difficult to conclude the likelihood of detecting new Early Mesolithic sites is sufficient to justify an archaeological survey. It is precisely this question that marine archaeologists are required to address when they evaluate whether the expected scientific benefits equal the resources required to produce them.

The necessity of incorporating research projects

Research projects offer an opportunity to investigate areas that would otherwise remain unexplored and are usually designed to examine specific research questions. A dedicated effort is required to coordinate targeted research projects with developer-led investigations in a way that can address the unan-

Fig. 2. Diving vessel in use at the underwater excavation in Aarhus Bay 2024 (Photo: Poul Madsen / Moesgaard Museum).

swered questions (e.g. points 1-3 above). Moreover, there is a pressing need to identify cultural heritage on the seabed so that as much as possible is preserved for posterity. Developer-led projects in Denmark are generally not used to develop new methods but to identify and investigate the heritage in a given area and preserve as much as possible for the future. It is therefore important to create research projects that can help maximize the returns from these efforts.

Research lacunae (example from Aarhus Bay)

Moesgaard Museum conducted four investigations in Aarhus Bay in the period 2017-2024 with the goal of assessing the role of coastlines. The first was a reconnaissance project in 2017 to determine if there were coastal settlements in a limited area near an earlier channel at a depth of 4-10 m. The investigation revealed the presence of worked flints on the seabed that could be typologically dated to the Maglemose-Kongemose transition. Subsequent underwater excavations took place in 2017, 2022,

2023, and 2024. These dives were able to demonstrate a presumed coastal settlement from the latest part of the Maglemose Period. It is still unknown how widespread coastal sites were at that time, but it is quite noteworthy that after only a few days of systematic searching a submerged one was found, whereas contemporaneous terrestrial sites are almost unknown in the Aarhus area despite years of archaeological research and collectors searching ploughed fields. This could well indicate that there is still a great deal to be discovered under water and that coasts were far more densely settled than many inland areas at this time. Of course, this could also reflect that preservation conditions are often better on the seabed compared to on land.

One of the main goals for investigating the site was to clarify whether the people who lived there relied on marine resources. All the material removed from the excavation units was therefore collected, sieved, and sorted, with the aim to recover and identify even the smallest fish bones and other artefacts. The preliminary zooarchaeological analysis confirms that most of the fish are marine or diadromous species, and as this is written a detailed evaluation of the importance of the

Fig. 3. Example of wooden object with unknown function. Found at the submerged Ertebølle site Hjarnø Sund in 2015 (Photo: Peter Moe Astrup).

individual resources is being prepared. Thanks to the generosity of the Augustinus Foundation and an EU-ERC synergy grant, a range of new underwater excavations will be conducted in the area in 2024-2029. The upcoming excavations are focused on recovering a large assemblage of faunal material from this Early Mesolithic coastal settlement. Hopefully, these animal remains can be used both to create a detailed understanding of the role of coastal areas in the subsistence economy of this period and reveal the fishing and other procurement methods that were employed. For example, did the well-documented fish fences and traps known from the Late Mesolithic have their roots in the Maglemose Period? Since the 1970s new types of tools have been discovered on submerged Stone Age sites because of the often excellent preservation conditions for organic materials. However, generally the same types of tools (e.g. leister prongs, paddles, bows, and wooden stakes) recur, despite the increasing number of sites that have been investigated in southern Scandinavia. There is a wide range of artefacts that presumably were used which have not yet been found, such as shoes, clothing, nets, containers, bowls, benches, and tables. With luck,

the coming years' excavations can provide a more complete picture of Stone Age material culture.

The upcoming work aims to create new knowledge about the subsistence economy at the coastal settlements. These results will then be used to determine the archaeological potential of other areas and target future survey work. There is no guarantee that conditions in Aarhus Bay 8,500 years ago exactly reflect those in other areas. However, it is expected that they will have relevance for accomplishing these goals. Therefore, as one thread in the research project SUBNORDICA the results from Aarhus Bay will be incorporated as one of many variables in a range of new models being developed to identify areas with high potential for Stone Age investigations in the North Sea.

Methods

Many preconditions must be met in order to identify a settlement on the sea floor. First, of course, is that there must have been people at that location that left traces of their presence. Next, the sediments with these traces cannot have been eroded away and there must be methodologies available that can identify and possibly excavate them under the extant conditions. We must improve upon the existing methods to ensure we are prepared for the expanding transition to green energy coincident with net zero goals that are driving increased development on the continental shelves. As part of the ERC synergy grant funded SUBNORDICA project, Moesgaard Museum will contribute to this process. As an example, Moesgaard will experiment with developing methods and technologies to identify exposed sites on the seabed with the help of machine learning/AI.

Final remarks

It is important to note that the rules for developer-led maritime archaeology in Denmark are likely to change in the coming years. These changes may alter the roles and tasks of the museums involved, which means that many of the fundamental principles in develop-led archaeology described in this article might not apply in the future. It is certain, however, that underwater archaeology will continue to provide an important source of answers to many of the open questions about prehistory facing us. Marine archaeological investigations must be organized in a manner that allows this potential to be realized. A project does not necessarily need to find new sites in an area where few have previously been identified to be successful. It is more important that individual projects/investigations are planned and prioritized based on serious evaluation of their potential to answer questions that are archaeologically important. It is for precisely this reason that it is essential to work within a problem-oriented and interdisciplinary research strategy with clear goals and expectations for what individual projects can contribute.

Peter Moe Astrup
Moesgaard Museum, Aarhus, Denmark
pma@moesgaardmuseum.dk

Bibliography

ASTRUP, P. M. 2018
Sea-level Change in Mesolithic Scandinavia. Long- and short-term effects on society and the environment (Jysk Arkæologisk Selskabs skrifter 106), Aarhus.

ANDERSEN, S. H. 1995
'Coastal adaption and marine exploitation in Late Mesolithic Denmark – with special emphasis on the Limfjord region', in *Man and the Sea in the Mesolithic. Coastal settlements above and below present sea level*, A. Fisher (ed.), Oxford, 41-66.

ANDERSEN, S. H. 2001
Oldtiden i Danmark. Jægerstenalderen, Copenhagen.

BOETHIUS, A. 2018
Fishing for ways to thrive Integrating zooarchaeology to understand subsistence strategies and their implications among Early and Middle Mesolithic southern Scandinavian foragers, Doctoral dissertation, Historical Osteology, Department of Archaeology and Ancient History Lund University, Acta Archaeologica Lundensia, Series altera in 8°, no. 70, Sweden.

FISCHER, A. 2001
'Mesolitiske bopladser på den danske havbund – udfordringer for forskning og forvaltning', in *Danmarks jægerstenalder – status og perspektiver*, O. Lass Jensen, S. A. Sørensen & K. Møller-Hansen (eds), Hørsholm, 59-71.

JENSEN, J. 2001
Danmarks Oldtid. Stenalder 13.000-2.000 f. Kr., Copenhagen.

LARSSON, L. 1990
'The Mesolithic of Southern Scandinavia', *Journal of World Prehistory* 4:3, 257-309.

LASS JENSEN, O. 2019

'Udgravning af anlæg', in *Strategi for ældre stenalders arkæologiske undersøgelser. Arkæologiske strategier for udgravninger i Danmark*, Slots- og Kulturstyrelsen, Nykøbing Falster, 19-25. Available at: https://slks.dk/fileadmin/user_upload/SLKS/Omraader/Kulturarv/Arkaeologi__Fortidsminder_og_diger/Arkaeologiske_strategier/PDF-udgaver/AEST_Strategi.pdf, Accessed May, 2025.

SARAUW, G. F. L., K. JESSEN & H. WINGE 1903

En Stenalders Boplads, Maglemose ved Mullerup, Sammenholdt med Beslægtede fund (Aarbøger for Nordisk Oldkyndighed og Historie), Copenhagen.

Marine Remote Sensing Techniques for the Study of Underwater Cultural Heritage Sites:

Case Studies from the Eastern Mediterranean Sea

Maria Geraga & George Papatheodorou

Abstract

The application of remote sensing techniques has become a fundamental tool for the protection of underwater cultural heritage sites. These techniques primarily use acoustic waves, making them non-destructive to archaeological materials. These marine geoarchaeological survey techniques typically involve Multibeam Echo-Sounders (MBES), Side scan sonars (SSS), Sub-bottom profilers (SBP), marine magnetometers (MM), Remote Operated Vehicles (ROVs), Autonomous Unmanned Vehicles (AUVs), and Unmanned Surface Vehicles (USVs). These tools produce geo-referenced data that record and reconstruct the seafloor's topography, texture, and stratigraphy, allowing for the detection, mapping, and documentation of archaeological sites on the seafloor or buried beneath sediments.

In this paper, we present applications of remote sensing techniques used in studying underwater cultural heritage (UCH) sites in the eastern Mediterranean Sea. The case studies focus on assessing coastal palaeogeographic evolution, mapping submerged ancient harbour remains, and detecting ancient and historic shipwrecks. In all instances, the remote sensing surveys were conducted by the Oceanus-Lab, Department of Geology, University of Patras, Greece.

Introduction[1]

The habitation of the eastern Mediterranean Sea started during the Palaeolithic, with the sea playing a vital role in the global human dispersal. Since then, the coastal zones of the sea have hosted settlements and great civilizations. Remnants of this human journey throughout time have been preserved on and in the seafloor and constitute valuable testimonies and archives for the evolution of humankind. As cultural heritage, the study, preservation and management of these sites is indispensable.

[1]   Acknowledgements: The authors would like to thank all the current and previous members and colleagues of the Oceanus-Lab which helped in the acquisition, processing and interpretation of the data. Special thanks go to Prof. G. Ferentinos, Dr D. Christodoulou, Dr A. Chalari, Dr E. Fakiris, Dr M. Iatrou, Dr S. Kordella, Dr M. Gkioni, M. Prevenios, Dr N. Georgiou, Dr X. Dimas and Dr D. Zoura. Furthermore, they would like to thank the Ephorate of Underwater Antiquities of Greece, particularly Dr Pari Kalamara and Dr Despina Koutsoumpa; the Hellenic Institute of Ancient and Medieval Alexandrian Studies, especially Charis Tzalas; the Centre d' Études Alexandrines – CEAlex-CNRS (France), particularly Dr J.-Y. Empereur; the French School of Athens and Aix-Marseille University, particularly Prof. Kalliopi Baika, and the Danish Institute at Athens, particularly Dr Bjørn Lovén, for providing Oceanus-Lab the opportunity to investigate the underwater archaeological sites referenced in this work and for their crucial assistance in interpreting the archaeological results. Finally, they would like to thank the

These underwater cultural heritage (UCH) sites include submerged coastal landscapes, settlements and facilities as well as ancient and historic shipwrecks. The coastal geography of the eastern Mediterranean Sea has changed several times in the past. Sea level changes attributed to large or short scale variations in climatic conditions and tectonic activity are the major factors that contribute to variations in the location and the extent of the ancient coastal zones. Just within the last glacial-interglacial cycle, the sea level has risen c. 120 m and has inundated large expanses of the past coastline together with possible traces of human activity. On the other hand, local or regional geological faulting activity has rapidly displaced the ancient shoreline several times, making prediction of its location even more complex. Furthermore, since antiquity, seafaring and the development of maritime trade among ancient civilizations as well as the strategic location of the eastern Mediterranean has given rise to a large number of ships transporting goods and joining naval battles. As a result, the seafloor hosts numerous known and unknown ancient and historic shipwrecks and remnants of battles.

UCH sites can be found from shallow to deep waters and on the seafloor or buried well beneath it. The challenges for their detection and mapping have given rise to the use of remote sensing techniques as meaningful tool in this approach. In this paper we will present briefly those techniques and their applications in selected underwater archaeological sites from the eastern Mediterranean, as investigated by the Oceanus-Lab (Laboratory of Marine Geology and Physical Oceanography, Department of Geology, University of Patras, Greece) and its colleagues.

Techniques

Remote sensing techniques are efficient for the detection, mapping, and documentation of the UCH sites.[2] They can collect comprehensive and efficient data over large areas of the seafloor, overcoming the depth limitations of conventional diving or other limitations related to environmental parameters such as light, water quality, and currents. Because they utilize acoustic energy, they do not destroy the archaeological material. The most common techniques are: (i) single and multibeam echo-sounders which emit sound beams aiming to map the seafloor bathymetry with high accuracy, (ii) side scan sonars, which provide records (sonographs) of the variation of the bottom return acoustic intensity allowing the mapping of seabed features, material, and textures, (iii) sub-bottom profilers which record the seismic or acoustic stratigraphy of the seafloor (seismic profiles), thereby locating potential archaeological sites buried beneath the sediments, and (iv) underwater visual inspection systems (cameras, underwater remotely operated ROVs or manned vehicles, and autonomous vehicles). Connecting all these geophysical instruments with positioning and navigation systems makes it possible to collect georeferenced data and construct detailed maps. The emission of sound waves usually covers a wide range of frequencies (1-900 kHz), giving the researcher the possibility of collecting data at a wide range of resolution.[3]

In a downscaling approach, underwater photogrammetry has emerged as a very effective metric documentation technique.[4] It produces high-resolution 3D models and 2D orthomosaics of underwater sites and artefacts. Recently, virtual reality (VR) and augmented reality (AR) systems improve the accessibility of the submerged archaeological sites leading to

Danish Institute at Athens, particularly its director Dr Sanne Hoffmann, Dr Athena Trakadas, and Dr Panagiotis Athanasopoulos, for organizing and supporting the lecture series at the Danish Institute at Athens and its publication.

2   Chalari et al. 2009; Papatheodorou et al. 2011; Geraga et al. 2020; Georgiou et al. 2021, and references within.
3   Geraga et al. 2015.
4   Calantropio & Chiabrando 2024.

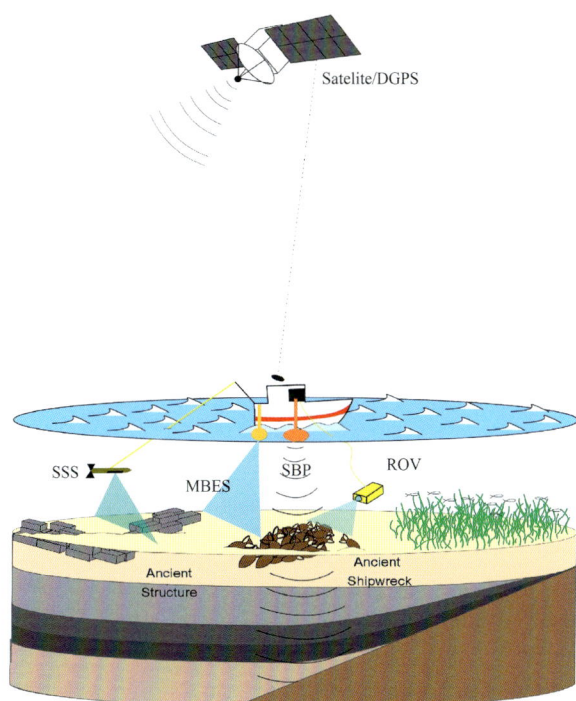

Fig. 1. Marine remote sensing techniques (SSS: side scan sonar, MBES: multibeam echosounder, SBP: sub-bottom profiler, ROV: remotely operated vehicles) (Modified from Georgiou et al. 2021).

better monitoring, conservation, and management.[5] Remote sensing surveys are usually organized in two distinct phases (Fig. 1).[6] First, a systematic survey of the seafloor is carried out using remote sensing techniques. The second phase consisted of visual inspection based on the results of the first phase.

The application of the remote sensing and related techniques covers a wide range of research, which include assessment of coastal palaeogeographic evolution, investigation of human dispersal potential, detection and mapping of submerged coastal artefacts and detection and mapping of ancient and historic shipwrecks and remains of naval battles.[7] In the

following text, selected case studies will be presented related to the above-mentioned applications.

Coastal palaeogeographic evolution case study: Coastal zone of Hellenistic Alexandria, Egypt

In the coastal zone of Alexandria, off the Eastern Harbour (Great Harbour – Μέγας Λιμήν), research has been conducted since 1999. Initially, this was in collaboration with the Hellenic Institute of Ancient and Medieval Alexandrian Studies and Charis Tzalas, and not long after with the Centre d' Études Alexandrines – CEAlex-CNRS (France) under the direction of Dr J.-Y. Empereur. The study area holds global cultural interest as it housed famous monuments of the ancient world such as the Lighthouse of Alexandria, the *Heptastadion*, Ptolemaic Royal Palace, and more. The coastal configuration of Hellenistic Alexandria presents exceptional interest.

Alexandria developed on a narrow land strip between Lake Mariut (Λίμνη Μαρεώτιδα) and the Mediterranean Sea (Fig. 2a). The island of Pharos in front of the city significantly influenced the structure of its port facilities. The *Heptastadion* (7 *stadia* long) connected Alexandria with the island and divided the coastal zone, forming two harbours (Fig. 2a): the eastern or Great Harbour and the western or Eunostos Harbour. Over the centuries, the *Heptastadion* was covered by sedimentary deposits, and part of the modern city of Alexandria was built on this area (Fig. 2b).

The purpose of the research was to map the coastal morphology during the Hellenistic Period and to identify potential archaeological sites of interest. A total area of 32.5 km² was surveyed using a 3.5 kHz sub-bottom profiling system and a dual-frequency EG&G 260 side scan sonar. Marine geophysical surveys provided detailed bathymetric, geological,

---

5   Bruno et al. 2020.
6   Papatheodorou et al. 2005.
7   Geraga et al. 2014; 2017; Papatheodorou et al. 2011; 2021.

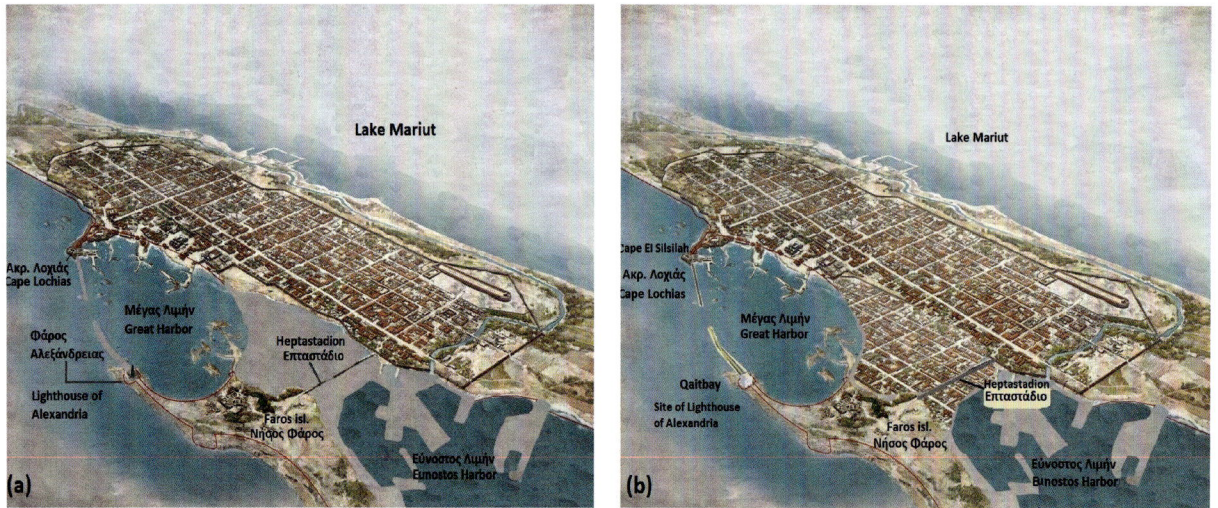

Fig. 2. Representation of the coastal configuration of Alexandria as seen from the north-west (a) in Hellenistic Period, and (b) today (modified from National Geographic).

and geomorphological maps for the examined area.[8] Based on these, models of the coastal zone were created, showing what it was like up to 8,000 years ago. Obvious emphasis was placed on the representation of the coastal configuration at the time when Alexandria was founded (331 BC).

The dominant seafloor feature revealed from the sub-bottom profiling and side scan sonar records was a well-shaped 3.5 km-long rocky ridge, 6-14 m high compared to the surrounding seafloor, and about 700 m wide (Fig. 3). The ridge lies about 1.0 km north of the Qait Bay Fort where the lighthouse (Pharos) used to stand, is almost parallel to the present shoreline, and has a dominant strike direction of about 45°. The ridge exhibits high reflectivity on the sonographs suggesting that it consists of hard (rocky) material in contrast to the surrounding

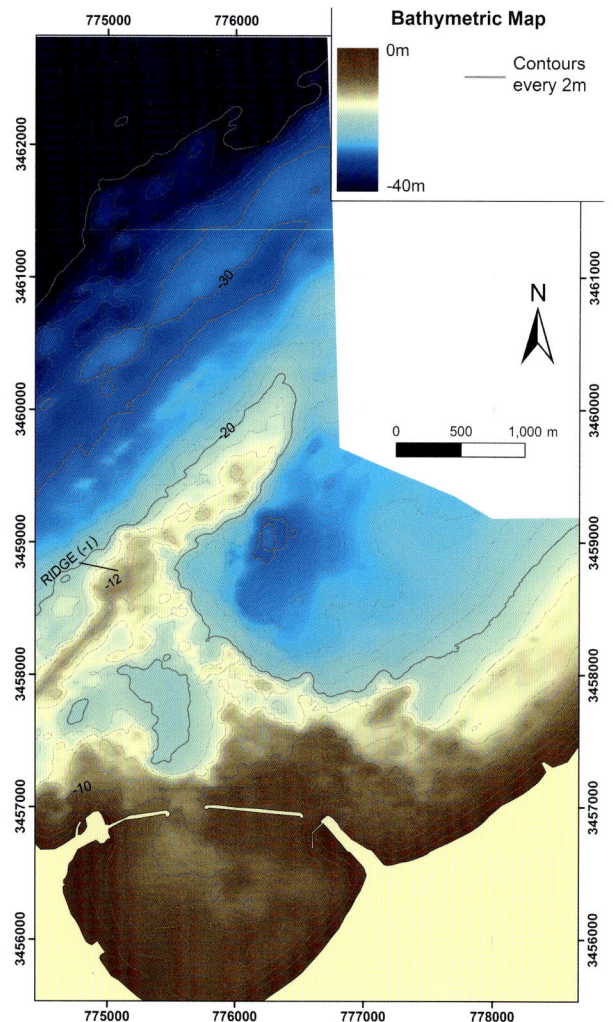

Fig. 3. Bathymetric map of the coastal zone of Alexandria showing a long rocky ridge (Ridge-I) running almost parallel to the shoreline (Oceanus-Lab [Laboratory of Marine Geology and Physical Oceanography]).

8   Chalari et al. 2008; 2009; Papatheodorou et al. 2015.

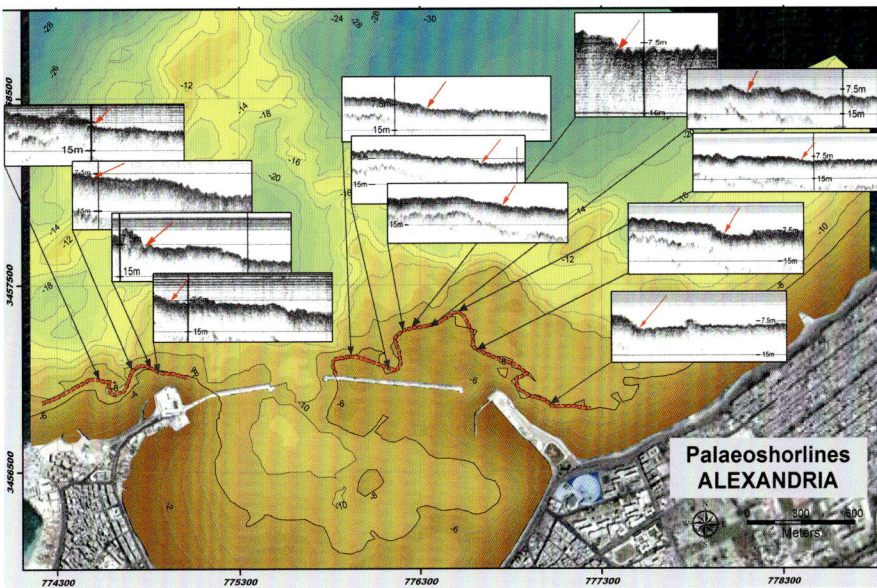

Fig. 4. Bathymetric map of the coastal zone of Alexandria, off the Great Harbour, showing (i) the palaeo-shoreline at a depth of 8 m below the present sea level (red line) and (ii) collection of representative sub-bottom seismic profiles, showing the location of the palaeo-shoreline at 8 m depth (red arrows) (After Papatheodorou et al. 2015).

sedimentary seafloor which presents low backscatter. The minimum water depth of the top of this ridge is 12 m, forming a narrow planar strip (Fig. 3).

In addition, the seismic profiles showed numerous small scarps which were attributed to sculptures on the rocky seafloor, as indicated by the wavy erosion at times of sea level stands. Therefore, these scarps were attributed as evidence of previous (palaeo-)shorelines. The scarps were clustered at 16 m, 14 m, 12 m, 10 m and 8 m depth (Fig. 4).

Among the above-mentioned groups of scarps, the one at 8 m depth is best recognized at the sites of Cape Silsilah (ancient Lochias Peninsula) and the Qait Bay Fort (see Fig. 4) and was considered a marker for the Hellenistic shoreline. Based on the data collected and combined with previous geological,[9] archaeological,[10] and tidal gauge data,[11] a local subsidence rate of 3.5 mm/yr was assumed.[12] It appears that the Hellenistic coastal zone was submerged by 8 m compared to today, likely due to subsidence episodes related to earthquakes and the simultaneous rise in sea level.

According to the 8 m subsidence scenario, the coastal configuration of Hellenistic Alexandria significantly differs from that of today. A clearly narrower passage led to the Great Harbour, while small rocky islets and extensive reefs developed in front of it, especially to the east towards the Lochias Peninsula, making navigation difficult, as described in Strabon's texts (Fig. 5).[13] Most of the Lochias Peninsula is now submerged, which is why many ancient architectural elements have been found on the surrounding seafloor. The Great Harbour seemed to be protected at the time of Alexandria's founding by a natural reef breakwater, the present rocky ridge, that ran parallel to the ancient coastline, 1 km north of today's Qait Bay Fort (at the location of the ancient Pharos) and the entrance to the ancient harbour. As the ridge's crest is now at a depth of 12 m, its crest was just 4 m below the sea's surface during the Hellenistic Period, based on the 8 m subsidence scenario. This acted as an effective natural reef breakwater for the harbour (see Fig. 5). However, it was also a hazardous area for sailors at the time, a hypothesis

9   Stanley 1988.
10 Frihy 1992; 2003; Empereur 1998; Jondet 1916.
11 El Fishawi & Fanos 1989.
12 Papatheodorou et al. 2015.
13 Strabon, *Geographica*, 17.1.6.

Fig. 5. 3D bathymetric reconstruction of the coastal configuration of Alexandria during the Hellenistic Period. The ancient coastline is indicated by the red line (Oceanus-Lab, after Papatheodorou et al. 2015).

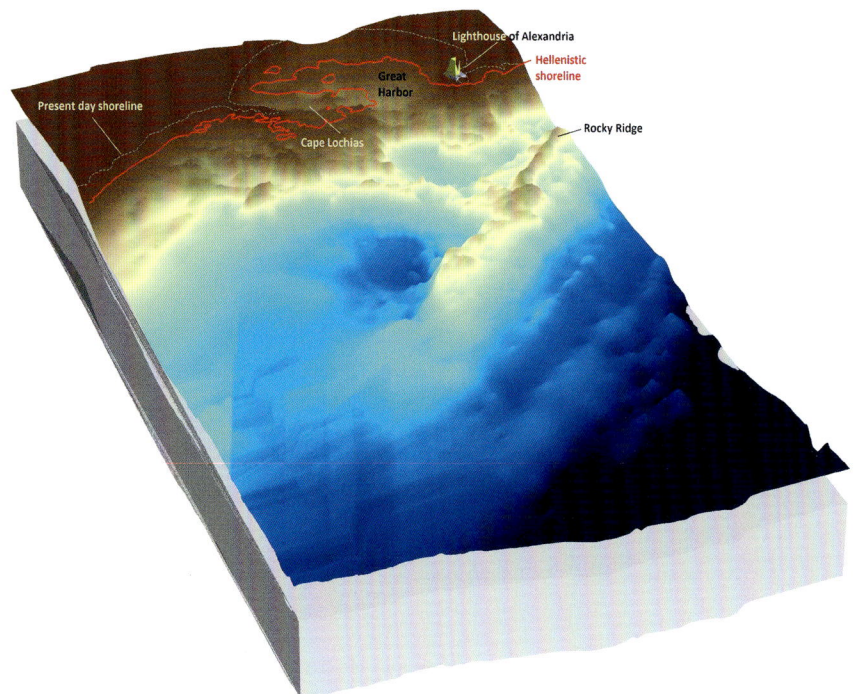

confirmed by the many ancient shipwrecks found here by J.-Y. Empereur.[14]

Additionally, numerous acoustic anomalies (targets) on the seafloor were visually confirmed and characterized as modern man-made items and items of historical or archaeological significance. Among them, the remains of an ancient shipwreck with amphorae were recorded.[15]

Human dispersal case study: The Ionian Sea

Archaeological data from the Ionian islands prove their habitation since the Middle Palaeolithic.[16] The question is whether the islands were part of the mainland and therefore then populated through land migration or were they already islands and their populating occurred by sea. The necessary data for

such a palaeogeographic reconstruction include the knowledge of vertical tectonic movements, the rate of sedimentation (i.e., the rate at which the seabed is covered with sediments entering the sea), and sea level changes. The analysis and processing of seismic profiles of shallow and deep penetration below the seabed from the area provided information about its tectonic and sedimentological regime (sedimentation rate, subsidence/uplift rate).[17] Based on these data and global sea level change data, possible models of the area's geomorphological evolution were examined. Since 125,000 years ago the sea level has been fluctuating between 20 and 120 m below its present level.[18]

Repeated marine geophysical surveys, over a long period of time, conducted by Oceanus-Lab in the Ionian Sea led to the collection of a large volume of data that allowed for the palaeogeographic reconstruction of an extensive marine area from Lefkada and Kefalonia Islands to Zakynthos Island.

14 Empereur 2000.
15 Chalari et al. 2006.
16 Galanidou et al. 2016, and references within.

17 Ferentinos et al. 2012.
18 Lambeck 1996.

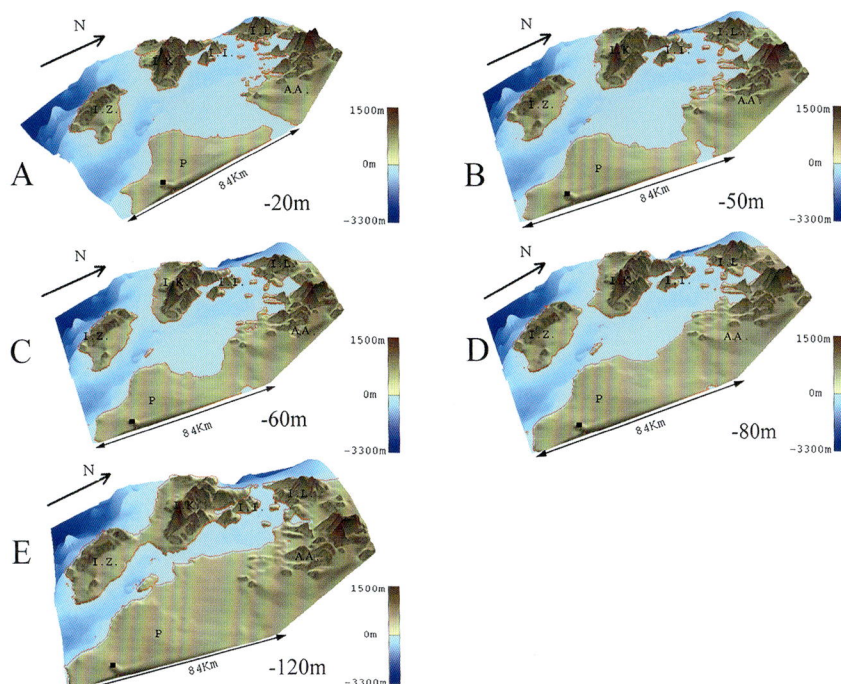

Fig. 6. 3D time-space models of palaeo-shoreline configuration in the southern Ionian Islands at 100, 60, 30, 18, 10 and 8 ka BP when the sea level was at -20, -80, -60, -120, -50 and -20 m below present, respectively. The perspective views are from a point in the Peloponnese marked by a solid square and from an elevation of 500 m. P: Peloponnese, AA: Aetolo-Akarnania, IZ: Zakynthos Island, IK: Kefalonia Island, IL: Lefkada Island (After Ferentinos et al. 2012).

The offshore and onshore geological data suggests that the study area is affected by compressional and extensional stresses[19] resulting in the formation of the Zakynthos, Kefalonia, and Lefkada basins, which cuts across the Kefalonia and Lefkada Islands. The seismic profiling data showed the presence of active and inactive faults with slip rates ranging between 1 to 5 mm/yr while the sedimentation rate in the basins was estimated between 1 to 3 mm/yr.

To investigate the possibility of insularity in the study area since the Palaeolithic, palaeogeographical evolution maps were made. The construction of these maps considered all possible scenarios of global sea level change, the current sea level and seabed bathymetry, the change in the tectonic regimes, and the change in sediment thickness over time.[20]

All examined cases concluded that Kefalonia and Zakynthos formed an island complex during the Middle Palaeolithic (Fig. 6) suggesting that seafaring activity in the southern Ionian Islands started some-time between 35,000 to 110,000 years ago. The short distances between the islands of the Ionian Sea at the time encouraged maritime movements (Fig. 7). Because of these dates, these geological findings suggest that the first voyagers who travelled to the Ionian Islands were Neanderthal hunter-gatherers. Additionally, based on the proposed palaeogeography of the Ionian Islands, the ability of Neanderthals to move by sea attributes new skills and new perceptions regarding their environmental management.[21]

Submerged port facilities case study: Shipsheds of Mounichia and Zea ancient harbours

Marine geophysical surveys at locations in the southern coastal zone of Attica have been conducted since 2006 in collaboration with the Danish Institute at Athens and the Ephorate of Underwater Antiquities of Greece at the ancient ports of Zea and Mounichia

19   Brooks & Ferentinos 1984; Kokkalas et al. 2006.
20   Ferentinos et al. 2012.

21   Ferentinos et al. 2012; 2014; Marshall 2012.

Fig. 7. Palaeo-shoreline reconstruction when the sea level was at -80 and -120 m, showing the most likely used short-range crossings to the islands from the Middle Palaeolithic to Mesolithic. P: Peloponnese, AA: Aetolo-Akarnania, IZ: Zakynthos Island, IK: Kefalonia Island, IL: Lefkada Island (After Ferentinos et al. 2012).

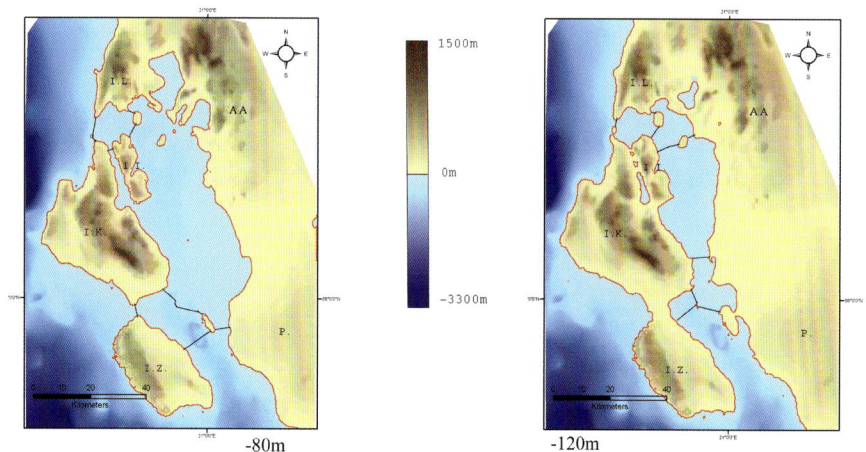

(or Mikrolimano). The analysis and processing of the collected marine geophysical data produced detailed maps for both the stratigraphy of the areas and the operational phases of the ancient ports, as well as their geomorphology. The seabed sonographs captured submerged sections of the ship sheds studied by Dr B. Lovén (Fig. 8).[22]

Additionally, the synthesis of the results provided information about the position of the ancient coastline inside Mounichia (Fig. 9). An area of higher reflectivity compared to the surrounding seafloor of the port probably represents the submerged (paleo-)shoreline. Similar information related to the position of the ancient shoreline and the submerged coastal installations was provided by the marine geological data collected nearby in Sounion and combined with the archaeological findings of the area.[23]

Submerged ancient port case study: Ancient Aegina harbour

The port facilities of ancient Aegina are frequently and extensively mentioned by ancient authors as elaborate and multifunctional. A detail remote sens-

ing survey was conducted in the wider area of the present-day port of Aegina, in the framework of "Aigina Harbour-City Project (2019-2023)" and "TECTONIC project" (TEchnological Consortium TO develop sustaiNabiIlity of underwater Cultural heritage, 2020-2025), a cooperation between the Ephorate of Underwater Antiquities of Greece, the French School of Athens and the Aix-Marseille University with the scientific support of six European partners.

The survey was designed and carried out by the Oceanus-Lab aiming to map the submerged remains of the famous ancient port. For the objectives of the study, the survey utilized: (i) an over-the-side ITER Systems BathySwath interferometric multibeam echo-sounder (MBES) which provides bathymetric and backscatter data of high resolution (up to 2 cm), (ii) a dual-frequency (100 & 400 kHz) side scan sonar (SSS) (EG&G 272TD) with an Edgetech 4200-P topside processor to acquire acoustic backscatter intensity, making it possible to assess the seafloor geomorphology and to detect and map targets of potential archaeological interest and (iii) a high resolution CHIRP type sub-bottom profiler system (SBP) to depict the acoustic stratigraphy of the seafloor with a maximum vertical resolution of 10 cm. To achieve high resolution and locational accuracy, the survey utilized: (i) a SMC IMU-108 motion sensor for the correction of the vessel movement (pitch,

---

22   Lovén 2011; Lovén & Schaldemose 2011.
23   Papatheodorou et al. 2014; Al-Hamdani et al. 2014.

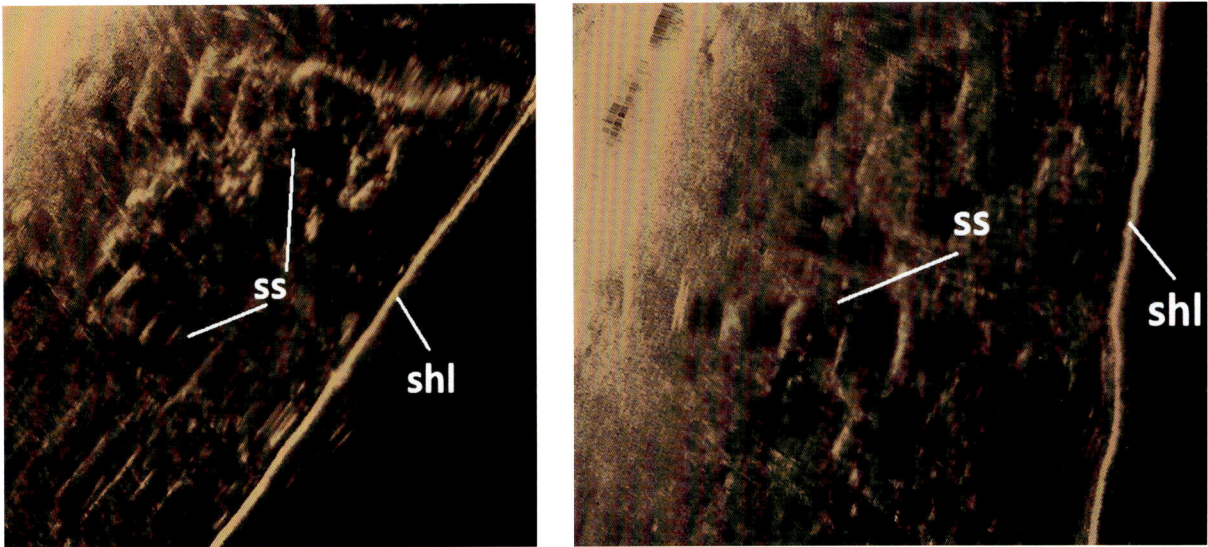

Fig. 8. Sonographs acquired in Zea Harbour showing submerged shipsheds (ss) (shl: shoreline) (Oceanus-Lab).

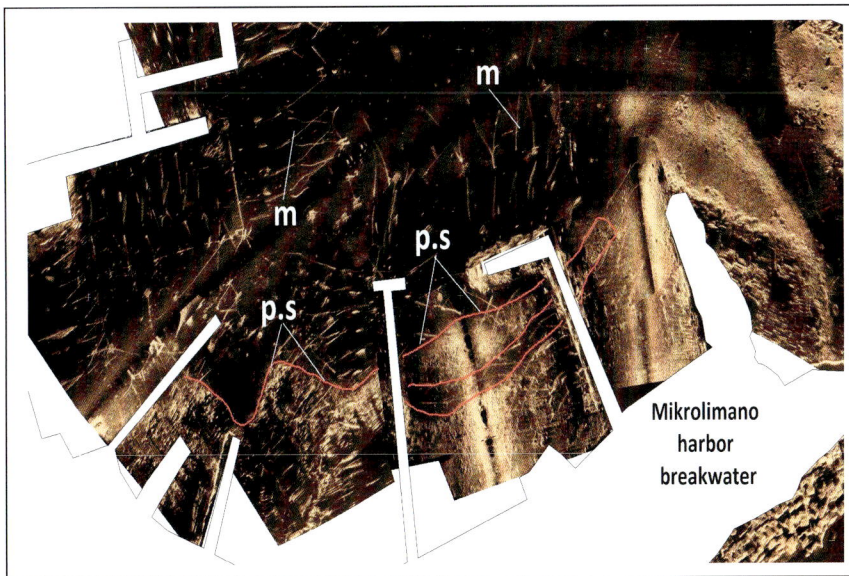

Fig. 9. Side scan sonar mosaic of the port of Mounichia showing part of the palaeo-shoreline (p.s) (m: moorings) (Oceanus-Lab).

roll, heave) with a resolution angle of 0.001° for pitch and roll and resolution heave of 1 cm, (ii) a Sound Velocity Profiler (SVP-Sea & Sun) to collect sound velocity profiles and use them as an input for the correction of the multibeam echo-sounder and (iii) a RTK GNSS positioning system that provided an accuracy of 10 mm.

In addition, a SubseaTech mini ROV was utilized for the optical inspection of regions of interest (R.o.I). The ROV was equipped with appropriately positioned cameras so that, with proper handling, it would be possible to capture high-quality video. The videos were processed using specialized software to produce photogrammetric images of the R.o.I.

59

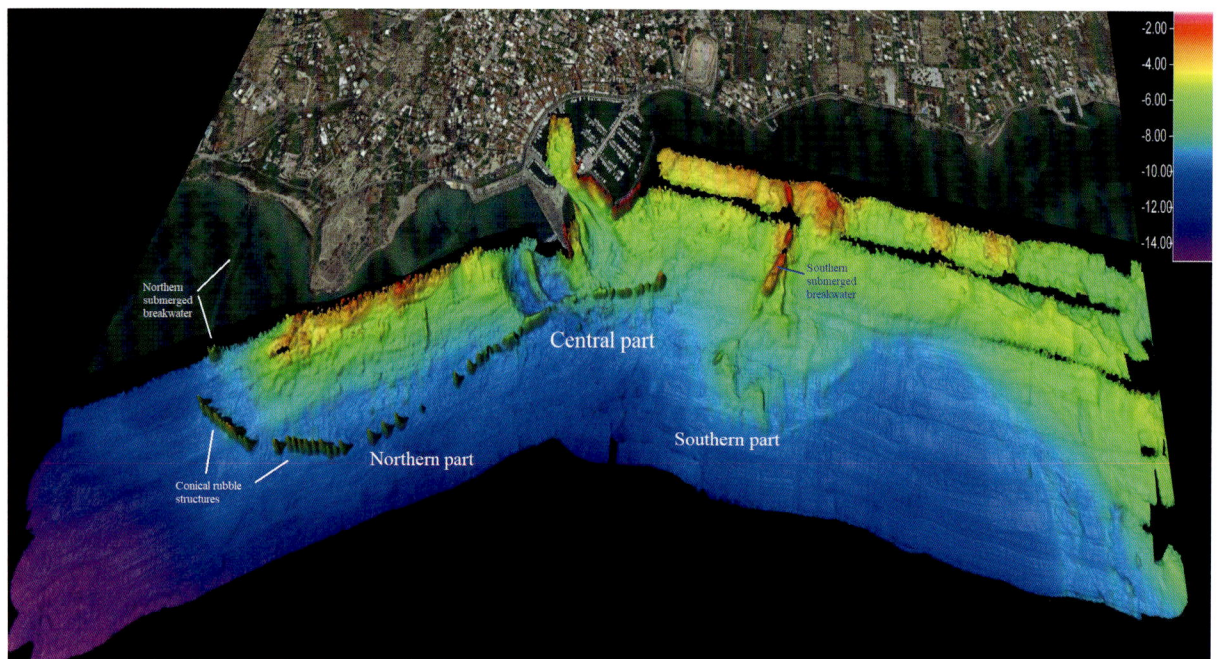

Fig. 10. Detail bathymetric map of the submerged ancient harbour of Aegina, based on multibeam data (Oceanus-Lab).

The marine remote sensing data showed that the submerged harbour can be separated in three different parts: (i) northern, (ii) central, and (iii) southern (Fig. 10).[24] The harbour is bounded, in the north, by a breakwater, which is an artificial submerged structure, linear, perpendicular to the coast, of at least 170 m in length. The southern end of the harbour is delimited by a 280 m long, E-W oriented curved breakwater with its concave facing the north. Undoubtedly, the most impressive feature of the ancient harbour is the series of submerged conical rubble structures (piles) that enclose it (Figs. 10, 11).[25] These piles were recorded in all acquired datasets providing valuable information regarding their spatial distribution, their shapes, and the seabed on which they were constructed. Each conical stone pile is made from stacked stones with curved surfaces (cobbles) carefully placed to ensure the durability and good preservation of the construction,

and indeed as it is proven today, lasting for thousands of years (Fig. 12).

The high-resolution bathymetric data acquired by multibeam echo-sounder and the photogrammetric data collected using ROV showed that these conical rubble structures consist of single or multiple conical piles. Sixty-seven percent of the piles' crests were found at a depth range of 3.6-4.1 m while the remainder ranged from 2.9-5 m. The height of most of the piles varied from 5.7-7.5 m while at the southern part they presented a minimum height of 3.6-4.1 m. The conical stone piles have been arranged in six clusters, leaving seven openings towards the ancient port facilities (Fig. 13).[26] The cluster of stone piles in front of the entrance to the modern harbour has suffered significant damage, likely during its construction or expansion in recent decades.

The stone piles are almost always placed at a water depth of about 10 or 11 m, with the six clusters arranged in a curve nearly parallel to the coastline.

24 Georgiou et al. 2021.
25 Georgiou et al. 2021.
26 Kalamara et al. 2023.

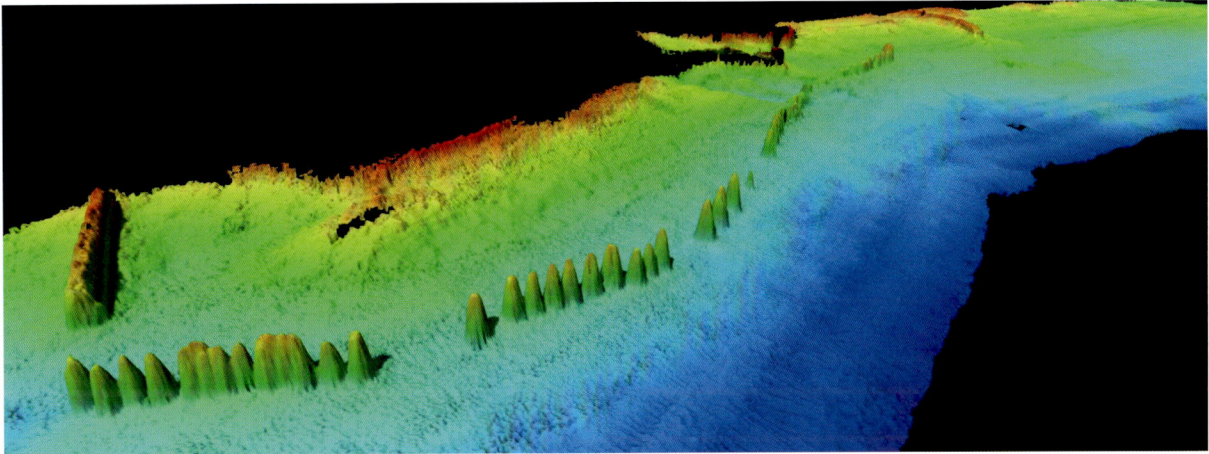

Fig. 11. 3D representation of a series of submerged conical rubble structures (piles) at the northern part of the sub-merged ancient harbour of Aegina, based on multibeam data (Oceanus-Lab).

Fig. 12. ROV photo showing the top of a conical pile consisting of stacked stones with curved surfaces (cobbles) (Oceanus-Lab).

Based on the estimated position of the ancient coastline, the series of conical piles was consistently 220 to 270 m away from it.

The good condition of the stone piles and their distribution in relation to the breakwaters indicate the abilities of ancient engineers and their knowledge of managing the marine environment. The importance of this offshore construction is highlighted by the following characteristics: (i) the average area covered by every single cone on average was 432 m² while in total an area of 35,000 m² is covered by the ancient structures and (ii) the average volume of each conical structure was estimated at 1,300 m³ while a rough estimation of 78,000 m³ total volume of construction material might have been used. Based on the most likely scenarios of sea level rise over the last 2,000 years, it is possible that the ancient port could

"re-emerge" in its ancient position and be system-atically studied for its functionality. In antiquity, the peaks of the conical stone piles would have almost touched the water surface, posing a hazard for ships. Pausanias mentions the difficulty of approaching the port of Aegina as dangerous reefs and skerries (rocks that barely protrude from the sea surface) had been constructed ('περί πάσαν καί χοιράδες άνεστήκασι').[27] The conical stone piles made access to the port difficult, playing their defensive role while possibly protecting the port facilities from storms. The palaeo-geographic reconstruction of the harbour will also allow the application of wave diffraction models to determine how these conical structures contributed to wave dissipation in antiquity.

---

27   Pausanias, *Ellados perigisis*, II.29.6.

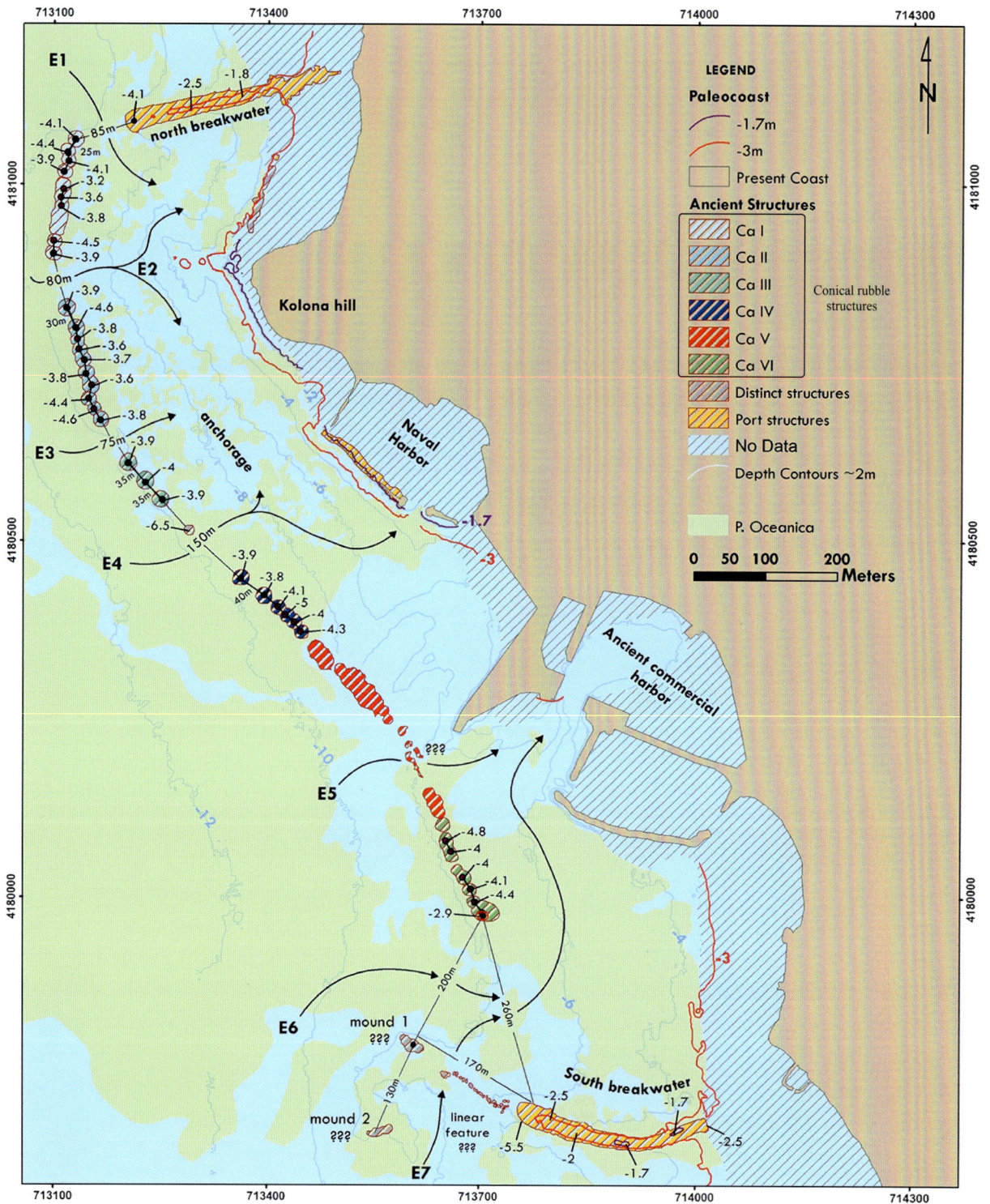

Fig. 13. Map showing the extent of the submerged structures (system of conical rubble piles) detected by the marine remote sensing survey and classification, the possible passages to the protected maritime area and their width, and the paleocoasts with depths of -3.8, -2.5, -1.7 m (purple, red, green) (Modified from Georgiou et al. 2021).

Detection and mapping of ancient and historic shipwrecks case study: Kefalonia Island, Ionian Sea

Shipwrecks appear in the bathymetric record as abrupt changes in the relief of the seafloor, in sonographs as features of certain geometry and higher backscatter intensity than the surrounding seafloor, and in the seismic profiling records as strong hyperbolic echoes. Although high resolution side scan sonar systems are considered as the most effective tools for wreck detection, integrated survey combining datasets from a wide range of acoustic systems (multibeam echo-sounders, side scan sonars, subbottom profilers, marine magnetometer) constitutes the most meaningful methodological approach for the detection and mapping of ancient and historic shipwrecks. The combination of multidisciplinary acoustic datasets is considered essential for the detection of unknown shipwrecks on the seafloor of Mediterranean Sea, since the acoustic anomalies produced by shipwrecks could mislead the researchers with other anomalies produced by common Mediterranean seafloor features and habitats such as rocky outcrops, coral formations, etc.

The systematic mapping of large areas of the coastal zone of Kefalonia Island, within the framework of the A.Pr.E.H. program (Interdisciplinary Aquaria for the promotion of Environment and History), led to the identification of significant cultural sites. These primarily include shipwrecks and remains of shipwrecks from World War II: (i) the British submarine HMS *Perseus*, (ii) the ship SS *Ardena*, and (iii) debris from an unknown shipwreck.[28]

The submarine HMS *Perseus* sank in the winter of 1941, south of Kefalonia Island, taking all sailors and officers to the bottom except for the stoker John Capes, who claimed to have escaped using a Davis escape apparatus. The shipwreck was record-

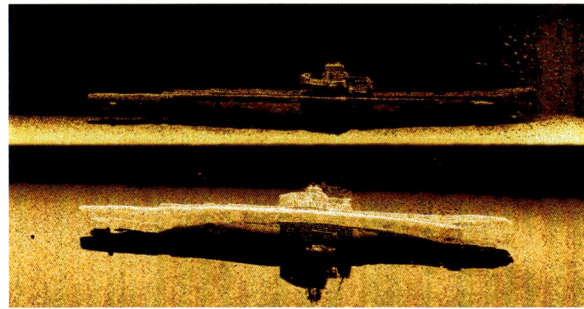

Fig. 14. Sonographs showing the HMS *Perseus* shipwreck (After Geraga et al. 2020).

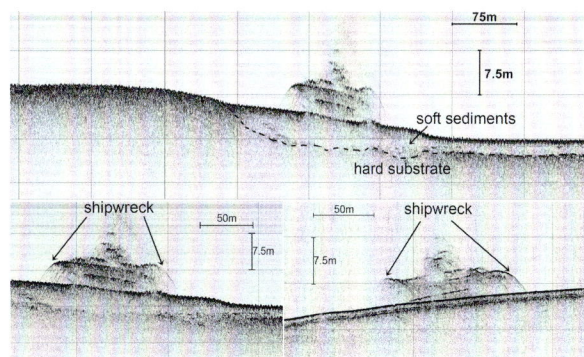

Fig. 15. High resolution seismic profiles showing the shipwreck of SS *Ardena* (hyperbolic echoes) resting on loose, sandy sediments (After Geraga et al. 2020).

ed clearly by all remote sensing systems. The wreck rests on a sandy seabed at a depth of 52 m, with an 18-degree inclination to starboard (Fig. 14).[29] The side scan sonar records showed that the shipwreck is intact without any debris field around it, with only a few unknown targets c. 10 m away. The high-resolution seismic profile shows the wreck rests on a thin layer of loose sandy sediments over a hard substrate, which ends about 75 m from the wreck site (Fig. 15). ROV ground truthing revealed extensive fishing nets covering the shipwreck.

The SS *Ardena* sank at the mouth of Argostoli Bay in September 1943, while transporting hundreds of Italian prisoners from the Italian "Acqui" division, most of who were dragged to the bottom. After the war, parts of the wreck were salvaged for metal recy-

28   Papatheodorou et al. 2013.

29   Geraga et al. 2020.

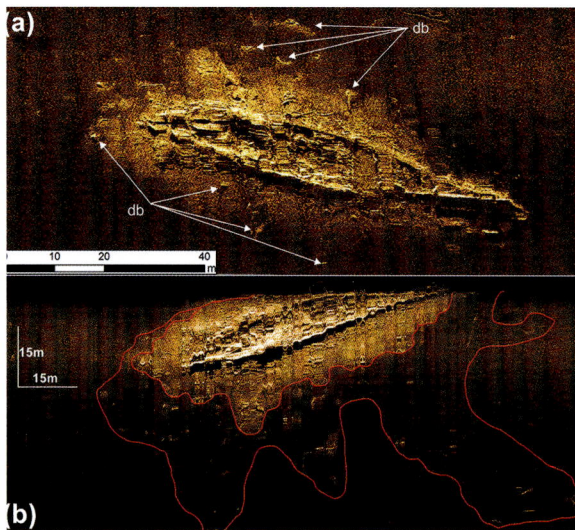

Fig. 16. Sonographs (a, b) showing the SS *Ardena* shipwreck (db: wreck debris, red lines show the debris field) (After Geraga et al. 2020).

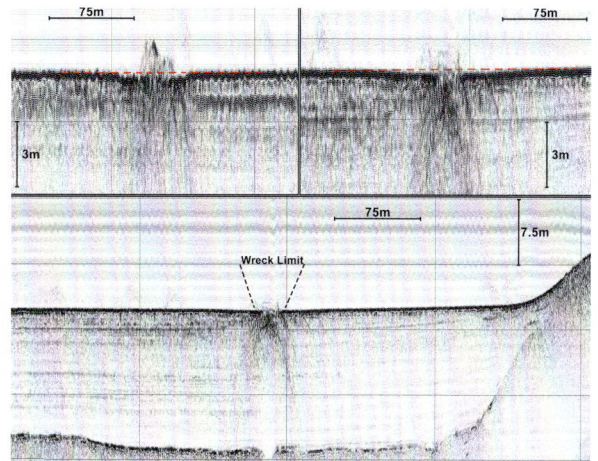

Fig. 17. High resolution seismic profiles showing cross section of the SS *Ardena* shipwreck (hyperbolic echoes) (After Geraga et al. 2020).

cling (scrap). Today, the wreck is located at a depth of c. 27 m. Side scan sonar revealed an extensive debris field around it, primarily lying alongside the wreck, extending up to 10 m on each side, with some debris scattered and average of 40 m away (Fig. 16). The low reflectivity of the sediments surrounding the wreck, combined with the acoustic properties from seismic profiles, suggests a seafloor composed of soft sediments, such as sandy to silty clay of about 15 m in thickness. The seismic profiles show that the keel has sunk into the soft sediments, and the shipwreck's extension above the seafloor is minimal, indicating significant deterioration (Fig. 17).

North of Fiskardo Bay, off Kefalonia Island and at a depth of 45 m, a large ancient shipwreck was discovered, containing a large concentration of Roman amphorae (Fig. 18). Based on high resolution sonographs, the shipwreck scatter is c. 30 m long, 12 m wide, and extends about 1.3 m above the surrounding seabed (Fig. 18). These dimensions make it one of the four largest shipwrecks in the Mediterranean Sea discovered so far, dating to from the period between the 1st century BC and the 1st century AD. The wreck is believed to be the same as that first dis-

covered during a research expedition conducted by the Ephorate of Underwater Antiquities of Greece in collaboration with a Norwegian research mission,[30] although researchers then reported different dimensions of the site (e.g. 25 m in length).

Based on seismic profiles, the concentration of amphorae appears to extend to a depth of about 2 m below the surface of the seabed, significantly increasing the estimated number of amphorae compared to initial calculations (Fig. 19a). Considering the dimensions of the ship and the amphorae, as well as the way they were stacked, an estimate of approximately 6,000 amphorae in the cargo cannot be ruled out. Additionally, the detailed marine remote survey provided information related to the conditions of the shipwreck and how it impacted the seabed (site formation processes).[31] The cargo of the shipwreck was divided into three parts, with the number of amphorae significantly decreasing from one part to the next (see Fig. 18). This seems to be the result of

---

30   Dellaporta et al. 2006.
31   Geraga et al. 2015; Ferentinos et al. 2020.

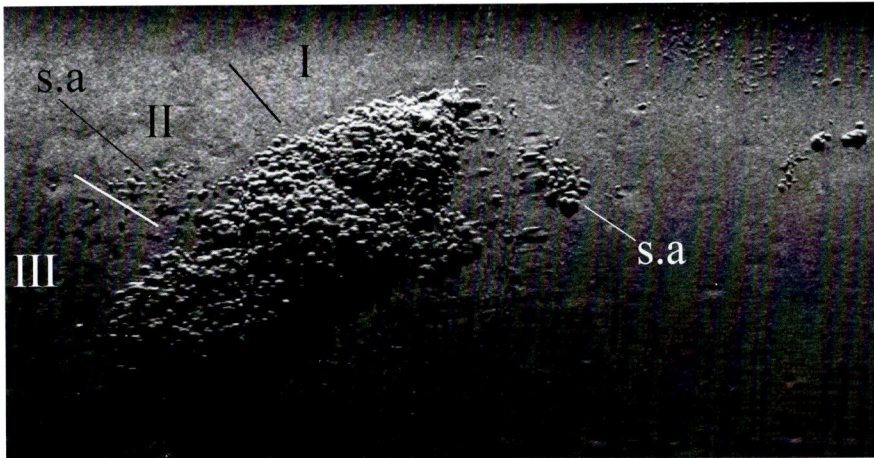

Fig. 18. High resolution sonograph showing the Fiskardo ancient shipwreck. The cargo (amphorae) of the ship has been divided into three parts (I, II, III) (s.a.: scattered amphoras) (Modified from Geraga et al. 2015).

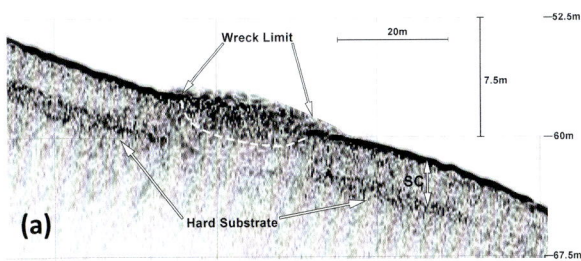

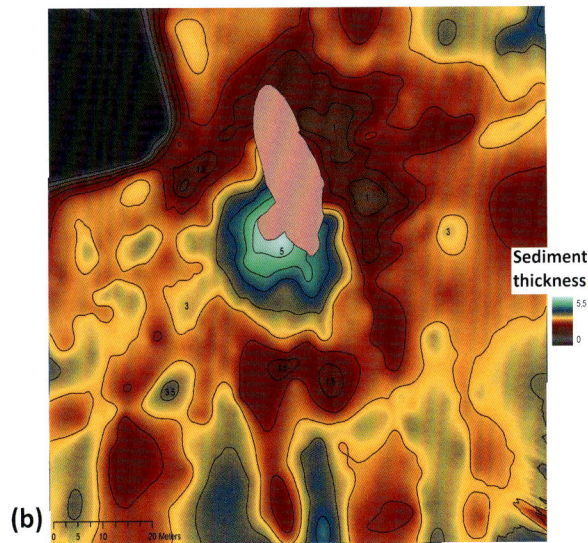

Fig. 19. (a) High resolution Chirp seismic profile acquired along the Fiskardo wreck site. The wreck site is represented by a chaotic acoustic pattern overlying an acoustically-transparent area and a high amplitude reflector (bedrock). (b) Map showing the thickness of the surface sediments above the bedrock around the shipwreck site (Modified from Geraga et al. 2015).

either the initial stacking method of the amphorae or the ship's collision with the seabed.

The scattered groups of amphorae next to the main bulk of the cargo is likely due to their fall during the violent impact of the ship with the seabed, the disintegration of the hull, or damage caused by the anchors of contemporary vessels (Fig. 18). Furthermore, seismic profiles showed variations in sediment thickness around the shipwreck, with significant sediment accumulation on the side of the wreck that is not exposed to currents, but not on the opposite side, where sediment accumulation was less due to continuous erosion (Fig. 19b). This indicates that the shipwreck acts as a low reef and causes modifications to the currents' flow patterns and consequently to the sediment deposition. Deep scars in the seabed, identified in the wider area by the side scan sonar, indicate that modern anchoring vessels pose a serious threat to the site's preservation and that an effective protection plan is required.

Maria Geraga & George Papatheodorou
Oceanus-Lab (Laboratory of Marine Geology and Physical Oceanography)
Department of Geology, University of Patras, Greece
m.geraga@upatras.gr
gpapathe@upatras.gr

Bibliography

AL-HAMDANI, Z., M. GERAGA, D. GREGORY, J. WUNDERLICH, G. PAPATHEODOROU, J. B. JENSEN, G. PANTOPOULOS, M. IATROU, D. CHRISTODOULOU, E. FAKIRIS, D. ZOURA, K. BAIKA, C. LIAPAKIS & V. BALIS 2014
'Design plan for surveying and monitoring coastal and underwater archaeological sites: A branch of the SASMAP project. EuroMed 2014', in *Digital Heritage: Progress in Cultural Heritage Documentation, Preservation and Protection*, M. Ioannides, E. Fink, A. Moropoulou, M. Hagedorn-Saupe, A. Fresa, G. Liestøl, V. Rajcic & P. Grussenmeyer (eds), Berlin, 547-56.

BROOKS, M. & G. FERENTINOS 1984
'Tectonics and sedimentation in the Corinth Gulf and the Zakynthos and Kefallinia Channels, Western Greece', *Tectonophysics* 101, 25-54.

BRUNO, F., M. RICCA, A. LAGUDI, P. KALAMARA, A. MANGLIS, A. FOURKIOTOU, D. PAPADOPOULOU & A. VENETI 2020
'Digital Technologies for the Sustainable Development of the Accessible Underwater Cultural Heritage Sites', *Journal of Marine Science and Engineering* 8, 955.

CALANTROPIO, A. & F. CHIABRANDO 2024
'Underwater Cultural Heritage Documentation Using Photogrammetry', *Journal of Marine Science and Engineering* 12, 413.

CHALARI, A., D. CHRISTODOULOU, G. PAPATHEODOROU, M. GERAGA, A. STEFATOS & G. FERENTINOS 2008
'Use of remote sensing and GIS in the reconstruction of coastal palaeogeography of Alexandria, Egypt', in *Proceedings of the 4th Symposium of the Hellenic Society for Archaeometry* (BAR International Series 1746), Y. Facorellis, N. Zacharias & K. Polıkreti (eds), Athens, 119-28.

CHALARI, A., G. PAPATHEODOROU, E. FAKIRIS, D. CHRISTODOULOU, M. GERAGA & G. FERENTINOS 2006
'A methodological scheme for the classification of side scan sonar targets with potential archaeological significance: A case study in the coastal zone of Alexandria', *8th Panhellenic Symposium of Oceanography and Fisheries, Thessaloniki*, Abstract Book, 134.

CHALARI, A., G. PAPATHEODOROU, M. GERAGA, D. CHRISTODOULOU & G. FERENTINOS 2009
'A marine geophysical survey illustrates Alexandria's Hellenistic past', *Zeitschrift fur Geomorphologie* 53, 191-212.

DELLAPORTA, K., M. E. JASISNSKI & F. SOREIDE 2006
'The Greek-Norwegian Deep-Water Archaeological Survey', *The International Journal of Nautical Archaeology* 35:1, 79-87.

EMPEREUR, J.-Y. 1998
Alexandria Rediscovered, New York.

EMPEREUR, J.-Y. 2000
'Underwater archaeological investigations of the ancient Pharos', in *Coastal management sourcebooks 2*, M. H. Mostafa, N. Grimal & D. Nakashima (eds), Paris, 54-9.

FERENTINOS, G., E. FAKIRIS, D. CHRISTODOULOU, M. GERAGA, X. DIMAS, N. GEORGIOU, S. KORDELLA, G. PAPATHEODOROU, M. PREVENIOS & M. SOTIROPOULOS 2020
'Optimal sidescan sonar and sub-bottom profiler surveying of ancient wrecks: The 'Fiskardo' wreck, Kefallinia Island, Ionian Sea', *Journal of Archaeological Science* 113, 105032.

FERENTINOS, G., M. GKIONI, M. GERAGA & G. PAPATHEODOROU 2012
'Early seafaring activity in the Southern Ionian Islands, Mediterranean Sea', *Journal of Archaeological Science* 39:7, 2167-76.

FERENTINOS, G., V. LYKOUSIS, G. PAPATHEO-DOROU & M. IATROU 2014
'Hellenic Shelf: Late Quaternary tectonics, Sea-level changes, sedimentation and Geo-hazzards', in *Continental Shelves of the World: Their Evolution during the Last Glacio-Eustatic Cycle*, F. L. Chiocci & A. R. Chivas (eds), London, 187-97.

EL FISHAWI, N. M. & A. M. FANOS 1989
'Prediction of sea level rise by 2100, Nile delta coast', *INQUA, Commission on Quaternary Shorelines, Newsletter* 11, 43-7.

FRIHY, O. E. 1992
'Sea-level rise and shoreline retreat of the Nile delta promontories, Egypt', *Natural Hazards* 5, 65-81.

FRIHY, O. E. 2003
'The Nile delta-Alexandria coast: vulnerability to Sea-level rise, consequences and adaptation', *Mitigation and Adaptation Strategies for Global Change* 8, 115-38.

GALANIDOU, N., C. PAPOULIA & G. ILIOPOULOS 2016
'The Palaeolithic settlement of Lefkas Archaeological evidence in a palaeogeographic context', *Journal of Greek Archaeology* 1, 1-32.

GEORGIOU, N., X. DIMAS, E. FAKIRIS, D. CHRISTODOULOU, M. GERAGA, D. KOUTSOUMPA, K. BAIKA, P. KALAMARA, G. FERENTINOS & G. PAPATHEODOROU 2021
'A multidisciplinary approach for the mapping, automatic detection and morphometric analysis of ancient submerged coastal Installations: the case study of the ancient Aegina harbour complex', *Remote Sensing* 13, 4462.

GERAGA, M., D. CHRISTODOULOU, ELEFTHE-RAKIS, G. PAPATHEODOROU, E. FAKIRIS, X. DIMAS, N. GEORGIOU, S. KORDELLA, M. PREVENIOS, M. IATROU, D. ZOURA, S. KEKEBANOU, M. SOTIROPOULOS & G. FERENTINOS 2020
'Atlas of shipwrecks in inner Ionian Sea (Greece): a remote sensing approach', *Heritage* 3, 1210-36.

GERAGA, M., E. KATSOU, D. CHRISTODOULOU, M. IATROU, S. KORDELLA, G. PAPATHEODOR-OU, V. MENTOGIANNIS & K. KOUVAS 2014
'Mapping natural and cultural marine heritage sites in Leros island, Greece', *Rapport Commission International de la Mer Méditeranée* 40, 847.

GERAGA, M., G. PAPATHEODOROU, C. AGOUR-IDIS, H. KABERI, M. IATROU, D. CHRISTODOU-LOU, E. FAKIRIS, M. PREVENIOS, S. KORDELLA, & G. FERENTINOS 2017
'Palaeoenvironmental implications of a marine geoarchaeological survey conducted in the SW Argosaronic gulf, Greece', *Journal of Archaeological Science: Reports* 12, 805-18.

GERAGA, M., G. PAPATHEODOROU, G. FEREN-TINOS, E. FAKIRIS, D. CHRISTODOULOU, N. GEORGIOU, X. DIMAS, M. IATROU, S. KORDEL-LA, M. SOTIROPOULOS, V. MENTOGIANNIS & K. DELAPORTA 2015
'The study of an ancient shipwreck using remote sensing techniques, in Kefalonia Island (Ionian Sea)', *Archaeologia Maritima Mediterranea* 12, 181-98.

JONDET, M. G. 1916
Les ports submergés de l'ancienne île de Pharos (Mémoires présentés à l'Institut Égyptien et publiés sous les auspices de Sa Hautesse Hussein Kamel, Sultan d'Égypte, Tome IX, Cairo.

67

KALAMARA, P., K. BAIKA & D. KOUTSOUMPA 2023
'What new facts come to light (ancient port of Aegina)', *Aeginaia* 32, 33-54.

KOKKALAS, S., P. XYPOLIAS, I. KOUKOUVELAS & T. DOUTSOS 2006
'Post-collisional contractional and extensional deformation in the Aegean region', in *Post-collisional Tectonics and Magmatism in the Eastern Mediterranean Region* (Geological Society of America, Special Papers 409), Y. Dilek & S. Pavlides (eds), Boulder, CO, 97-123.

LAMBECK, K. 1996
'Sea-level change and shoreline evolution in Aegean Greece since Upper Palaeolithic time', *Antiquity* 70, 588-610.

LOVÉN, B. 2011
The Ancient Harbours of the Piraeus, Volume I.1 – *The Zea Shipsheds and Slipways: Architecture and Topography* (Monographs of the Danish Institute at Athens, 15.1), Aarhus.

LOVÉN, B. & M. SCHALDEMOSE 2011
The Ancient Harbours of the Piraeus, Volume I.2 – *The Zea Shipsheds and Slipways: Finds, Area 1 Shipshed Roof Reconstructions and Feature Catalogue* (Monographs of the Danish Institute at Athens, 15.2), Aarhus.

MARSHALL, M. 2012
'Neanderthals were ancient mariners', *New Scientist,* 2854.

PAPATHEODOROU, G., M. GERAGA, A. CHALARI, D. CHRISTODOULOU, M. IATROU, E. FAKIRIS, S. KORDELLA, M. PREVENIOS & G. FERENTINOS 2011
'Remote sensing for underwater archaeology: Case studies from Greece and Eastern Mediterranean Sea', *Bulletin of the Geological Society of Greece* 44, 100-15.

PAPATHEODOROU, G., M. GERAGA, A. CHALARI, D. CHRISTODOULOU, M. IATROU & G. FERENTINOS 2015
'Hellenistic Alexandria: A palaeogeographic reconstruction based on marine geophysical data', in *Alexandria under the Mediterranean, Archaeological studies in memory of Honor Frost* (Etudes Alexandrines 36), G. Soukiassian (ed.), Alexandria, 27-62.

PAPATHEODOROU, G., M. GERAGA, D. CHRISTODOULOU, E. FAKIRIS, M. IATROU, N. GEORGIOU, X. DIMAS & G. FERENTINOS 2021
'The Battle of Lepanto Search and Survey Mission (1971-1972) by Throckmorton, Edgerton and Yalouris: Following Their Traces Half a Century Later Using Marine Geophysics', *Remote Sensing* 13:16, 3292.

PAPATHEODOROU, G., M. GERAGA, D. CHRISTODOULOU, M. IATROU, E. FAKIRIS, S. HEATH & K. BAIKA 2014
'A marine geoarchaeological survey, Cape Sounion, Greece. Preliminary results', *Mediterranean Archaeology and Archaeometry* 1, 357-77.

PAPATHEODOROU, G., M. GERAGA, D. CHRISTODOULOU, M. IATROU & V. MENTOGIANNIS 2013
'Marine geophysical survey for the mapping, protection and management of the marine cultural heritage around Kefallinia Island (Greece) and Santa Maria al Bagno (Italy)', *International Conference A.Pr.E.H "Interdisciplinary Aquaria for the promotion of Environment and History", Kefalonia, 2-4 July 2013*, Abstract Book, 26-8.

PAPATHEODOROU, G., M. GERAGA & G. FERENTINOS 2005
'The Navarino Naval Battle site, Greece – an integrated remote sensing survey and a rational management approach', *International Journal of Nautical Archaeology* 34:1, 95-109.

STANLEY, D. J. 1988
'Subsidence in the northeastern Nile delta: rapid rates, possible causes and consequences', *Science* 240, 497-500.

Tree-ring Science for Maritime Archaeology:

What Timber in Ships Can Tell Us

Aoife Daly

Abstract

Dendrochronology – analysis of the tree rings – of ships' timbers reveals not only the precise date of the ship. As the pattern of tree growth is particular to the region in which the tree grew, dendrochronology is also a powerful tool in identifying the origin of timber found at a wreckage. As timber was increasingly a traded commodity, and as ships large enough to carry this bulk product were built, ships often were built of timber from several sources. Therefore, we must analyse extensively to unravel the often-complicated story from the ship's timbers. This has allowed a detailed timeline of the changes in timber usage, exploitation, and quality across Northern Europe, from coastal traders to ocean-going ships that traversed the globe. In this paper, using a selection of case studies, I will present this narrative.

Introduction[1]

Throughout more than a century of archaeological investigation, numerous findings of shipwrecks represent an enormous research resource. In Northern Europe, the preservation of the organic parts of these vessels allows us to study the changes, over time, of building traditions and technology that past people used and developed. While study of the ways in which timber was shaped and joined to build these complex structures gives us detailed insight into the building process, study of the wood and timber, as a

raw material, brings us insight into the exploitation of this resource, through time and geography.

One of the most utilized scientific techniques in studying preserved timber remains from our archaeological record is the technique of dendrochronology. The core of this discipline is to record the annual variation of the tree's growth by measuring the tree rings in each timber. The pattern of wide and narrow rings is formed as the tree grows, and trees from the same region, growing at the same time, display very similar growth patterns. Through analysis of thousands of timbers from forests, historical buildings, and archaeological sites in a region, and finding how each of the timbers match each other, a record of tree-ring growth for a region, a master chronology, is built (Fig. 1). When we then analyse timbers from a shipwreck, we can test its tree-ring pattern against these regional chronologies, to identify, to annual precision, when the tree used to build the ship grew. Furthermore, once the dating of the

1   Acknowledgements: I wish to thank all the archaeologists, researchers and curators who have allowed me to analyse the wooden structures that they have discovered, excavated and researched, over my many decades as a dendroarchaeologist. Furthermore, I wish to thank those dendrochronology colleagues that have shared their tree-ring data to allow our discipline to grow and thrive, and to be secured for future generations.

Dendrochronology

ILLUSTRATION: **HENRIK KIÆR** © AOIFE DALY & HENRIK KIÆR 2021

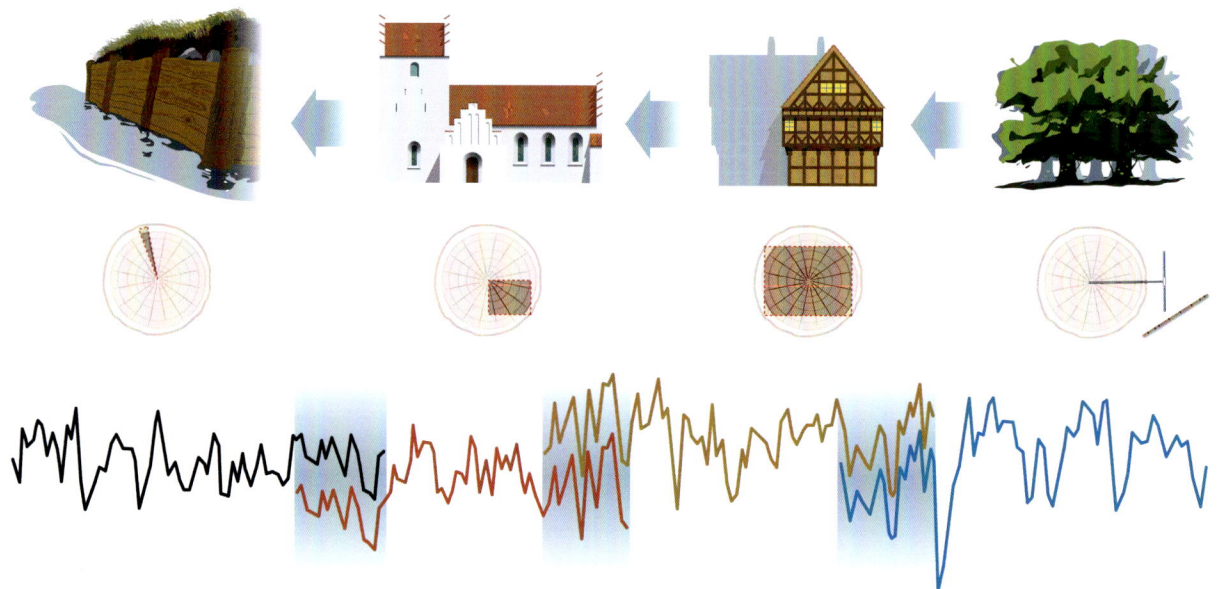

Fig. 1. The technique of building a dendrochronological master chronology. The growth variation of the tree can be seen in the pattern of wide and narrow rings. To build a master tree-ring chronology we must take samples from living trees, historic buildings and from timber structures preserved under water or under ground. The tree-ring widths from inner to outer in a long uninterrupted series are measured on each sample. These long tree growth patterns are matched together and once the chronological connections between all these are found, the dataset is finally averaged to a master chronology, which is a record of annual tree growth over time for a region (Illustration: Henrik Kiær).

timber is found, we can also identify the region of origin of that timber, by examining which regional chronologies the timbers' tree-ring pattern fits best. That trees preserve a mathematical code into their past growth is a fascinating phenomenon that we can exploit when researching the material remains from our human past.

Dendrochronology of numerous shipwrecks provides the discipline of maritime archaeology with the strict chronological framework in which we can study these remains, but the identification of the place where the trees grew can point us also to the place where a ship was built. This is a way more complicated aspect of the study of timber, however,

because, as the growth of some economies exerted pressure on the local timber supply, increasingly timber had to be brought in from regions with surplus. So as the science of dendrochronology has developed over the last several decades, the complicated question of the exploitation of the timber resource for shipbuilding has become exceedingly nuanced. We might categorize this narrative as a timeline, where the timber supply story in Northern Europe develops and evolves, and where economic growth and resource exploitation attains a shifting geography. Let us look at a few case studies to illustrate this story.

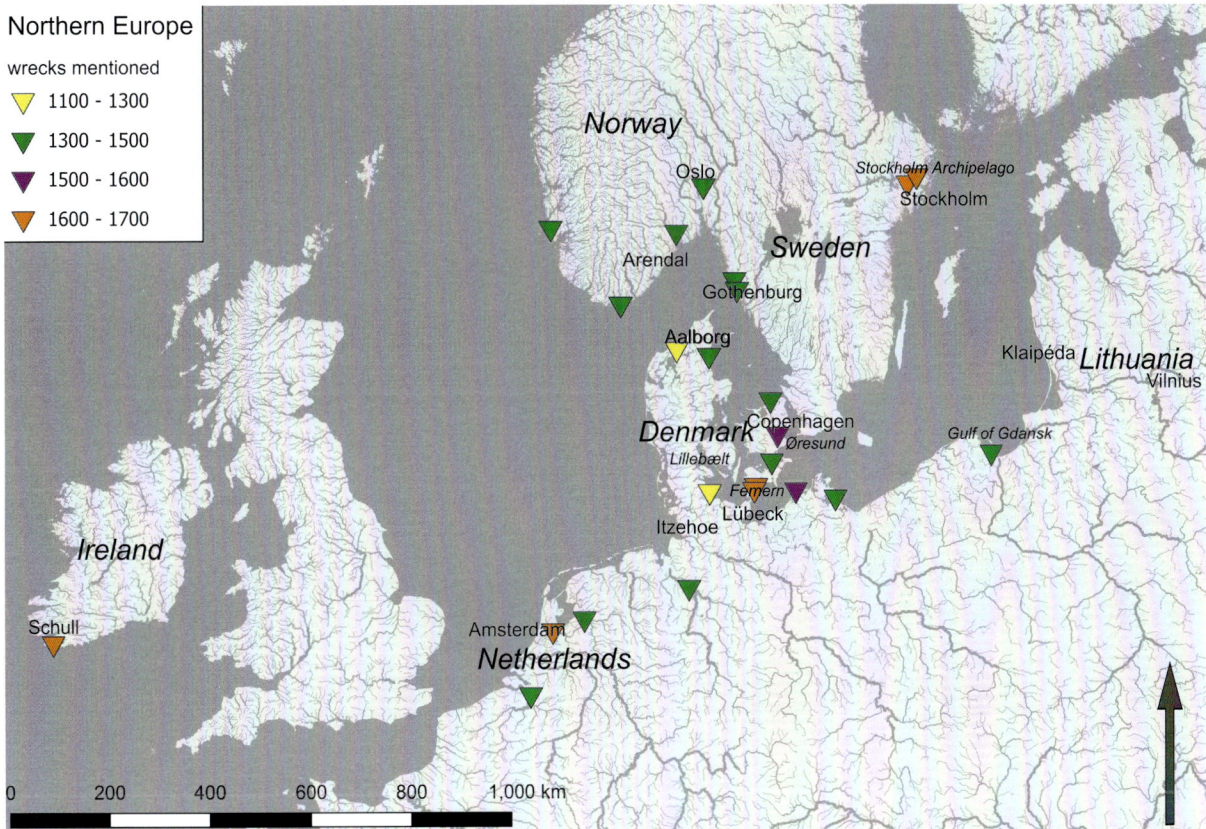

Fig. 2. Map of Northern Europe with the regions and towns mentioned in the text. The shipwreck locations mentioned are also marked and coloured according to their dating. The background map is from the Global Administrative Areas project (gadm.org: https://geodata.ucdavis.edu/gadm/gadm4.1/work/, Downloaded January, 2023). The river data is from Lehner & Grill 2013: www.hydrosheds.org, Accessed March, 2020). The map is generated using QGIS.org, 2021. QGIS Geographic Information System. QGIS Association. http://www.qgis.org (Illustration: Aoife Daly).

High medieval period, c. 1100-1300 AD

Beginning our narrative in the high medieval period, in terms of timber for shipbuilding, the dendrochronological evidence comes from a period of transition, where the Nordic ship-type is gradually replaced by new ship-building traditions, particularly with the appearance of the "Bremen Type", often referred to as a "Cog". The Karschau ship, found in the Schlei – the channel of water that connects Hedeby to the North Sea (Fig. 2) – is dendrochronologically dated to c. 1145 AD, and it was built in the Nordic

tradition.[2] The tree-ring patterns from the 17 dated timbers from the Karschau find are very similar to each other, demonstrating that the ship is built with trees from the same source.[3] This suggests that the ship was built near where the trees were felled, and the dendrochronology (Fig. 3) suggests that the trees grew on the island of Funen in Denmark, on the eastern side of the Lillebælt Sound.[4]

---

2   Englert 2015.
3   Daly 2007a.
4   Daly 2007a.

Fig. 3. Anton Englert carefully saws a plank from the Karschau ship for dendrochronological analysis (Photo: Aoife Daly).

But a new building style was beginning to be adopted in Northern Europe at the same time. A ship form that is constructed with abutting planks in the lower hull strakes, and with an angled transition from keel to stem and stern posts, has been named the Cog, referring to historic sources that use this term.[5] The ship can also be termed the Bremen Type, as the many common building features were described archaeologically from this find, which is dendrochronologically dated to 1378 AD. The angled sternpost allows for the fixing of an aft-placed rudder, which is also a technological transition away from the side rudder that was used in the ships of "Nordic Type". The oldest example of this building tradition identified archaeologically was found at Kollerup, in northern Jutland (Denmark).[6] It is dendrochronologically dated to c. 1150 AD, in other words, by and large at the same time as when the Karschau ship was built.[7] The oak for this new ship type had grown in southern Jutland, matching best with medieval timber structures from the town of Haderslev which lies of the western side of the Lillebælt Sound (Fig. 2).

A ship of the Bremen Type, the Doel 1, found in Belgium, dates to 1325/26 AD.[8] This ship was built of oaks from the lands around the Weser River and although it is a half-century older than the Bremen ship, the tree-ring data from these two cross-match with significant correlation, suggesting that these were built with oaks from the same region.[9]

These are just three examples to illustrate this period, in terms of the dendrochronological evidence. The homogeneity of the timbers used for each ship, and the tree-ring evidence from terrestrial structures from the period, indicates that the transport of bulk building timber is the exception. Ship builders are using the resources locally available, and the traditions in use are probably based on local boat-building knowledge. Even as shipbuilding technology changes, it is causing little impact in the timber resources needed for boat building.

A century of transition, c. 1330 to 1500s AD

From around the mid-14th century AD, we begin to see the appearance of Baltic oak in western Europe. It is a phenomenon that increases over this period that I have called a century of transition, and the Baltic oak comes to dominate the Northern European overseas timber supply for several centuries. In this period, we see several ships built exclusively of Baltic oak. These include the medieval shipwrecks from Norway: Avaldsnes in west Norway,[10] the Bøle wreck (trees felled c. 1376-96 AD, dendroprovenance around the Gulf of Gdansk) that was carrying whetstones from Telemark, southern Norway (Fig. 4)[11] and the Skjernøysund

---

5   e.g. Crumlin-Pedersen 2000.
6   Kohrtz Andersen 1983.
7   Daly 2007b; 2015.

8   Haneca & Daly 2014.
9   See below and Belasus & Daly 2022.
10   Alopaeus & Elvestad 2006; Daly 2007b.
11   Daly & Nymoen 2007.

Fig. 4. Pål Nymoen of the Norwegian Maritime Museum sampling the keel of the Bøle wreck in Norway, by boring a core from the timber. Note the tree rings visible on the end of the timber (Photo: Aoife Daly).

3 wreck[12] (winter 1389-90 AD, oak provenance coastal current-day Poland) from southern Norway which included timber planks, of the same provenance as the ship timbers, in its cargo.[13] From Sweden the Skaftö wreck (late 1430s AD) is also of Baltic oak (provenance present-day Poland),[14] and it contained metal ingots, lime, tar, timber planks as well as bricks and roof tiles.[15] From Denmark the Vejby wreck is another example of a ship of the Bremen Type also of Baltic oak, more specifically from coastal current-day Poland.[16] From the Gulf of Gdansk, the so-called Copper Wreck also belongs in this period. It contained a large cargo of oak planks of various dimensions, clearly illustrating that this product was destined for a foreign market.[17]

Common to these wrecks, in terms of the dendrochronology, is that both framing and planking from these ships are of Baltic oak, and where a precise provenance is indicated, these are all from trees that grew in coastal current-day Poland.

When we see Baltic oak in western Europe in the built heritage it is almost exclusively in the form of planking, boards, and wainscots – not as bulk timber. The dendrochronological evidence strongly indicates that the product that began to be shipped from the east was already converted into planks and boards at the source, before loading onto ships for transport to the markets in the west. Thus, the ships mentioned above, that are all built with southern Baltic oak, probably represent ships built in Gdansk, which at the time was a thriving trading port under the control of the Teutonic Knights. These ships then took part in the trade of wood, and of course other products, across the growing western and Scandinavian economies of the time.

There are also boats and ships from this period of transition that were built using a mix of Baltic wood and wood from other sources. One of the boats found during excavations in Oslo, the so-called Barcode 17,[18] was built in the 1350s AD with a mixture of oak and pine planking. The dendrochronology shows that this boat was built from trees from several sources. Two oak planks are from around the Gulf of Gdansk while the pine planks are from Scandinavia.[19] In Denmark, a boat found in the moat

12   Auer & Maarleveld 2013.
13   Daly 2011b; 2020a.
14   Linderson 2004.
15   Von Arbin et al. 2022.
16   Bonde & Jensen 1995; Daly 2007b.
17   Ossowski 2014a; 2014b.

18   Wickler & Falck 2020.
19   Daly 2016.

around Vordingborg castle is also built with Baltic planking, felled c. 1355-1366 AD around the Gulf of Gdansk.[20] These examples appear to be very early evidence for the shipping of planking from Gdansk to western Europe, to be used as planking for boat building.

From this period of transition there are a couple of ships that tell us a very different story, in terms of the timber supply. A ship of the Bremen Type, found on the western Swedish coast north of Gothenburg at Mollö, dates to around 1365 AD. This is built of oak that grew in southern Scandinavia, in that the material cross-matches master and site chronologies from sites in Denmark.[21] At the time of sampling, it was noticed that many of the timbers had large knots in their growth. This was not specifically quantified, however, but observations of the same thing on another Bremen Type ship, the Bremen Ship itself, led the author to wonder about this phenomenon. The dendrochronological analysis of the Bremen ship demonstrated that oaks local to the town of Bremen were used for her construction.[22] The presence of large knots in the wood used for the planking indicate that the trees used had large side branches, that would indicate trees that had grown in an open landscape, where they had little competition for light.[23] Does the evidence from these two Bremen Type ships demonstrate that shortage of trees for planking was a catalyst for the growth in the trade of long straight-grained oak boards and planks from the densely forested regions in the southern and eastern Baltic?

From around 1400 AD the appearance of ships that, through dendrochronological analysis, are shown to have been built of a mixture of oaks from Baltic and other sources herald the emergence of this new practice. Found in the Netherlands, the IJsselkogge,[24] yet another example of the Bremen Type, is built with oaks and even some pine planks from a range of sources in the Baltic region while the framing timbers are oaks from Westfalia.[25] A similar pattern is seen in around 1420 AD, in the case of a clinker-built vessel found at Peenemündung Ostsee VII, Fpl 105.[26] For this ship, Baltic timber is utilised for planking while the framing is from southern Scandinavia.[27]

A clinker vessel from Denmark, found at Vejdyb, illustrates a similar wood procurement story, dating to around 1465-75 AD.[28] The planks from this wreck enable a date for the ship to be identified, and the provenance of these is Baltic, but this time a more eastern provenance is suggested, in that these planks are correlating best with a group of tree-ring datasets that are called "Baltic 1" which is a dataset based on analysis of panel paintings, and the oak of these seem to come from coastal Lithuania.[29] There are two strands of evidence to suggest that this boat was not built in the eastern Baltic. Three frames from the Vejdyb ship were also analysed, and these could not be dated. They were from very fast-grown trees, with average ring widths at around 4 mm, and they thus each contained less than 50 tree rings. Furthermore, the clinker planks were joined using a combination of iron nails and wooden dowels.[30] This fastening method has been observed in a handful of ships found in the Netherlands, all dating to the first few decades of the 16th century AD.[31] The Vejdyb find is thus very probably a Dutch-built ship, where framing timbers are acquired locally, while the planking is imported from the eastern Baltic. It illustrates the pattern that the

---

20   Daly et al. 2021b.
21   Von Arbin & Daly 2012.
22   Daly 2017; Belasus & Daly 2022.
23   Belasus & Daly 2022.
24   Waldus et al. 2019.
25   Domínguez-Delmás et al. 2017.
26   Dalicsek et al. 2018.
27   Daly 2019.
28   Daly 1997.
29   Daly & Tyers 2022.
30   Bill 1997.
31   Overmeer 2007.

long, straight grained oaks from the Baltic region are valued as raw material for planking, while the gnarly fast-growing oaks of the open landscape are more than suitable for the frames. This case also illustrates the importance of accounting for all the wood in a shipwreck, when selecting the long-lived timbers for dendrochronology. Because dendrochronology needs generally more than 100 rings in a sample, to be able to find the correct dating of its tree-ring pattern, there is a real danger that bias is introduced into the corpus of material, already at the sampling phase of any tree-ring research.

Growing economies and abundant evidence c. 1500 to 1600 AD

The frequency of ship finds dating to 1500 AD onwards allows study of the growing diversity of details in ship-building technology and to relate this to the evidence from determining the origin of the timbers used. It is in this period that ships built using the carvel technique appear in Northern Europe, but as the precise dating of many wrecks has shown, the clinker tradition continues to thrive in places, and we also see wrecks where both clinker and carvel layers are combined.[32]

In terms of the timber supply for this period, there are several wrecks that allow a detailed analysis of the timber source because of extensive dendrochronological sampling. Numerous relatively small clinker-built ships from Oslo Harbour attest to the continued use of the clinker boat-building tradition. The oaks from these ships grew in southern Norway, around Oslo Fjord, or in western Sweden, and often the internal correlation (the cross-match between each timber with each other) demonstrates a homogeneous source for the timber for each ship. Some of these small ships probably represent coastal

Fig. 5. The Køge 2 wreck, during excavation by Museum Sydøstdanmark (Museum of Southeast Denmark), in 2018 (Photo: Aoife Daly).

vessels, built in different ports along the coast of the region, and small enough to be able to sail all the way into Oslo Harbour. The oaks used in these ships are predominantly slow-growing, long-lived trees, and dendrochronologically we can link the exploitation of the resource in the region also to the export of this material. For example, oaks felled in winter 1532-33 AD and in spring/summer 1558 AD that were used to build two waterfronts excavated in Copenhagen in Denmark, also come from western Sweden (at this time under the Danish Crown), attesting to the surplus of timber from the region and to the transport of large amounts of bulky, squared timber being carried as ship cargo in the 16th century AD.[33]

A wreck found in Denmark in 2018, in Køge, just south of Copenhagen, illustrates a quite different timber supply for this century (Fig. 5). Archaeologically, this clinker ship displayed features that suggested a Dutch-built ship. The clinker planks were joined to each other with a mixture of iron nails and wooden dowels. In other words, the ship is built using similar construction details as the Vejdyb, mentioned above. Extensive dendrochronological analysis of the timbers of this ship showed a build

---

32   e.g. Auer et al. 2010; and listed in Falck 2024, 141.

33   Daly 2024.

phase from trees felled between spring/summer 1525 AD and winter 1526-27 AD and a modification of the forward end of the vessel in 1539 AD. The analysis demonstrated that two main sources of oak were utilised, one source for the framing timbers and another for the planking. The planks present as a highly homogeneous group and represent imports to the Low Countries[34] from coastal Lithuania, in that they correlate best with the tree-ring datasets for Klaipeda and with Daly & Tyers' so-called Baltic 1 groups.[35]

The abundant evidence for the growth of the shipbuilding industry in the Low Countries demonstrates that this region had developed an enormous timber import industry to enable this extensive activity.

Towards the end of this century, dating to around 1590 AD, a wreck off the island of Darss (the so-called 4AM wreck), Mecklenburg-Vorpommern, Germany, was found. It had a clinker planking layer, but a second layer of carvel planks completed the hull.[36] The oak for these two layers shows very different sources. The clinker planks and two of the framing timbers are from trees that grew in southwest Sweden, while the carvel planks and a third frame are from the Mecklenburg region. This ship was probably built in the clinker tradition around the Danish Sound and was modified, by the addition of a carvel outer hull, on the southwestern Baltic coast.[37]

A global reach, c. 1600-1700 AD

While not forgetting that ships small and large continue to be built for serving domestic and wider trading needs, this century is characterised in Northern Europe also by the emergence of huge ships, built for status and for conflict. When we examine the timber used for these ships with a view to analyse the exploitation of this resource, it is useful to consider the contrast between ships built in regions that have a shortage of domestic timber resources and those built in regions with extensive dense forestry. We can, for example, examine ships that were built for the Danish Crown. The wreckages of *Delmenhorst* (excavated by the Viking Ship Museum in Roskilde, Denmark) and *Lindormen*[38] were found in the Femern Belt, and identified as two Danish ships that had sunk during the Battle of Femern in 1644 AD. *Delmenhorst* was built in Arendal, in Norway, while *Lindormen* was built at Itzehoe, Holstein.[39] Both ships are built with oak from Norway, as the dendrochronological analyses demonstrate,[40] but they were built in very different locations. Norwegian oak was exploited for the Danish timber needs, and indeed oak from Norway was shipped to Copenhagen and Aalborg in Denmark[41] and to Scotland[42] and the Netherlands[43] for buildings on land.

The building of ships in Sweden in this century reflects quite a different story. The large, forested regions of Sweden in the 17th century AD would have represented an abundant resource of oak trees for the needs of shipbuilding. An illustration from the end of this century even depicts the way bulk logs could be transported (Fig. 6).[44] A large open barge is depicted containing three logs, while a fourth is being lifted out with a crane, suggesting that this material was transported piecemeal, not

---

34 The coastal lowland region of northwestern Europe: modern-day Netherlands, Belgium, and Luxembourg.
35 Daly & Tyers 2022; Færch-Jensen & Daly 2024.
36 Auer et al. 2010.
37 Daly 2011a.

38 Hyttel et al. 2015.
39 Probst 1996.
40 *Delmenhorst* was analysed by Daly (2020b), *Lindormen* was analysed dendrochronologically by Dr Karl-Uwe Heußner at the Deutsches Archäologisches Institut who kindly shared the tree-ring data.
41 Daly 2007b.
42 Crone & Mills 2012.
43 Domínguez-Delmás et al. 2011.
44 Rålamb 1691, pl. I.

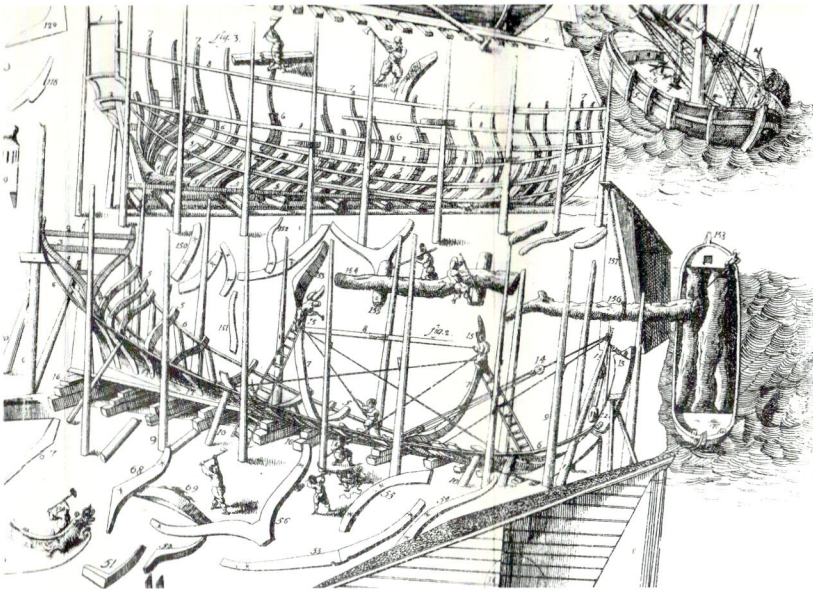

Fig. 6. Timber being loaded from a barge, illustration of a Swedish shipyard from the late 17th century (After Rålamb 1691, pl. I).

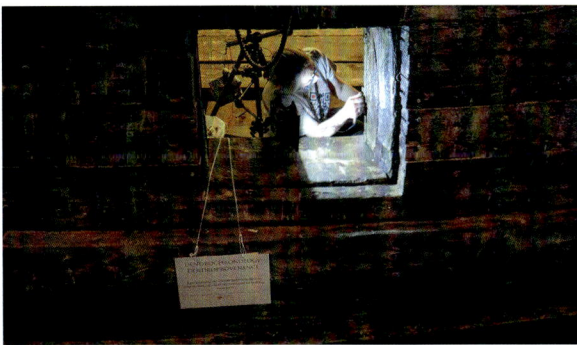

Fig. 7. Aoife Daly analysing timbers at one of the gun-ports of *Vasa* (Photo: Fred Hocker).

in huge cargo quantities. The purchase records for the building of *Vasa* state that while extensive purchases of oak timber were made from estates west and south of Stockholm, which would make perfect sense, oak planks were also purchased in Königsberg and in Amsterdam.[45] *Vasa* was a warship built for King Gustav II Adolf of Sweden, launched in 1628, but which capsized after sailing less than 2 km, in Stockholm Harbour. Extensive dendrochronological analysis of the timbers of this huge ship, lifted out of the harbour in 1961 and now housed at the Vasa Museum in Stockholm, allowed the timbers of

different provenance to be identified (Fig. 7).[46] One group, consisting exclusively of planks from the ship, matches strongly with a chronology named "Baltic 3", which is built from tree-ring data from painted panels[47] and which represents trees that grew in the region around Vilnius in Lithuania. A second group correlates very strongly with chronologies from the western coastline of Sweden, which is most probably the source of the timber that was then purchased in Amsterdam. Two more oak groups, which represent the majority of the timbers that were analysed, correlate with southern Scandinavian oak datasets, and most probably represent the timber purchased in the region west and south of Stockholm. Dendrochronologically however, there are no oak datasets from buildings on land for eastern Sweden from the period that the tree-ring groups from *Vasa* cover. The evidence currently suggests that the use of oaks in the eastern Swedish region was reserved for shipbuilding at this time.

When maritime archaeologists from Vrak – Museum of Wrecks discovered a warship in the Stockholm Archipelago that had been deliberately sunk

45 Cederlund 1966; Hocker 2011.

46 Daly 2021.
47 Daly & Tyers 2022.

Fig. 8. Painting of Lisbon. To the left, in the middle-ground, sugar boxes can be seen being weighed. Dirk Stoop, *Terreiro do Paço no séc. XVII*, 1662 (Museu da Cidade, Lisboa, Portugal. MC.PIN.261. © Museu da Cidade – Câmara Municipal de Lisboa. Public domain, via Wikimedia Commons: https://commons.wikimedia.org/wiki/File:Terreiro_do_Pa%C3%A7o_em_1662.jpg).

as a defensive barrage to protect Stockholm from attack from the sea, the tree-ring patterns from the timbers of the newly-found wreck correlated extraordinarily well with the two eastern Swedish *Vasa* groups, and two timbers, one from each ship, even matched so well that they might have come from the same tree. The tree-ring pattern that the two eastern Swedish *Vasa* groups have are so characteristic that it could be used to identify, without a doubt, that the new discovery was *Vasa*'s sister ship, *Äpplet*. Other wrecks that have been identified by the archaeologists at Vrak – Museum of Wrecks are also dated using the large dataset from *Vasa*, but none of these are so similar to *Vasa*'s timber as the *Äpplet* oaks.

The global reach of the 17th century, where Northern European shipping is truly expanding to all corners of the globe, can be demonstrated through study of the remains of a ship that was launched in exactly the same year as *Vasa*. The Dutch-built *Batavia* set sail for its colony in Java, Indonesia, but due to navigational error, in 1629, hit a reef off the east coast of Australia[48]. The remains

of this ship were located and lifted in the 1970s and are now housed at the Western Australian Maritime Museum's Shipwreck Galleries in Fremantle.[49] The dendrochronological study of the remains of *Batavia* clearly identified the oak as Northern European, and as we have seen in Dutch-built ships from the previous century (above), timbers for the bulky frames were from Twente/Westphalia in the eastern Netherlands and north-western Germany, while the planks were transported greater distances, with sources around Lübeck and Vilnius.[50]

Evidence of the increasingly global world of the 17th century reaching Europe is also seen in shipwreck remains. A wreck off the coast of Ireland, near Schull in West Cork, was found and excavated by Julianna O'Donoghue in 2012. Timbers from the ship itself, and from the large wooden chests that were found, did not belong to a Northern European flora and remains of coconuts and Iberian ceramics attested to the exotic nature of the remains. Staves and heads from barrels were of oak, and dendro-

48   Pelsaert 1649.

49   Green 1989; Van Duivenvoorde 2015.

50   Daly et al. 2021a.

chronological analysis of these placed the ship in the 1620s or 1630s[51] – a very similar date as Dutch *Batavia* and Swedish *Vasa*. One thin board from the ship was identified as *Gallesia* sp., which in English I have seen termed "Garlic wood" but in Brazil it is called *Pau d'alho*. This wood is from the neotropics, from western South America to Brazil. The large wooden chests were made from wood from the Laurel family (*Lauraceae*) and from the legume family (*mimosoid* or *caesalpinioid Leguminosae*), that are predominantly from warm-temperate and tropical climates (identification to genus level was not possible). The wood evidence points us towards the South American continent and the size and form of the chests are similar to sugar boxes, as depicted, for example, in a painting of Lisbon by Dirk Stoop (1662), *Terreiro do Paço no séc. XVII* (Fig. 8).[52] Brazil had, by the turn of the 16th century, become the dominant producer of sugar, channelled through Portugal and onwards to the Low Countries for distribution to European markets.[53] The finds of *Batavia* and the Schull wreck truly emphasise the global reach of the 17th century.

Conclusions

This short article doesn't allow for a more detailed immersion into the complexity of the topic, but with the above narrative on past exploitation of the oak timber resource for shipbuilding in Northern Europe I hope that I have demonstrated the shifts, through time and geography, that such studies reveal. It is a rare privilege that such extensive remains of wood are preserved for study in this region, and it is a privilege to be entrusted with the dendrochronological analyses of these many spectacular archaeological structures.

---

51   Daly 2014.
52   Stoop 1662.
53   Strum 2013.

Aoife Daly
Dendro.dk, Copenhagen, Denmark
dendro@dendro.dk

Bibliography

ALOPAEUS, H. & E. ELVESTAD 2006
'Avaldsnesskipet – et "nordisk" skip fra Polen?' in *Tormod Torfæus mellom Vinland og "Ringenes Herre"*, A. Kongshavn (ed.), Karmøy, 73-86.

VON ARBIN, S. & A. DALY 2012
'The Mollö Cog re-examined and re-evaluated', *International Journal of Nautical Archaeology* 41:2, 372-89.

VON ARBIN, S., T. SKOWRONEK, A. DALY, T. BRORSSON, S. ISAKSSON & T. SEIR 2022
'Tracing Trade Routes: Examining the Cargo of the 15th-Century Skaftö Wreck', *International Journal of Nautical Archaeology* 51:1, 112-44.

AUER, J., M.-L. GRUE, B. GRUNDVAD NIELSEN, S. FAWSITT & C. THOMSEN 2010
Fieldwork Report Ostsee IV, FPL 77 [4AM Wreck] (Esbjerg Maritime Archaeology Reports 2), Esbjerg.

AUER, J. & T. MAARLEVELD 2013
Fieldwork Report, Skjernøysund 3 Wreck 2011 (Esbjerg Maritime Archaeology Reports 5), Esbjerg.

BELASUS, M. & A. DALY 2022
'Timber Resources for the 'Bremen Cog', *International Journal of Nautical Archaeology* 51:2, 207-31.

BILL, J. 1997
Small scale seafaring in Danish waters AD 1000-1600, PhD thesis, University of Copenhagen, Denmark.

BONDE, N. & J. JENSEN 1995
'The dating of a Hanseatic cog-find in Denmark. What coins and tree rings can reveal in maritime archaeology',

in *Shipshape. Essays for Ole Crumlin-Pedersen. On the occasion of his 60th anniversary February 24th 1995*, O. Olsen, J. S. Madsen & F. Rieck (eds), Roskilde, 103-21.

CEDERLUND, C. O. 1966
Stockholms skeppsgård 1605-1640. Personalens struktur och organisation (SSHM internal report), Stockholm.

CRONE, A. & C. M. MILLS 2012
'Timber in Scottish buildings, 1450-1800: a dendrochronological perspective', *Proceedings of the Society of Antiquaries of Scotland* 142, 329-69.

CRUMLIN-PEDERSEN, O. 2000
'To be or not to be a cog', *International Journal of Nautical Archaeology* 29:2, 230-46.

DALICSEK, D., D. DIEZ MERIDA & F. STEFFENSEN 2018
Evaluation of Anomalies in Temporary Exclusion Zones M_R39_07049 and R40_10085, Nord Stream 2 (Landesamt für Kultur- und Denkmalpflege, Mecklenburg-Vorpommern), Schwerin.

DALY, A. 1997
'Dendrokronologisk undersøgelse af skibsvrag fra Vejdyb ved Hals, Aalborg amt', *Nationalmuseets Naturvidenskabelige Undersøgelser, rapport 1997/12*, Copenhagen.

DALY, A. 2007A
'The Karschau Ship, Schleswig-Holstein: Dendrochronological Results and Timber Provenance', *International Journal of Nautical Archaeology* 36:1, 155-66.

DALY, A. 2007B
Timber, Trade and Tree-rings. A dendrochronological analysis of structural oak timber in Northern Europe, c. AD 1000 to c. AD 1650, PhD thesis, University of Southern Denmark, Esbjerg. https://doi.org/10.5281/zenodo.3349667, Accessed October 2025.

DALY, A. 2011A
'Dendro-geography – mapping the Northern European historic timber trade', in *Tree rings, art, archaeology-Proceedings of an international conference, Brussels, Royal Institute for Cultural Heritage*, P. Fraiture (ed.), Belgium, 107-24.

DALY, A. 2011B
'Dendrochronological analysis of oak from a shipwreck, Skjernøysund 3, Mandal, Norway', in *Fieldwork Report, Skjernøysund 3 Wreck 2011, Esbjerg Maritime Archaeology Reports* 5, J. Auer & T. Maarleveld, Esbjerg, 58-68.

DALY, A. 2014
'Dendrochronological and wood-anatomical analysis of ship and cargo wood from the Colla Wreck, Co. Cork, Ireland', *Dendro.dk report*, 2014:10. https://doi.org/10.5281/zenodo.15535014, Accessed October 2025.

DALY, A. 2015
'Dendrochronological analysis of large cargo ships from Danish waters', in *Large Cargo Ships in Danish Waters, 1000-1250* (Ships and Boats of the North, Vol. 7), A. Englert, Roskilde, 356-74.

DALY, A. 2016
'Dendrochronological analysis of samples from shipwreck BC17 found at Barcode, Oslo', *Dendro.dk report*, 2016:4. https://doi.org/10.5281/zenodo.4353487, Accessed October 2025.

DALY, A. 2017
'Dendrochronological analysis of timbers from the Bremen Ship, Germany', *Dendro.dk report*, 2017:46, 13. https://doi.org/10.5281/zenodo.4925871, Accessed October 2025.1

DALY, A. 2019
'Dendrochronological analysis of timbers from a shipwreck found at Peenemündung, Germany – Ostsee VII, Fpl 105', *Dendro.dk report*, 2019:42.

https://doi.org/10.5281/zenodo.4355264, Accessed October 2025.

DALY, A. 2020A
'Ships and their timber source as indicators of connections between regions', *AmS-Skrifter* 27, 133-43. https://doi.org/10.31265/ams-skrifter.v0i27.264, Accessed October 2025.

DALY, A. 2020B
'Dendrochronological analysis of timbers from a shipwreck found at Femern, Denmark', *dendro.dk report*, 2020:44. https://doi.org/10.5281/zenodo.15535116, Accessed October 2025.

DALY, A. 2021
'Timber supply for Vasa – new discoveries', in *Open sea, closed sea: Local traditions and inter-regional traditions in shipbuilding, Proceedings of the Fifteenth International Symposium on Boat and Ship Archaeology (ISBSA 15),* G. Boetto, P. Pomey & P. Poveda (eds), Paris, 263-8.

DALY, A. 2024
'Timber supply through time – Copenhagen waterfronts under scrutiny', *Dendrochronologia* 83, 126164.

DALY, A., M. DOMÍNGUEZ-DELMÁS & W. VAN DUIVENVOORDE 2021A
'Batavia shipwreck timbers reveal a key to Dutch success in 17th-century world trade', *PLoS ONE* 16:10, 0259391.

DALY, A., A. JOUTTIJÄRVI, L. MELDGAARD SASS JENSEN, T. NICOLAJSEN & M. RAVN 2021B
'The Vordingborg Boat: Investigation, Presentation and Interpretation of a 14th-Century Boat-Find from Vordingborg Castle, Denmark', *International Journal of Nautical Archaeology* 50:1, 97-115.

DALY, A. & P. NYMOEN 2007
'The Bøle Ship, Skien, Norway – Research history, dendrochronology and provenance', *International Journal of Nautical Archaeology* 37:1, 153-70.

DALY, A. & I. TYERS 2022
'The sources of Baltic oak', *Journal of Archaeological Science* 139, 105550.

DOMÍNGUEZ-DELMÁS, M., J. F. BENDERS & G. L. G. A. KORTEKAAS 2011
'Timber supply in Groningen (northeast Netherlands) during the early modern period (16th-17th centuries)', in *Tree rings, art, archaeology. Proceedings of an international conference, Brussels, Royal Institute for Cultural Heritage,* P. Fraiture (ed.), Brussels, 151-73.

DOMÍNGUEZ-DELMÁS, M., Y. VORST & R. A. VÁZQUEZ RUIZ DE OCENDA 2017
'Dendrochronological research of samples from the Kampen cog shipwreck (The Netherlands)', *Universidad de Santiago de Compostela Report* nr.:2017001, Lugo.

VAN DUIVENVOORDE, W. 2015
Dutch East India Company shipbuilding: The archaeological study of Batavia and other seventeenth-century VOC ships, College Station, TX, USA.

ENGLERT, A. 2015
Large Cargo Ships in Danish Waters, 1000-1250 (Ships and Boats of the North, Vol. 7), Roskilde.

FALCK, T. 2024
The Becoming of Boats. Craft Practices in Southern Norwegian Boatbuilding (1050-1700 CE), PhD thesis (Stockholm Studies in Archaeology 86), Stockholm University.

FÆRCH-JENSEN, J. & A. DALY 2024
'Køge 2. A Clinker-built Shipwreck from the Medieval Harbour of Køge, Zealand, Denmark', *Acta Archaeologica* 94:1, 97-131.

GREEN, J. N. 1989
The loss of the Verenigde Oostindische Compagnie retourschip Batavia*, Western Australia 1629: An excavation report and catalogue of artifacts*, Oxford.

HANECA, K. & A. DALY 2014
'Tree-Rings, Timbers and Trees: a dendrochronological survey of the 14th-century cog, Doel 1', *International Journal of Nautical Archaeology* 43:1, 87-102.

HOCKER, F. 2011
Vasa. Medströms Bokförlag and National Maritime Museums in Sweden, Stockholm.

HYTTEL, F., B. S. MAJCHCZACK, J. DENCKER & M. SEGSCHNEIDER 2015
Fehmarn Belt Fixed Link. The Excavations on the Wreck of Lindormen, Schleswig.

KOHRTZ ANDERSEN, P. 1983
Kollerupkoggen, Thisted.

LEHNER, B. & G. GRILL 2013
Global River Hydrography and Network Routing: Baseline Data and New Approaches to Study the World's Large River Systems, *Hydrological Processes* 27:15, 2171-86.

LINDERSON, H. 2004
'Dendrokronologisk analys av Skaftövraket (I), Bohuslän', *Department of Quaternary Geology, Lund University, Rapport* 2004:26, Lund.

OSSOWSKI, W. 2014A
'The Copper Ship excavations', in *The Copper Ship. A medieval shipwreck and its cargo*, W. Ossowski (ed.), Gdansk, 77-120.

OSSOWSKI, W. 2014B
'The copper ship's cargo', in *The Copper Ship. A medieval shipwreck and its cargo*, W. Ossowski (ed.), Gdansk, 241-300.

OVERMEER, A. B. M. 2007
'Searching for the missing link? A research on clinker-built ships in the 15th and 16th centuries', in *Symposium voor onderzoek door jonge archeologen (SOJA) Bundel 2006*, M. Kerkhof, R. van Oosten & F. Tomas (eds), Amsterdam, 63-72.

PELSAERT, F. 1649
Ongeluckige Voyagie van 't Schip Batavia, Utrecht. https://nla.gov.au/nla.obj-39984464/view?partId=nla.obj-39984478, Accessed November, 2024.

PROBST, N. M. 1996
Christian 4.s flåde den danske flådes historie 1588-1660 (Marinehistoriske skrifter 26), Copenhagen.

RÅLAMB, Å. C. 1691
Skeps byggerij eller adelig öfnings tionde tom (Sjöhistoriska Museet Faksimileditioner I). Facsimile from 1943 after the original printed in Stockholm 1691, Stockholm.

STOOP, D. 1662
Terreiro do Paço no séc. XVII. Painting. Museu da Cidade, Lisboa, Portugal. MC.PIN.261. © Museu da Cidade – Câmara Municipal de Lisboa. Dirk Stoop, Public domain, via Wikimedia Commons https://commons.wikimedia.org/wiki/File:Terreiro_do_Pa%C3%A7o_em_1662.jpg, Accessed November, 2024.

STRUM, D. 2013
The Sugar Trade: Brazil, Portugal and the Netherlands (1595-1630), Stanford.

WALDUS, W. B., J. F. VERWEIJ, H. M. VAN DER VELDE, A. F. L. VAN HOLK & S. E. VOS 2019
'The Ijsselcog project: from excavation to 3D reconstruction', *International Journal of Nautical Archaeology* 48:2, 466-94.

WICKLER, S. & T. FALCK 2020

'The social context of boats and maritime trade in late medieval Norway: case studies from northern and southern peripheries', in *IKUWA 6. Shared Heritage: Proceedings of the Sixth International Congress for Underwater Archaeology: 28 November-2 December 2016, Western Australian Maritime Museum Fremantle, Western Australia*, J. A. Rodrigues & A. Traviglia (eds), Oxford, 49-59.

Methodology Against Budget:

A Compromised Business

George Koutsouflakis

Abstract

Underwater archaeologists operating across the Mediterranean today engage with a diverse range of environments and site types, adopting varying research interests and methodological approaches. Despite these differences, they share a common challenge: the persistent struggle with limited resources. This constraint is an inherent aspect of conducting field research at sea, requiring archaeologists to balance ideal project goals with the practical limitations imposed by unpredictable and often unstable conditions.

As in other areas of archaeological research, methodology in underwater archaeology plays a critical role in ensuring the systematic survey, excavation, and preservation of underwater cultural heritage in accordance with established standards and principles. Nevertheless, restricted budgets frequently pose substantial obstacles. A central challenge for contemporary underwater archaeologists lies in the prioritization of research objectives through careful pre-calculation of both flexible (elastic) and fixed (inelastic) costs. This prioritization must also ensure adherence to stringent safety protocols for team members and incorporate strategies to minimize project costs while maintaining the highest possible quality of outcomes.

Methodology in this context should be regarded as a dynamic set of guiding principles designed to facilitate effective work rather than a rigid framework resistant to adaptation. Crucially, methodological rigor must support, rather than hinder, the primary objective of archaeological interpretation, avoiding its reduction to an end in itself.

Introduction

Underwater archaeology, a field of immense significance for understanding human history, has undergone transformative development from its early days as a "nascent discipline" to its current status as a science governed by clearly defined principles, rules, and ethics. Initially, discoveries at sea were largely random and incidental, with deliberate and systematic recovery of antiquities left to individuals lacking specific academic qualifications.[1]

In a large part of the 20th century, underwater archaeology was more closely associated with salvage than with scientific research. Diving, considered incompatible with the academic qualifications expected of archaeologists, relegated archaeological directors to the surface. As described by G. Bass,

---

1 Frost 1963, xi-xiv, 9-26; Throckmorton 1964, 34-9; du Plat Taylor 1965, 34-118; Bass 1966, 63-81; 2005, 10-8; Blot 1996, 37-51; Theodoulou 2011, 16-20.

archaeologists "stayed on deck and gratefully accepted the artifacts handed up to them by hired divers".[2] This absence of academic oversight often led to destructive excavation methods and poorly documented findings. For example, Albert Falco, chief diver for Jacques-Yves Cousteau, recounted the Grand Congloué excavation,[3] during which thousands of amphorae were recovered without detailed documentation, underscoring the trial-and-error nature of early underwater archaeology. The conveyor-belt style of artefact retrieval prioritized quantity over scientific precision, highlighting the need for methodological reform.

A turning point came in the late 1950s and early 1960s, when George Bass introduced terrestrial excavation methodologies to underwater sites, setting new standards for systematic research. His groundbreaking work on the Late Bronze Age Gelidonya wreck and the subsequent excavation of the Yassı Ada wreck demonstrated the importance of applying accepted archaeological principles to underwater contexts.[4] These projects established new norms for underwater research, emphasizing careful planning, meticulous documentation, and interdisciplinary collaboration.

However, these advancements were not universally adopted across the Mediterranean, and variations in methodological rigor persisted to the turn of the 21st century. Part of this inconsistency is due to logistical constrains but also on the very fact that the Mediterranean's underwater sites present diverse challenges influenced by depth, visibility, water currents, and the fragility of materials. These environmental factors demand site-specific methodologies tailored to address unique conditions. For example, rapid prototyping and iterative adjustments are often required to navigate unpredictable underwater environments. This diversity underscores the importance of adaptability in methodology to balance scientific objectives.

Underwater archaeology today remains further complicated by limited budgets and logistical stresses. This dynamic tension between methodological ideals and budgetary constraints necessitates creativity and strategic resource allocation. Methodology, therefore, is both a guiding framework and a flexible tool. Effective underwater archaeology demands methodologies that accommodate unpredictable underwater environments and constrained resources. A rigid adherence to standardized protocols may not always be feasible. Instead, methodological adaptability ensures that critical research objectives are met without compromising the integrity of the final interpretation of a site.

This paper emphasizes exactly the interplay between methodological requirements and financial limitations. By addressing these dual challenges, it seeks to provide insights into how archaeologists can navigate the complexities of underwater research while preserving its scientific and cultural value. Through an understanding of past shortcomings and modern innovations, this discussion aims to highlight the strategies that can help practitioners achieve methodological rigor within the realities of constrained budgets.

The resource challenge

In underwater archaeology, methodology provides the essential framework for addressing research objectives, outlining the approaches, techniques, and processes that guide a project from inception to completion. It encompasses not only the methods employed during fieldwork but also project design, financial planning, timetabling, safety protocols, conservation strategies, and the dissemination of

---

2   Bass 2011, 6.
3   https://archeologie.culture.gouv.fr/archeo-sous-marine/en/grand-congloue-experiment, Accessed May, 2025.
4   Bass 1961, 268-9; 1966; 1982, 9-31; 2011, 6-7; Bass & Throckmorton 1967, 20-39.

results.[5] The chosen methodology must align closely with the project's objectives and address the unique challenges of working under water, where varying site conditions necessitate tailored approaches. However, despite its theoretical underpinnings, methodology is deeply intertwined with practical considerations, often incurring significant costs that influence project execution. These costs arise from the personnel, tools, and specialized equipment required in implementing the methodological plan. Furthermore, methodological decisions must navigate a myriad of external constraints, from logistical challenges to unpredictable environmental factors, making it essential to adapt theoretical principles to real-world conditions.

Fieldwork, particularly on-site documentation, is central to underwater archaeological projects and forms the primary focus of this discussion. Documentation has long now replaced artefact recovery in the concept of modern research as the element that differentiates archaeology from mere salvage. For the scope of the paper, projects have been classified into two categories—surveys and excavations—each presenting distinct levels of human intervention, documentation demands, and challenges. Surveys emphasize the identification and mapping of submerged sites, requiring more often than not sophisticated remote sensing tools, while excavations involve direct interaction with the seabed to recover artefacts and study stratigraphy. Both approaches require careful planning and robust methodologies to achieve their objectives effectively.

No matter if survey or excavation, each underwater project must establish a clear framework: objectives are defined, personnel and tools selected, a timeframe established, and a budget created.[6] Open-ended strategies can rarely be an option and projects must have clear beginnings and ends, as well as measurable goals. The resource-intensive nature

of underwater archaeology often pushes these plans to their limits.

Securing long-term funding is among the most significant hurdles. Despite the much pronounced UNESCO Rules 17-19 for Activities directed at Underwater Cultural Heritage,[7] project directors typically operate on short-term budget approvals, often relying on funds that have yet to be disbursed or may be released during an ongoing campaign. This uncertainty is compounded by external factors such as financial crises, extreme weather events, bureaucratic delays, or even pandemics, which can derail timelines and create significant stress for project teams. Delays in funding, coupled with restrictions on how funds may be used (very common among projects funded by the EU), pose further challenges, leaving directors to make difficult choices about how to proceed.

In Greece, the funding for underwater archaeological research is rarely, if ever, provided by a single entity. In collaborative projects that involve multiple stakeholders, the Ministry of Culture typically contributes with machinery and equipment, but the actual financial resources are usually sourced from other public or municipal bodies. Additional funding may also come from participation in European programmes, sponsorships from institutions, and donations from both companies and individuals. However, managing these diverse sources of funding can be challenging. The overlap of different sponsors, each with their own terms and conditions, often leads to a complex web of logistical and administrative obstacles. This intricate funding structure can delay project timelines, as well as create additional layers of accountability, making it difficult to ensure smooth coordination among all involved parties. Such challenges, while common, require careful navigation to maintain the integrity and success of the research efforts.

---

5   Bowens 2009, 34-7; Maarleveld et al. 2013, 111-9.
6   Maarleveld et al. 2013, 61-75; Underwood 2011, 135-8.
7   Maarleveld et al. 2013, 127-50.

Fig. 1. Late Roman ship-wreck off Makronisos Island, located in the 2011 survey. Lying 2 miles off-shore at a depth of 40-45 m it would have been impossible to locate without crucial information from local divers (Photo: V. Mentogiannis).

Prioritizing research objectives is a critical step in ensuring the successful execution of underwater archaeological projects, especially when working within the constraints of limited resources. This process involves identifying the primary goals of the project and aligning them with the realities of available funding, equipment, and personnel. By focusing on the most significant research questions, archaeologists can maximize the impact of their work while minimizing unnecessary expenditure.

A notable example of prioritization comes from the survey of the southern Euboean Gulf, conducted in Greece by the Ephorate of Underwater Antiquities and the Hellenic Institute of Marine Archaeology (HIMA) during the years 2006-2016.[8] In a vast area allotted for research and with limited existing funds, it was a strategic decision not to go "by the book".[9] Instead of following blind survey lines that might lead or not to discoveries, archaeologists initially focused on locating ancient shipwrecks according to available information provided by local divers and fishermen (Fig. 1). This prioritization allowed the team to locate several shipwrecks during the first years of the project, when resources were at the minimum, announce the results to the public and stimulate the interest of sponsors. With more adequate funding available in the following years, the project was able to allocate resources effectively while extending the survey to vast tracts of sea where no information from the locals existed, locating several more unknown shipwrecks and laying the groundwork for future phases of exploration and documentation. Meanwhile, the core of the research team gained experience and self-confidence, retrained in advanced diving qualifications and became ready to extend the survey lines deeper from the initial diving comfort zones.

Risk assessment also played a crucial role in setting priorities in the Southern Euboean Gulf Project. Applied in a very dynamic environment, the survey required careful planning to address local weather conditions, strong currents and varying visibility. By identifying key areas for investigation based on statistic weather records and improvising a "plan B" for every environmental challenge or technical failure, the project minimized time-loss and augmented the team effectiveness. This approach reduced risks

---

8   Koutsouflakis 2013; 2017; 2018.
9   Bowens 2009, 114-7; Green 2004, 51-7.

to divers and equipment while ensuring that the project's objectives remained as much as possible achievable. Cost compression strategies further enhanced the ability to prioritize effectively. Collaborations with local diving centres and individual divers reduced significantly the research cost and provided access to specialized tools and expertise. Public engagement, such as offering educational programs or inviting citizen scientists to participate in the team, also supplemented funding while raising awareness about the project.

Ultimately, prioritization requires archaeologists to strike a balance between ambition and pragmatism. While it is tempting to pursue comprehensive investigations, resource limitations often necessitate difficult choices. By focusing on the most critical objectives, underwater archaeologists can ensure that their work contributes meaningful insights to the field while remaining sustainable in the long term.

Funds are not adequate. Now what?

Setting strict priorities in the objectives of a project, might help to ensure the minimum loss of time and resources, but does not necessarily guarantee its final implementation, if funds are not available in time. Funding is indeed the most critical precondition for any field research. As stated in the UNESCO Manual, "A project's financial needs must be fully covered by the appropriate sources of funding before starting its implementation. The funds have to actually be available (i.e. in the bank account) before the start of each phase of the project".[10] This rather strict approach presumes that accounting can be very precise, that the project manager can freely regulate the flow of cash from a bank account and that no serious fluctuations appear in prices of goods and services during the preparatory year. Project management

and finances, however, are much more unsteady and trickier and a project director, most probably an archaeologist, is not a banker, an accountant or a fortune teller.

If a project director finds himself in this predicament, and if this insufficiency pops out in the final stages of preparations, there are still some formulas of action. One possible response to funding shortfalls is obviously to postpone the project to the next season in anticipation of adequate and better secured resources. This rigid approach of "zero compromise" ensures that the project remains faithful to its original objectives but often results in significant aftermaths. Large-scale projects, particularly those involving international collaboration, are particularly vulnerable to such disruptions, as the execution of fieldwork is directly dependent on the availability of personnel. The coordination of individual schedules and agendas—already a complex task—can be severely affected by the cancellation of a field season. Furthermore, a prolonged absence from fieldwork can weaken the team's cohesion, impact collaborative ties and estrange archaeologists from the localities.

From a more optimistic standpoint, a flexible approach entails scaling back the project's objectives and realigning priorities to match with available funding. If the implementation of a comprehensive master plan is unfeasible, the objectives should be adjusted to reflect what can be achieved within the constraints of existing resources. Further on, a director can either shorten the duration of the field period or downsize the research team (and it is not rare will he need to do both).

Underwater archaeology projects vary widely in their aims, organizational structures, and logistical demands. The costs of such projects are influenced by factors such as the distance from base operations, the size of the team, and the duration of the campaign. Secondary costs, including vessel rentals, fuel, and gases, can significantly add to the financial burden. Depth is another critical factor, as operations in

---

10   Maarleveld et al. 2013, 134.

Year	Research Type	Duration in days	Mob-Demob in days	Days lost from technical failures and weather conditions	Personnel	Total Cost (in Euros)
2015	Survey	13	3	2	12	17,000
2016	Survey	26	4	4	24	31,000
2017	Survey	25	5	5	29	33,000
2018	Survey	24	4	9	30	36,000
2020	Survey	20	4	3	18	28,000
2021	Excavation	26	6	6	28	48,000
2022	Excavation	25	7	8	29	52,000
2023	Excavation	25	7	9	33	61,000
2024	Excavation	27	6	2	28	68,000

Table 1. The Phournoi survey (2015-2020) and excavation (2021-2024) in numbers (prices in the last column after rounding).

deeper waters require more specialized equipment and greater support and resources.

The reduction in staff size can lead to the formation of smaller, more cohesive teams, which, under certain conditions, may be more efficient and productive than larger groups where logistical challenges and communication breakdowns can impede progress (Fig. 2). However, this approach also places

Fig. 2. The 12-member crew that conducted the 2011 survey on Makronisos Island, downsized from the original 22 due to financial constraints (Photo: V. Mentogiannis).

greater demands on individual team members, often requiring extended working hours, an additional burden of multiple and cumbersome tasks for each one participant and extraordinary effort to meet objectives.

Shortening the duration of fieldwork, while another possible solution, comes as well with distinct challenges. The ongoing project at the Phournoi archipelago (2015-present) exemplifies the intricate interplay of methodology, project priorities and budgetary constraints. Initially designed to document ancient, medieval, and modern shipwrecks, the project has since 2021 shifted its focus to the excavation of a Roman-period shipwreck.[11] Except for the year 2015, each campaign was planned to last around 25 days (Table 1); however, preparatory activities, such as travelling and mobilizing equipment, anchoring support vessels, assembling airlifts, completing trials and setting up outdoor conservation labs, takes around five days at the beginning of each excavation campaign. An additional two days are required for packing and demobilization. As a result,

---

11 Viglaki et al. 2019, 146-225; Campbell & Koutsouflakis 2021, 271-90.

Expenses	Cost (in Euros)	Percentage	Type of expense	Priority
Transportation & Shipping	3,500	5.2%	inelastic	high
Accommodation	10,000	14.8%	elastic	high
Support Vessel Charter	15,000	22.5%	inelastic	high
Food	12,500	18.5%	elastic	high
Compensation of personnel	10,000	14.8%	elastic	low
Fuels, lubricants, filters, oxygen, etc	6,000	8.8%	inelastic	high
Purchase of equipment	3,000	4.4%	elastic	low
Maintenance & Service of gear	2,500	3.7%	inelastic	high
Others	5,000	7.4%	elastic	low

Table 2. Analytical cost per category of expenses of the 2024 Phournoi Expedition. Prices are rounded and correspond to 28 crew members.

only 18 days remain for actual fieldwork. Adverse weather conditions frequently result in a reduction of effective working days by 30-40%, thereby further constraining the time available for uninterrupted seabed operations. Although published records rarely highlight the impact of weather-related delays, this is a common challenge for exposed sites in the Aegean, as documented in other projects.[12]

These constraints underscore the challenge of reducing research duration without jeopardizing project outcomes. Mobilization and demobilization represent fixed logistical requirements, while unpredictable factors such as adverse weather further curtail the time available. This raises critical concerns about the viability of shortening research campaigns as a cost-saving strategy, particularly given the substantial resources and effort already invested.

Therefore, the methodology adopted for underwater archaeological projects must strike a balance between theoretical ideals and the practical realities of budgetary and logistical limitations. These challenges emphasize the importance of careful planning and the need to adapt methodologies to the specific conditions of each project.

An intermediate solution between reducing staff and shortening the duration of the fieldwork is cost compression. Research budgets are typically divided into various categories of expenses (transportation and shipping, accommodation, food, support vessel charter, personnel compensation, fuels and lubricants, equipment purchases, service and maintenance of equipment, miscellaneous expenses, etc).

Fig. 3. The main and supporting vessels of the Phournoi 2022 excavation, essential for operations in remote areas, where chartering boats constitutes a significant and not negotiable portion of the budget (Photo: S. Pappas).

Fig. 4. Outdoor documentation of raised artefacts by students, during the Phournoi 2016 survey (Photo: G. Koutsouflakis).

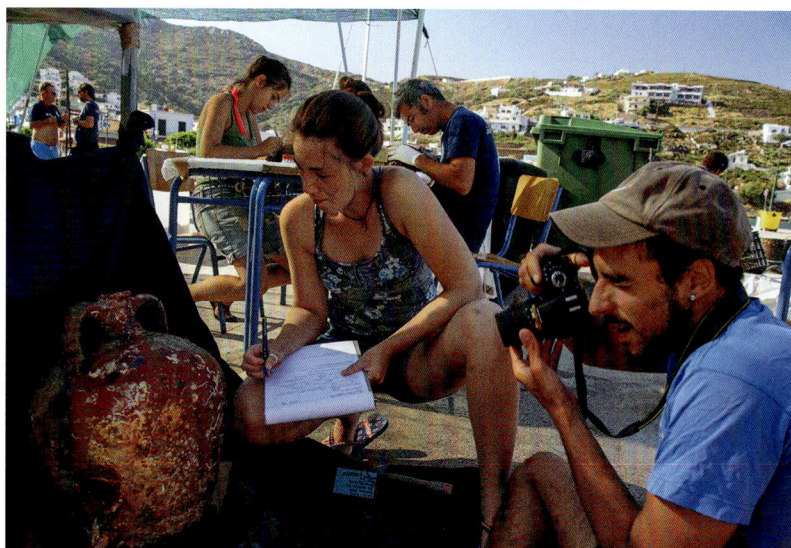

These categories can be further divided into elastic and inelastic costs (Table 2). For instance, transportation costs are inelastic, as are the costs associated with chartering a support vessel for research and diving activities (Fig. 3). Distinguishing between elastic and inelastic costs is another vital strategy in compressing expenses and re-prioritizing objectives. As already noted, the duration of a survey or the extent of an excavation can be adjusted based on the budget. Inelastic costs, extend also further to non-negotiable and less defined expenses such as compliance with safety protocols, the cost of which is incorporated in a variety of cost categories. Recognizing these distinctions enables archaeologists to make informed decisions about how to allocate funds.

One often-overlooked aspect of fieldwork organization is ensuring that the team has adequate rest, food, and appropriate facilities for completing archaeological logs, diaries and data processing (Fig. 4). When budgets are constrained, human comfort is typically the first area to be sacrificed. Practically, this may involve adding extra beds to double rooms or squeezing research partners to live in self-organized camps or boats not originally intended for accommodation. While these arrangements can foster strong team bonds, they may also generate tension and conflict, especially during the later stag-es of a project. Food is less negotiable to shortcuts and the adage "an army marches on its stomach" is equally applicable to archaeological teams (Fig. 5). It is important to consider that factors influencing a team's physical well-being will progressively affect daily productivity, potentially leading to a decline in archaeological standards over time.

In Greece, various research programs have adopted strategies to reduce costs associated with underwater projects. For instance, the directors of the HIMA underwater archaeological survey in the Argosaronic Gulf have scheduled fieldwork during late autumn, avoiding the peak summer months when most Aegean projects typically occur.[13] This approach significantly reduces accommodation expenses, allowing resources to be allocated to other priorities. However, this scheduling decision entails challenges such as lower ambient temperatures, more frequent adverse weather conditions, and reduced daylight hours. Similarly, the Kasos Project (2019-present), carried out by the Ephorate of Underwater Antiquities in collaboration with the National Hellenic Research Foundation, chose to operate later in the season, specifically in October 2022. While this scheduling helped reduce accom-

13   Agouridis 2007, 12; Agouridis & Michalis 2017, 76-7.

Fig. 5. Makeshift dinner aboard during the Levitha survey (2019). Cooks are often deemed the "most important team members" in remote projects (Photo: H. Barda).

modation costs, extended periods of adverse weather led to a suspension of diving activities for several weeks, causing significant time loss and continued expenses.

Surveys against excavations

In general, underwater surveys are more susceptible to budgetary constraints than excavations. Surveys can have different aims and objectives, but they share in common the process of exploring, locating and documenting a site or a wider area.[14] They can be applied in relatively well-known areas or in completely archaeologically uncharted waters. Underwater survey methodology involves essential preparatory ac-

tions, including consolidating local knowledge from divers and fishermen, and consulting archives, libraries, historical cartography, aerial photography, toponymy, and land-based archaeological data. While these tasks are time-consuming, they generally incur minimal costs and do not significantly impact a project's budget. Significant expenses arise once fieldwork begins.

While it is crucial to adhere to accepted archaeological standards to ensure the validity and credibility of findings, there must also be room for innovation and adaptation. For example, while advanced geophysical surveys using technologies like side scan sonar or sub-bottom profilers are ideal for large-scale site assessments, their high cost may make them impractical for smaller projects. In such cases, archaeologists might rely on lower-cost alternatives, such as diver-led surveys, which can still

14   Bowens 2009, 103-16; Green 2004, 50-84.

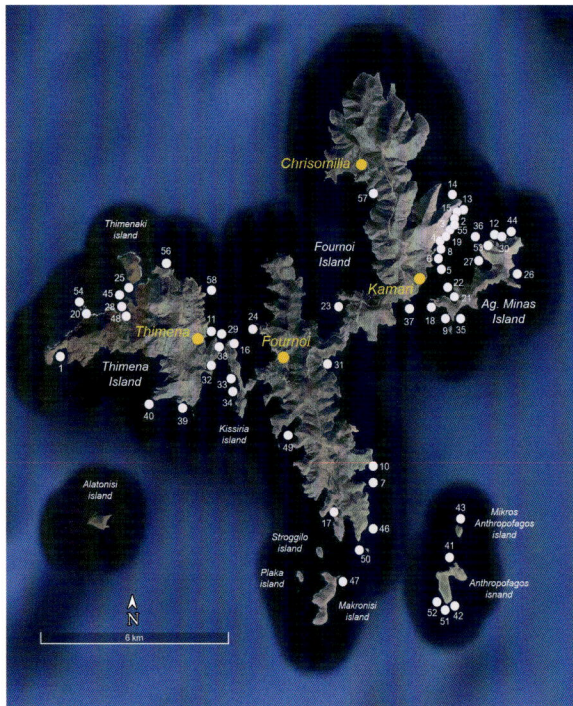

Fig. 6. Distribution map of located shipwrecks around the insular complex of Phournoi (Edit: F. Vlachaki).

ship between time, cost, and quality of results. While high-quality documentation can be achieved with low financial investment, it may be time-consuming, whereas high-quality results in a short timeframe are likely to be costly. Alternatively, a project may produce quick results at a low cost, but this often comes at the expense of documentation quality. The archaeologist must prioritize project objectives and determine which compromises are acceptable.

In some cases, the primary goal of a survey may be to locate shipwrecks within a specific area, with documentation limited to essential information in a very elementary level: coordinates, depth, terrain type, site description, cargo identification, condition assessment, and chronology. This was the case of many underwater surveys conducted in Greece during the last 20 years when the protection of underwater heritage became a national priority in earnest. The spotting and elementary documentation of ancient shipwrecks was at the heart of this effort as it was considered for long the Achilles' heel of maritime archaeology in Greece.[16] Gibbins, in a most profound essay about Hellenistic shipwrecks, stated, quite explicitly back in 2001, the lack of published shipwreck records in Hellenic territorial waters as "the greatest lacuna in Mediterranean shipwreck data".[17] Since the turn of the 21st century, more than 150 shipwrecks have been documented in the national archives through the collaborative efforts of the Ephorate of Underwater Antiquities, HIMA, and strategic partnerships with third parts. Regardless of the different methodological approaches employed, these surveys typically followed standard archaeological research steps. More detailed documentation, such as high-accuracy ortho-photomosaics, 3D models, or core sampling, may have been postponed until later stages after the declaration of newly-spotted shipwrecks as protected underwater archaeological sites.

yield valuable data while conserving resources. The use of simple hand-drawn site plans or community-sourced diving assistance may be more practical in certain contexts than expensive, technology-driven solutions. Diving to conduct an extensive survey is the most common (and the most successful so far) approach to underwater site assessment and documentation in Greece. Although diving patterns, such as parallel line surveys often described in maritime archaeology manuals,[15] are effective in shallow, flat waters, they are less suitable for the steep and complex underwater terrains typical of the Aegean. Therefore, instead being a rigid set of rules, methodology must be flexible enough to adapt to the unique characteristics of each site.

Despite the ideal that minimal technical resources should be used to achieve optimal results, the reality is that underfunded projects face a clear relation-

---

15   Green 2004, 51-5.

16   Parker 1992, 7, table 2.

17   Gibbins 2001, 280.

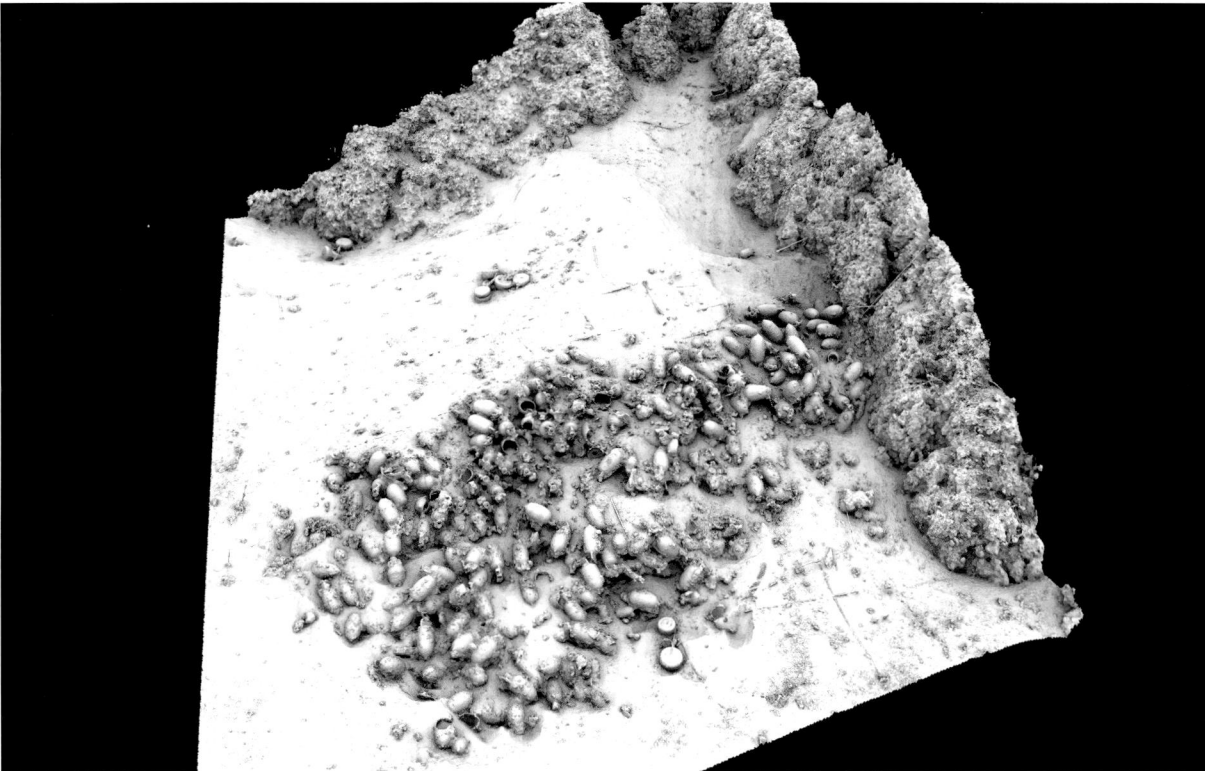

Fig. 7. Ground plan of Shipwreck 15 in Phournoi. The amphorae cargo lies in the depth zone of 42-50 m (Photogrammetry: K. Yamafune).

The survey at Phournoi (2015-2018) accordingly focused on completing the survey lines, with documentation initially kept to an elementary level.[18] Accurate measurements and ultimate precision could wait. A subsequent campaign in 2020 was dedicated to refining the mapping and documentation once the survey had been completed and 58 underwater sites spotted (Fig. 6). Surveys, by definition, provide opportunities for the researcher to be more flexible in processing times and methodological protocols. Instead of going by the manual, they can choose to follow the evidence and they can stop the research at any time, without any impact on the archaeological field, precisely because the entire approach is based on minimal or zero human intervention.

Excavations, in contrast, require more stringent adherence to methodology, as they are intrusive and destructive processes that demand continuous and repeatable documentation. Although again the methodology can be differentiated according to the specific conditions of each individual site, a typical excavation process at sea includes (in small words) a pre-disturbance documentation, the gradual removal of the sediments that alternates with photogrammetric documentation at all stages of the excavation, and the retrieval of finds or their *in situ* protection. The pace and progress of the excavation is directly dependent on the environmental conditions and on the depth at which it is carried out. Technical requirements and supporting services aside, the most intricate and time-consuming process is that of underwater documentation.

The ongoing excavation of a Late Roman shipwreck at Phournoi (Shipwreck 15), situated on a steep, rocky seabed at depths ranging from 42 to 50 m, offers a significant case study in excavation meth-

18   Campbell & Koutsouflakis 2021, 281-4.

Fig. 8. Short briefing and updating information between divers at the 6 m decompression station (Photo: S. Kontos).

odology under budgetary constraints (Fig. 7). As on any other excavation under the 40 m zone, diving logistics are highly regulated, significantly influencing the pace and progress of the excavation. Two key methodological challenges are outlined below.

The excavation proceeded in phases, with the dive time per team set at 48 minutes: 2 minutes for descent, 20 minutes for direct work on the wreck, and 26 minutes for ascent and decompression stops, using a modified oxygen mixture (50%) from 21 m and pure oxygen at depths of 6 m and 3 m. In the case of a second dive on the same day, these bottom times are further reduced. Thus, for every approximately 50 minutes of diving, only 20 minutes are spent on the seabed itself. In theory, this schedule allows for successive dives every 20 minutes, with airlifts running continuously and handed off between consecutive diving teams.

However, in practice, this ideal sequence of continuous diving is unfeasible. Methodology dictates that a basic level of communication and understanding must exist between consecutive teams to facilitate instruction, draw attention to important details, and exchange critical information. These are fundamental principles for a controlled excavation. Indisputably, the most effective communication occurs in dry conditions, yet this substantially impacts the excavation's pace, limiting it to one dive per hour.

Moreover, each excavation stage requires photographic documentation of progress, and photogrammetry should be periodically applied to capture the entire excavation zone. This necessitates pauses in the excavation process for the sediments to settle down and allow clean shootings. Ideally, photogrammetry would be conducted after each dive to comprehensively document every phase of the ex-

Fig. 9. Photogrammeter Kotaro Yamafune, completing photogrammetric documentation at the end of a working day (Photo: S. Kontos).

cavation but if these protocol-driven procedures are adhered to fully, the projected total excavation time for Wreck 15 – initially estimated at a minimum of ten years – could be significantly prolonged to the double. Consequently, the question arises: are there feasible ways to expedite the process?

In the context of diver communication, a pragmatic approach involves transmitting information under water during the handover of airlifts between teams. However, practical tests have revealed that this method is only partially effective. Divers ascending to the surface prioritize adherence to strict decompression protocols over spending additional time exchanging shorthand notes, especially given the potential impact of nitrogen narcosis. Consequently, the exchange of information was shifted to either the 21 m stop or the 6 m decompression station (Fig. 8). The use of shorthand note exchanges has demonstrated satisfactory effectiveness, particularly among divers familiar with the wreck and the specific requirements of the project. This communication system enables the doubling of dives within an hour and facilitates the potential for further acceleration of the work pace.

In the realm of photographic and photogrammetric documentation, the potential for compromise is significantly constrained. Archaeological excavation inherently involves the destruction of an information repository, necessitating high-resolution recording of each excavation phase to enable the digital reconstruction of the wreck's contextual relationship with its surrounding environment—an association that, once disrupted, cannot be restored. Nevertheless, it is crucial to acknowledge the practical limitations of documenting every minute detail, such as the removal of each grain of sand. For Shipwreck 15, photogrammetric surveys are conducted at the end of each working day, contingent on favourable lighting and visibility conditions, or at the start of the following day (Fig. 9). Despite the slow progress of excavation, this methodology ensures comprehensive documentation of the site with minimal data loss. In instances where particularly sensitive data are encountered during excavation, operations are temporarily halted to perform *in-situ* photogrammetry of the specific area before resuming work.

Conclusions

Methodological flexibility is a cornerstone of a successful underwater archaeological project. In a field where environmental conditions and resource availability can vary widely, the ability to adapt methodologies to suit specific circumstances is critical. Flexible methodologies allow archaeologists to tailor their approaches to the specific challenges of a site. One of the primary advantages of methodological flexibility is its ability to accommodate the unique challenges of underwater environments. While it is crucial to adhere to accepted archaeological standards, there must also be room for innovation and adaptation. It is up to each individual director to balance the needs of a project and align them with an accepted methodological framework. Methodology in underwater archaeology must serve as a practical tool that enables researchers to reach interpretive conclusions, rather than being an end goal in itself. A rigid adherence to standardized processes can sometimes overshadow the ultimate aim of archaeology: to uncover and interpret the stories embedded in underwater cultural heritage. The biggest challenge for a modern underwater archaeologist is therefore to prioritize research objectives, to remain in compliance with specific safety protocols and to estimate how the cost of a project can be aligned to the objectives with the smallest possible impact in the quality of the result. As a generation, we are lucky enough to operate in the digital era and technological advantages in underwater photography and photogrammetric software together with the fact that this innovative technology has become much more user-friendly and is offered with a substantial cost reduction, can ease such considerations in the future.[19]

Finally, methodology should be seen through an ethical lens. Researchers have a duty to balance precision and cost-efficiency while ensuring that the cultural heritage they study is preserved for future generations. Over-emphasis on sophisticated methodologies at the expense of interpretation or preservation could be considered a failure to meet this ethical obligation.

George Koutsouflakis
University of Thessaly, Greece
geokoutsgr@yahoo.gr

Bibliography

AGOURIDIS, C. S. 2007
Ἐνάλια αρχαιολογική έρευνα Αργολικού. Ερευνητική περίοδος 2005', *Enalia* 10, 12-30.

AGOURIDIS, C. S. & M. MICHALIS 2017
Ἐνάλια Αρχαιολογική Έρευνα στον Αργοσαρωνικό, 2009: Ανασκαφή Μυκηναϊκού Ναυαγίου στη νησίδα Μόδι', *Enalia* 12, 76-94.

AGOURIDIS, C. S. & M. MICHALIS 2021
'The Arduous Voyage of Underwater Research on the LBA Shipwreck off Modi Islet', in *Under the Mediterranean*, I. *Studies in Maritime Archaeology on the Anniversary of the Centenary of Honor Frost's Birth*, S. Demesticha & L. Blue (eds), Leiden, 22-41.

BASS, G. F. 1961
'The Cape Gelidonya Wreck: Preliminary Report', *American Journal of Archaeology* 65, 267-76.

BASS, G. F. 1966
Archaeology Under Water, London.

BASS, G. F. 1982
'The Excavation', in *Yassı Ada*, Volume I. *A Seventh-Century Byzantine Shipwreck*, G. F. Bass & F. Van Doorninck (eds), College Station, 9-31.

---

19 McCarthy et al. 2019; Demesticha & Blue 2021, 15; Diamanti et al. 2024; 2025.

BASS., G. F. 2005
'Introduction. Reclaiming Lost History from Beneath the Seven Seas', in *Beneath the Seven Seas. Adventures with the Institute of Nautical Archaeology*, G. F. Bass (ed.), London, 10-28.

BASS, G. F. 2011
'The Development of Maritime Archaeology', in *The Oxford Handbook of Maritime Archaeology*, A. Catsambis, B. Ford & D. L. Hamilton (eds), Oxford, New York, 3-22.

BASS, G. F. & P. THROCKMORTON 1967
'The excavation', in *Cape Gelidonya: A Bronze Age Shipwreck* (Transactions of the American Philosophical Society 57), G. F. Bass (ed.), Philadelphia, 21-39.

BLOT, J.-Y. 1996
Underwater Archaeology, Exploring the World Beneath the Sea, London.

BOWENS, A. (ED.) 2009
Underwater Archaeology. The NAS Guide to Principles and Practice (The Nautical Archaeological Society, Second Edition), Portsmouth.

CAMPBELL, P. & G. KOUTSOUFLAKIS 2021
'Aegean Navigation and the Shipwrecks of Fournoi. The Archipelago in Context', in *Under the Mediterranean*, I. *Studies in Maritime Archaeology on the Anniversary of the Centenary of Honor Frost's Birth*, S. Demesticha & L. Blue (eds), Leiden, 271-90.

DEMESTICHA, S. & L. BLUE 2021
'Under the Mediterranean' in the 21st century. Constants, trends and perspectives in Mediterranean Maritime Archaeology', in *Under the Mediterranean*, I. *Studies in Maritime Archaeology on the Anniversary of the Centenary of Honor Frost's Birth*, S. Demesticha & L. Blue (eds), Leiden, 9-19.

DIAMANTI, E., M. YIP, A. STAHL & Ø. ØDEGÅRD 2024
'Advancing Data Quality of Marine Archaeological Documentation Using Underwater Robotics: From Simulation Environments to Real-World Scenarios', *Journal of Computer Applications in Archaeology* 7:1, 153-69.

DIAMANTI, E., Ø. ØDEGÅRD, V. MENTOGIANNIS & G. KOUTSOUFLAKIS 2025
'Underwater drones: a low-cost, yet powerful tool for underwater archaeological mapping', *Journal of Computer Applications in Archaeology* 8:1, 10-24.

FROST, H. 1963
Under the Mediterranean, London.

GIBBINS, D. 2001
'Shipwrecks and Hellenistic Trade', in *Hellenistic Economies*, Z. H. Archibald. J. Davies, V. Gabrielsen & G. L. Oliver (eds), London, 273-312.

GREEN, J. 2004
Maritime Archaeology, A Technical Handbook (second edition), San Diego, London.

KOUTSOUFLAKIS, G. 2013
Ναυσιπλοΐα και εμπορευματική διακίνηση στον Νότιο Ευβοϊκό από τον 6ο αι. π.Χ. έως τον 14ο αι. μ. Χ., Unpublished PhD dissertation, National Kapodistrian University of Athens.

KOUTSOUFLAKIS, G. 2017
'Υποβρύχια Αναγνωριστική Έρευνα στον Νότιο Ευβοϊκό (2010-2016). Μέρος Α΄: Πεταλιοί, Μακρόνησος', *Enalia* 12, 32-75.

KOUTSOUFLAKIS, G. 2018
'Υποβρύχια Αναγνωριστική Έρευνα στον Νότιο Ευβοϊκό, 2010-2016. Μέρος Β΄: Λαυρεωτική – Νότια Καρυστία', *Enalia* 13, 18-47.

MAARLEVELD, T., U. GUÉRIN & B. EGGER (EDS) 2013
Manual for Activities directed at Underwater Cultural Heritage, Guidelines to the Annex of the UNESCO 2001 Convention, Paris.

MCCARTHY, J. K., J. BENJAMIN, T. WINTON & W. VAN DUIVENVOORDE (EDS) 2019
3D Recording and Interpretation for Maritime Archaeology (Springer Open: Coastal Research Library 31), Cham.

PARKER, A. J. 1992
Ancient Shipwrecks of the Mediterranean and the Roman provinces (BAR International Series 580), Oxford.

DU PLAT TAYLOR, J. 1965
Marine Archaeology: developments during sixty years in the Mediterranean, London.

THEODOULOU, T. 2011
'Συνοπτική Αναδρομή στην Υποβρύχια Αρχαιολογική Έρευνα στην Ελλάδα', *Αριάδνη* 17, 13-84.

THROCKMORTON, P. 1964
The lost ships. An adventure in undersea archaeology, Boston, Toronto.

UNDERWOOD, C. 2011
'Excavation Planning and Logistics: the HMS Swift Project', in *The Oxford Handbook of Maritime Archaeology*, A. Catsambis, B. Ford & D. L. Hamilton (eds), Oxford, New York, 133-60.

VIGLAKI, M., G. KOUTSOUFLAKIS & P. CAMPBELL 2019
Κορσιητῶν νῆσοι. Αρχαιολογικά ευρήματα και μία προσέγγιση της ιστορίας των Φούρνων Κορσεών, Athens.

Preservation

Underwater Perspectives:

Dialogue with Heritage Conservators

Angeliki Zisi

Abstract

"In 2020, almost 25 years after the excavation of the Roskilde shipwrecks, we still have ship timbers in our treatment tanks, awaiting a future in the museum storages".[1] At the same time as the Roskilde shipwrecks were being brought to light, in 1997, I was initiating my future *as a heritage conservator. I was an avid member of the – then new – generation of students. Could I also be the future the Roskilde shipwrecks were awaiting? Can one draw on one's experiences and condense personal thoughts in order to derive and communicate a perspective meaningful beyond oneself? Without claiming to be comprehensive, this short paper touches on practising conservation under water and on-site and how we, heritage conservators, approach this fieldwork, what our contribution is, how we care, how we collaborate, how we compromise, and how we can manage underwater finds and sites. Answers are presented by exemplifying the work in progress at Lechaion Harbour, Ancient Corinth's main harbour, placing it at the centre of the elaboration. As a dialogue under water is a rather quiet one, what follows is, I hope, to 'sound' some of those possible answers mulling over in the mind of those heritage professionals, as to why we do what we choose to do.*

"The other is that all these things, which thou seest, change immediately and will no longer be; and constantly bear in mind how many of these changes thou hast already witnessed. The universe is transformation: the life is opinion [as in perception]." - Marcus Aurelius, Meditations, 4.3

All measures and actions aimed at safeguarding tangible cultural heritage while ensuring its accessibility to present and future generations. […] Conservation is complex and demands the collaboration of relevant qualified professionals. In particular, any project involving direct actions on the cultural heritage requires a conservator-restorer.[3]

Definition[2]

In 2010, the 25th ICOM General Assembly defined the term "conservation" as:

---

1 Strætkvern & Hjelm-Petersen 2021, 48.

2 Acknowledgements: The author wishes to warmly thank Sophia Palos for her precious edits on an earlier version of this manuscript and the anonymous reviewer and editors of this MoDIA volume for the kind comments and useful communication. Warm thanks are extended to colleague, conservator, Margrethe Gjedboe Felter and friend, geophysicist, Mark Vardy, for their support.

3 ICOM 2010, 6.

The definition resonates well with the team working on the Lechaion Harbour Project (LHP) in 2017 as an example. This team consists of 14 archaeologists, of which two are also illustrators; *a conservator*; one dive master who is also the underwater- and on-land photographer; one geomorphologist; one architect; and, last but not least, two team-members contributing with technical support. To make it more complex, the team is represented by six nations – Greece, Denmark, Slovenia, France, Germany, and the United Kingdom, fortunately communicating in one language, English.

Object: Lechaion Harbour, Corinth

Based on our recent findings, the harbour basins of Lechaion were in use from the Late Bronze Age to Late Antiquity. This corresponds to a life span of roughly over 2,000 years, from c. 1380 BC to 1300 AD.[4] The reason why the harbour was active during this historical period is because it was needed. Whatever was broken during its use was repaired, so as to maximise the investment. Because in a then innately sustainable society, commodities such as time needed to build such infrastructure and a great deal of resources, including human lives, could not but *be* valued. It was only time and nature that could take over. It should be noted that Ancient Corinth – the city to which the harbour belonged – lies in a highly seismogenically active area. During the Roman Period the inner harbour was becoming too costly to maintain and by the 13th century AD, the same problem impacted the outer, artificial harbour. Ancient Corinth then lost its primacy but persevered through time. With no humans keeping it afloat, nature continued claiming back her reach, immersing the harbour into her underwater realm. Nature, time and luck have been the rulers of the rate of decomposition of this once vibrant and vital Greek harbour. Still, not yet enough time, nature or bad luck have gone by to fragment and fully dissolve all evidence of existence.

It is these remains that caught the eye of the archaeologist and left them with an urge to poke the surface. There are also scholars, like the team's geomorphologist, who shifts the focus and recognises a once-active river outlet, the beginning of the unravelling of a fascinating geological sequence. As for the conservator, a challenge is about to be met. Highlighted in Fig. 1 is the harbour's infrastructure during the Roman Period, here covering an area of a merely 0.7 km². In this on-site 'conservation laboratory', the conservator is now confronted with the task of safeguarding one very large, complex, exposed and ever-changing *object*.

With the help of the team's illustrator and archaeologist, one can start to imagine what this 'object' looked like in the past. There is an entrance channel with small boats temporarily anchored and a view to the inner harbour's basins and magazines along its shore; Lechaion's wooden caissons – parallels to wooden crates – used as a foundation to artificially raise the seabed and so add the moles to this artificial outer harbour, are also present. Preserved is also a wooden bulwark, a retaining wall defined by wooden pilings in a line, pushed into the seabed sediment tightly alongside the stone mole. This acts to hold the side of the mole in place due to damage or for additional support, and therefore signifies a repair at some stage during its use. The evidence for proving that the remains located in the middle of one of the harbour's main inner basins could have formed the harbour's lighthouse given their location and size, is still to be found.

Then, after c. 2,000 years or, put in perspective, in less than a twinkling of an eye, we are excavating this 'object' and documenting what is left from it; a circumstance not to be taken lightly since it is the first time such remains have been found in the warm Greek seas exposed to direct sunlight; conditions

4   Chabrol et al. 2023.

Fig. 1. Superimposition (approximation) of archaeological data (in red) on an aerial photograph of the Lechaion Harbour site in Corinth, highlighting the harbour remains from Late Antiquity, used here just for illustrating purposes (Data: Athanasopoulos et al. 2023, 606, fig. 2, Map Data: Google, ©2014 CNES, Maxar Technologies).

which are rather unfavourable for the preservation of organic material. Unequivocally it is about a real harbour, monumental for its kind. It requires methodical work, a careful area-by-area unravelling, to document and conserve the historical evidence.

Conservation under water

Lechaion Harbour remains are exposed to the forces of powerful winds, longshore drift and strong swells due to the shallow waters and waves. Fortunately, there are moments of rest which make temporary covering of wooden remains *in situ* a calming and fairly easy task in these very shallow waters of less than half a metre in some instances (Fig. 2); although, at the cost of a challenge to maintain in this highly dynamic burial environment.

Because conditions for underwater conservation are certainly far less challenging at significant depths for practising archaeology, like the Mazotos shipwreck, the Late Classical period (4th century BC) merchant ship, which was still fully loaded with ceramic transport amphora, as found off the coast of Cyprus resting quietly at a depth of 45 m on a flat, sandy/clayish and fairly anaerobic seabed, out in the open. That the shipwreck's wooden hull is at last coming to light,[5] was righty foreseen during the early days of its documentation.

Anything but flat is the case of the Late Bronze Age (late 13th/12th century BC) shipwreck at Modi, a rocky islet just off of the island of Poros, Greece.[6] The remains of this shipwreck, rich in a ceramic cargo and embedded with sherds of fine pottery which

---

5   Manning et al. 2022.
6   Agouridis & Michalis 2021.

Fig. 2. Temporary *in situ* protection of Caisson Area 1, Lechaion Harbour. Wide and long strips of non-woven geotextile (300 g/m² and made from polyester fibres) were laid on top of the exposed parts of the wooden remains (see middle image: finger points between a caisson's plank and an upright's cross-section, both camouflaged due to biofouling) and were pinned on the ground with custom-made (30 x 50 cm) hessian sacks (highest quality, i.e. thick weave) filled with inert quartz sand (0.1-0.4 mmᵒ), to such an amount as to allow manipulating the sack and fully snuggle around the remains. Loose seabed rocks were fitted together to anchor the covering on the seabed (Snapshots from videos. Video: Frederik Vingaard Rasmussen, © Lechaion Harbour Project).

trickled down on it from the remains of the settlement from the late phase of the Late Helladic III B2 period, atop the islet, lie at an average depth of 25 m and follows the islet's natural rocky slope. Indeed, a rocky burial slope needs a temporary retaining wall built to secure us from rubble crumbling on our heads whilst working and certainly from smashing the artefacts, too. Conservation work to extract these artefacts with a mallet and chisel from this rocky, conglomerative burial context is a sort of meditative sculpturing, reshaping the already shaped, both under water and aboard the research vessel.

Fig. 3. Building the artificial wall parallel to Caissons 5's west side (top photograph) and north side (bottom photograph), whilst creating a c. 0.30 m ditch to be laid with geotextile before pouring in the fine quartz sand in the process of reburying after excavation. Mole L-M3, Area 1, Lechaion Harbour (© Lechaion Harbour Project).

Conservators need a broad skill set and to be inventive, because working under water is ambitious – *in situ* protection is not as *easy* as excavation, because it *should* last. Take, as an example, Caisson 5 of Mole L-M3 at Lechaion Harbour: a very large organic material 'object', measuring from what has been excavated so far, as c. 4 m along its north side and another 4 m along its west side and with a preserved height of about 0.7 m. Since full excavation, removal, storage and conservation of the caisson is not an option, as yet, our approach to rebury it was to build a strong wall along its north and west sides by stacking small-sized polypropylene (PP) bags filled with sieved sand from the beach at a distance of c. 0.30 m, in essence creating a ditch, architecturally executed by one of our Danish senior maritime archaeologists (Fig. 3).[7]

The ditch was then laid with thick non-woven geotextile and filled with fine inert quartz sand, to promote an anaerobic and sterile environment in proximity to the organic matter. The ditch was levelled with the seabed and then sealed with another piece of geotextile, fully concealing and pinned down by layering, flat and densely, large PP bags filled with sand from the beach and interlocking with big stones lying abundantly on the seabed.

The wooden pilings were first wrapped individually in thick geotextile, tightened with wide bandage strips. A wall, which was as long and as high to cover all the pilings, was built close against the pilings, this time using dense-weaved hessian sacks filled with fine quartz sand. The dredgers were reversed and the extensive trench was backfilled with the same material that had been removed during the excavation.

7   Zisi forthcoming *a*.

109

Fig. 4. Excavating deeper down the trench, whilst using plastic bags filled with beach sand in order to hold up the trench from collapsing (© Lechaion Harbour Project).

Yet, the number of plastic bags used for reburying Caisson 5 was alarming to the Greek authorities and to us for environmental reasons, since all this plastic was (re)buried too. This also included the bags used to cover the wooden remains fully exposed on the seabed, as well as the numerous bags the archaeologist laid out ingeniously to hold up his 'nest' from collapsing whilst excavating deeper down the remainder of the mole (Fig. 4) Therefore, in 2016 we decided to discontinue the use of plastic bags and in 2017 we started replacing first all those non-buried plastic bags with hessian sacks filled with quartz sand. The sand from the removed plastic bags was released back to the beach. It should also be noted that removing sand from the beach can have legal consequences in many places around the world.

Since 2016, LHP uses custom-made hessian sacks of the highest quality (dense weave) when associated with wooden remains, filled with the inert, fine quartz sand and of the next, lower quality when associated with non-organic material for supporting trench sides. These sacks are filled with fine limestone gravel from the local quarry in modern Corinth.[8]

Contribution ongoing excavation

Our contribution as conservators in the field, as well as in the laboratory, stems from our training in material science, material degradation and technological aspects. We have a trained eye capable of tracing and identifying degradation and distinguishing it from the actual construction of an object. We are, therefore, able to derive or at the very least, suggest a deterioration sequence and therefore, a likely sequence of events (history). A very simple example: observing the cross-sections of Caisson's 5 upright wooden pilings, we see they are fully perforated by *Teredo* (shipworm), in contrast to the caisson's large beams, forming its framework, whose wood cross-sections have not been attacked. It is easy to derive that these beams were originally covered and never exposed until today.[9]

From our knowledge of materials and technology, we can spot tool marks and work out construction designs, as, for example, joining the upright wooden

8   Zisi forthcoming *a*.

9   Zisi & Athanasopoulos 2021; Brandon 2014, 214, fig. 8.59.

pilings to the main caisson frame. The existence of just one random nail hit inversely, from the outside of the caisson inwards, in contrast to the rest of the archaeological evidence, can mark a quick fix before launching. Perhaps the upright did not quite fit upon assembly; could this further indicate the involvement of semi-skilled, young carpenters or time pressure and fast production?

Moreover, there is evidence supporting that not all pilings of the retaining wall were originally uniform in thickness or in profile. The condition assessment excluded natural degradation from being the cause of this. What we can observe, instead, is that some pilings have been adzed rectangularly, whilst others are round. In contrast to the adzed pilings, which preserve sapwood only at their corners – if at all – the round profiled pilings clearly preserve the sapwood layer circling the heartwood. Given that the existence of the sapwood layer defines roughly the end of a tree's life before being cut for use, it was possible to securely conclude that not all pilings had equal original thicknesses. It could be suggested that pilings were used based on local availability and/or are placed here in secondary use. The latter can possibly explain, at first glance, the reason some of the pilings look and feel considerably more battered than others, as it could be possible that their preserved condition was already compromised from previous use and thus were more prone to degradation/erosion than others, now being under water. Some could have also been replaced with 'fresh' wood pilings during service.[10]

Measured during condition assessment, preserved piling diameters, in most cases with sapwood, so far are between c. 0.11 m and 0.28 m. Since this is oak wood[11] – that is, from a tree that grows to a large dimension – could these pilings be a result of pollarding? This is a form of pruning trees in order to increase the yield – with oak this means more food for animal stock, i.e. acorns.

Collaboration

Conservators are a flexible, adjustable, practical and very easy-going kind of people, always open to collaborations with fellow colleagues all around the world representing all sort of professions and together, operate in a multidisciplinary mode.

Experience from various underwater excavations has shown that what seems to make the project work smoothly and efficiently (especially when it is multilingual), is small teams with all essential professions for its operation present at all times and led by equally skilled, inspiring and inclusive archaeologists-leaders. It is also important to mention that full employment in comparison to volunteering, secures more work and consistent work being done within the same period of time, because the team can remain on-site for the whole excavation season. Financial security can, furthermore, help to ensure that the same team which now has experience with the site, returns (hopefully) the next year. This approach allows commitment from team-members, which is also important when dealing with this kind of working experience. That said, there must always be room for wisely distributed voluntary work and internships, for it is essential for training, experience purposes and continuation, as well as dissemination and public engagement: the *raison d'être*.

Managing underwater challenges

At Lechaion Harbour, the most challenging archaeological remains, from a preservation point of view, are the rare organic wooden remains. A substantial amount of these remains, if not still fully buried in the sediment, is visible on the seabed, lying under

---

10   Zisi & Athanasopoulos 2021; Athanasopoulos et al. 2023, 610-2; Athanasopoulos 2024, 815-8.

11   Zisi forthcoming *b*.

Fig. 5. The map of the observable Universe. We are here: at the tip of the map, inside the Milky Way that is simply one of the dots forming the pale blue region with all the spiral-type galaxies (highlighted in blue circle). There are about 2 billion light-years from us to the next yellowish and brighter region with the elliptical-type galaxies and 13.7 billion light-years to the edge of the observable universe where the first flash of radiation was emitted soon after the Big Bang (Visualization by B. Ménard & N. Shtarkman, Johns Hopkins University, modified by the author. For a detailed version see Mapofthe-Universe: https://mapoftheuniverse. net/, Accessed November, 2025).

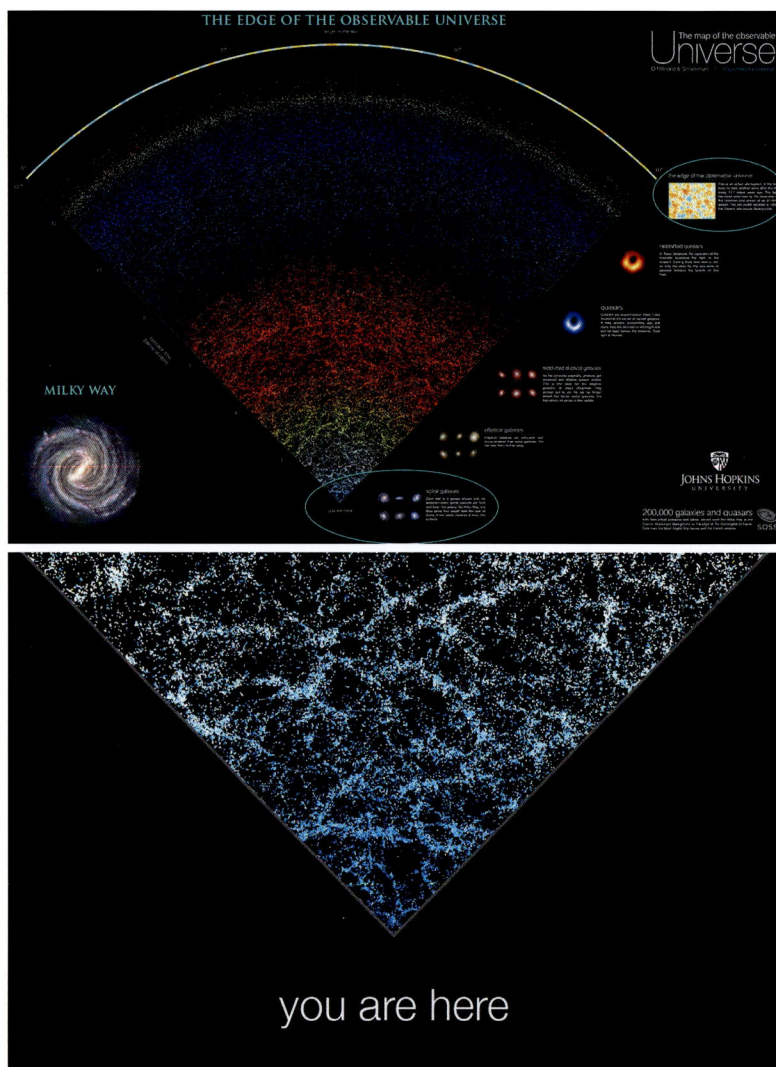

shallow waters, exposed to the sun, public bathing and a very dynamic and changing underwater environment. All these parameters make their excavation, documentation and especially long-term protection, a great undertaking – if not, at times, futile – in all earnest and even if funding has been secured.

Ethics in conservation direct that, unless we know and can better here and now, then we protect what is, as is, *in situ*, for future generations, because, as human progress proves, the future holds better solutions allowing generation after generation to resolve challenges based on technological and intellectual human progress and needs of their time. This makes the 'past' a source for perpetual progress. What mat-

ters is that Lechaion Harbour is there to harbour, bring us together and through our effort to study it and safeguard it, it evolves us, not itself *per se*; like the carcass of a once-travelling whale. Barely savoured by her surface predators, it will not take long until her body begins to sink to the depths below, to the earth's abyssal bed. Sea creatures sense her arrival and even in the total cold darkness, breakdown of her still giving body by the large supercentenarian predators and the minute bacteria shall continue until the perishment of this, once, evidence of existence. Yet, now fully utilised, it allows continuation for the species living even at those depths.

Fig. 6. In this mosaic image stretching 340 light-years across, Webb's Near-Infrared Camera (NIRCam) displays the Tarantula Nebula star-forming region in a new light, including tens of thousands of never-before-seen young stars that were previously shrouded in cosmic dust (Image and caption credits: NASA, ESA, CSA, STScI, Webb ERO Production Team. Tarantula Nebula (NIRCam Image)).

Heritage advancement

International consensus has via ICOM, set as its mission to ensure access to world heritage to present and future generations. But is there really a difference between present and future generations? The Greek physicist and writer, Giorgos Grammatikakis, writes in his book '*Η Κόμη της Βερενίκης*'[12]: "what surrounds us belongs to the distant past or the recent past". But since we are surrounded by the past light travelling to us, then, for the past light, we are the future (Fig. 5). We are the present generation as we are the future too. For the phrase 'for future generations' which lately, many so seemingly passively ruminate as the ultimate reasoning for all present action, like it is an action unrelated to us, is not an abstract term. The future cannot be preserved if one does not preserve oneself in the present.

Like a fraction of a Big Bang, *so* minuscule that is almost non-existent, we all too came into being by an explosion, that is our birth. In an interesting way, one could say that energy was released from this birth too. Although most likely not condensed in the same infinite magnitude and way as was the mass of the universe inside its spawning singularity, but instead comparing to the time scale of our Universe of which each one of us is momentarily a part of, then we do live a very, *very* condensed life, inside our spawning body and therefore, perhaps as significant as the Big Bang. Within it every human expression has a substance to give to its irrevocable continuance, even if carried in a perishable body.

Grammatikakis writes: "The humans' perception of the structure and function of the Cosmos reflects in every great civilisation and religion". There exists definitely 'something' great for us to draw from in search of meaning. Fig. 6 contains a merely 340 light-years across it[13] and if one light-*second* is equal to 384,400 km and this is the distance from the Earth to the Moon, one can reflect how great this something is. But as 'infinitely' great as it is, a primordial part of it, from the moment of its birth, is forged into our own bodies. Even if (literally) elemental, it is powerful in a way to initiate an inner dialogue; to stimulate our life choices; to make us pick the remains of hu-

---

12 Grammatikakis 2023, 35. The title refers to Coma Berenices, "Lock of Bernice", a small constellation with seven stars in the northern hemisphere. In modern times, apparently 'tangled' at Coma Berenices, are to be observed several supernovae, during whose luminous *death* only, the heavy elements necessary for *life* creation can be produced.

13 A light-year is the distance a beam of light travels in vacuum in a year on earth, which equates to approximately 9.5 trillion km.

man expression and preserve the evidence of our existence, as an anchor in the vastness of our Universe.

Given the creativity and level of ingenuity we humans have been and still are capable, or even in need of producing within our short and condensed cosmic lives, it is vital that we preserve its expression as, more often than not, we seem to want to forget and therefore repeat painful mistakes and hinder human advancement. The conservation of our common repository of museums and monuments both on land and under water and the whole cultural expression and wisdom, is significant to provide us evidence, truth, perspective, comfort, confidence, a sense of belonging and continuation. A human advancement aligned with that of our Universe.

Grammatikakis adds: "Awe amplifies when scientific knowledge is added to the experience. For it is the scientific knowledge which unravels the depth or the extension of all those things that the eye perceives".[14] Because it is the personal uplift sourcing from human culture that evidences existence.

Angeliki Zisi

Museum of Cultural History, University of Oslo, Norway

angeliki.zisi@khm.uio.no

Bibliography

AGOURIDIS, C. & M. MICHALIS 2021
'The Arduous Voyage of Underwater Research on the LBA Shipwreck off Modi Islet', in *Under the Mediterranean*, I. *Studies in Maritime Archaeology on the Anniversary of the Centenary of Honor Frost's Birth*, S. Demesticha & L. Blue (eds), Leiden, 22-41.

ATHANASOPOULOS, P. 2024
'Ἀρχαῖο Λιμάνι Λεχαίου: Χρήση ξύλου στην κατασκευή λιμενικῶν ἔργων κατά την Ὕστερη Ἀρχαιότητα', in *Proceedings of the Third International Scientific Meeting- Archaeological Work in the Peloponnese, AWOP 3*, M. Xanthopoulou (ed.), Kalamata, 811-9.

ATHANASOPOULOS, P., D. KOURKOUMELIS, B. LOVEN & P. MICHA 2023
'The Lechaion Harbour Project (2013-2018): Excavations at the Harbour of Lechaion in Corinth, Greece' in *ENTRE MARES, Emplazamiento, infrastructuras y organizacion de los puertos romanos*, Vol. II, M. Urteaga & A. Pizzo (eds), Rome, Bristol, 603-14.

BRANDON, C. J. 2014
'Roman formwork used for underwater concrete construction', in *Building for Eternity: the History and Technology of Roman Concrete Engineering in the Sea*, J. P. Oleson, R. L. Hohlfelder, C. J. Brandon & M. Jackson (eds), Oxford, 189-222.

CHABROL, A., H. DELILE, S. BARON, C. BOURAS, P. ATHANASOPOULOS & B. LOVÉN 2023
'Harbour geoarchaeology of Lechaion (Corinth area, Greece) sheds new light on economics during the Late Bronze Age/Early Iron Age transition', *Marine Geology* 465, 107-67.

GRAMMATIKAKIS, G. 2023
Η Κόμη της Βερενίκης, 6th edition, Herakleion.

ICOM 2010
Resolutions adopted by ICOM's 25th General Assembly, Shanghai, China, 2010, Paris. Available at: https://icom.museum/wp-content/uploads/2018/07/ICOMs-Resolutions_2010_Eng.pdf, Accessed May, 2025.

MANNING, S. W., B. LORENTZEN & S. DEMESTICHA 2022
'Dating Mediterranean shipwrecks: the Mazotos ship, radiocarbon dating and the need for independent chronological anchors', *Antiquity* 96:388, 968-80.

14   Grammatikakis 2023, 43.

STRÆTKVERN, K. & A. HJELM-PETERSEN 2021
'Standing on the shoulders of our predecessors – A base and a viewpoint. Fifty years of working with conservation of waterlogged archaeological shipwrecks in Denmark', *TINA Maritime Archaeology Periodical* 13, 46-68.

ZISI, A., FORTHCOMING A
'*In situ* conservation actions at Lechaion Harbour during excavation seasons 2015-2017', in *The Ancient Harbour of Lechaion: The use of wood in harbour construction during Late Antiquity* (Monographs of the Danish Institute at Athens), P. Athanasopoulos (ed.), Aarhus.

ZISI, A., FORTHCOMING B
'Wood identification of waterlogged wood samples from Lechaion Harbour, Greece', in *The Ancient Harbour of Lechaion: The use of wood in harbour construction during Late Antiquity* (Monographs of the Danish Institute at Athens), P. Athanasopoulos (ed.), Aarhus.

ZISI, A. & P. ATHANASOPOULOS 2021
'The Ancient Harbour of Lechaion in Corinth, Greece: Preliminary Results from the Excavation, Documentation, and Conservation Actions of its Submerged Wooden Structures', in *Maritime Archaeology Graduate Symposium, Book of Abstracts,* Aix-en-Provence, Marseille, 14. Available at: https://generic.wordpress.soton.ac.uk/mags/?page_id=154, Accessed May 2025.

Out of the Water Perspectives:

Dialogue with Heritage Conservators

Kristiane Strætkvern

Abstract

It's a fascinating sight when old wooden shipwrecks are exposed in underwater or water-saturated environments. Upon recovery, they appear with stories burning to be told and shared. Waterlogged archaeological wooden artefacts often appear to be in good condition, so why not take them out of the water and make them available to everyone?

Essential properties in archaeological, degraded wood from underwater or water-saturated environments diverge considerably from those of fresh or undegraded wood. Once removed from the underwater/water- saturated environment, a chain of destructive processes starts – unless they are met with precautions, definite plans, and resources to secure the future of the excavated artefacts. Understanding the differences between fresh or undegraded wood and archaeological waterlogged wood and its requirements are crucial for everyone involved in the excavation of waterlogged wooden finds and an introduction to the special properties of waterlogged wood is given in the opening of the paper. The paper then outlines some of the necessary steps when waterlogged archaeological shipwrecks are removed from the submerged environment until being in stable condition in appropriate storage or exhibition. Some steps are supplied with examples from work carried out by the National Museum of Denmark, where shipwreck projects in the field and in the laboratory have produced valuable research and experiences. Still, with the knowledge, experience, and equipment at hand, the process from exposure to exhibition of large archaeological finds – such as shipwrecks – continues to spark discussions, challenges, compromises, and unfortunately, loose ends. The paper discusses some of the unintended and unfortunate situations that occur over time when the long-term projects lose momentum, managers' attention, and resources.

Waterlogged archaeological wood

Irrespective of species, the cell structure in wood is composed of lignin and various types of celluloses. When a dry piece of wood is wetted or immersed in water it will swell. If the immersion of the wood in water or in a wet site continues, the wood pores are filled with water and the wood becomes waterlogged. Artefacts of wood buried in the right environmental conditions can survive for thousands of years.

Crucial for the survival of wooden artefacts is the presence of water and the absence of oxygen, as only very few wood degrading insects, microorganisms and bacteria survive in wet and anoxic conditions. The surviving 'Erosion bacteria' degrade and alter the celluloses and hemi-celluloses in the cell lumen. They are, however, unable to break down the lignin in wooden cell walls. The interior cell structure in heavily degraded wood has lignin as a main component (Fig. 1).

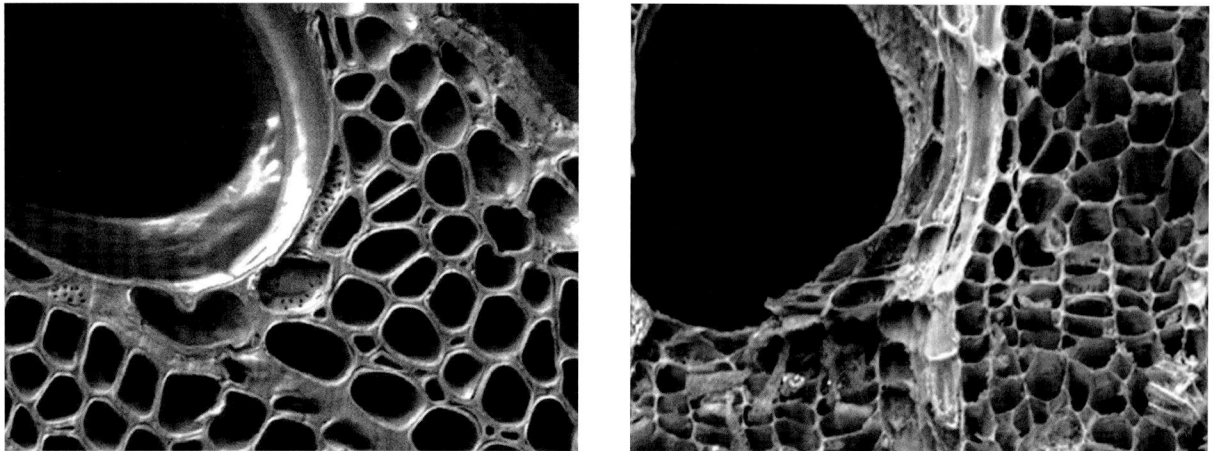

Fig. 1. LV-SEM pictures of undegraded (left) and heavily degraded (right) ash wood. Note the extremely thin 'lignin' cell walls and lack of celluloses in the degraded wood (Photos: Ulrich Schnell).

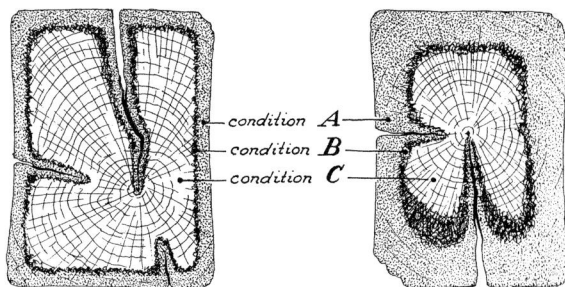

Fig. 2. Degradation patterns in waterlogged archaeological wood. The zones marked 'A' indicate heavily degraded wood suffering from substantial loss of material where strength and cohesion are considerably reduced. The zones marked 'B' have a mix of heavily degraded and almost undegraded wood. The zones marked 'C' consist of wood with little or no degradation. In the wood cross-section to the left, only the surface is heavily degraded and the less degraded core parts dominate. In the section to the right, heavy degradation dominates the wood condition. The difference in degree of degradation is not obvious until further examinations have been executed (Illustration: B. Brorson-Christensen).

Unless attacked by shipworm (e.g. *Teredo navalis*), waterlogged archaeological wood often appears undegraded and in perfect condition. Even then, the un-attacked parts of the ship timbers look perfect on the macroscopic level, but on the microscopic level,

as shown in Fig. 1, the view is different. Archaeological wood buried in oxygen-free waterlogged environments has typically been degraded by erosion bacteria, starting at the surface of the object, continuing towards the centre of the object at various rates (Fig. 2).[1] Some objects might be completely degraded and soft all the way through, whereas others have a more complex degradation pattern.[2] The degradation pattern depends on the wood species, the environment, the dimensions, and the geometry of the object and can therefore vary considerably for the elements in a find. As the wood surfaces may have tool marks, carvings, pigments, imprints, etc., important information is easily lost unless precautions are taken in the field.

As the fragile wood structure is only supported by water, the degree of degradation is rarely apparent upon exposure and most waterlogged archaeological wood appears in good shape and a well-preserved condition. However, once water evaporates uncontrolled from the degraded cells, the wood will de-

---

1 The degradation mechanisms and patterns and properties of degraded waterlogged are described by several experts, such as Björdal et al. 2021; Pedersen 2015; Gregory et al. 2012.
2 Brorson-Christensen 1970.

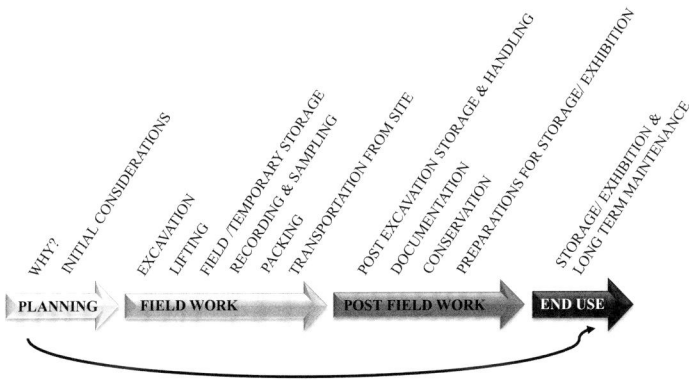

Fig. 3. Steps to consider and prepare for when planning an excavation where a shipwreck is to be removed from its marine environment. The ideal process considers and secures all steps including the end-use (Illustration: author).

form and shrink, creating irreversible damage. and very soon become unsuitable for documentation, research, conservation, and exhibition. Once exposed and excavated, a stable condition of the wood can only be achieved by reburial in a controlled, anoxic waterlogged environment or by conservation.

Any archaeological excavation leads to a change of the hitherto protective environment that has caused the survival of the wood. Therefore, excavations of archaeological shipwrecks require exceptional planning, resources, and long-term commitment, all of which will be described on the following pages.

Planning

Why excavate?

Article 2.5 of the UNESCO 2001 Convention on the Preservation of the Underwater Cultural Heritage stresses *in situ* preservation of cultural heritage as the first option.[3] Excavation forever disturbs the context, the environment, and the authenticity of the historical event. Nevertheless, there can be several reasons for disturbance, exposure, and excavation of archaeological sites. In spite of its small areal extent,

Denmark has a relatively long coastline (8,750 km), 400 islands, and a long tradition of coastal-based activities (seafaring, local sea transport, fisheries, a naval fleet, etc.). Moreover, if we go 5,000 to 7,000 years back, to the early settlements in Denmark, the sea level was considerably lower and rich remains from settlements in Danish pre-history still exist submerged beyond the current coastline. Therefore, almost any harbour expansion, bridge- or tunnel construction work on the seabed or coast around Denmark will produce cultural heritage remains.

The majority of excavations and investigations in Denmark are driven by development and construction projects. In most cases, when shipwrecks are removed from their environment, it is due to their location on a construction site. Some sites, in particular the prehistoric ones, are exposed and threatened due to changes in currents and sediment transport; some sites may be threatened by looting and on very rare occasions, underwater sites are excavated as part of research projects.

When *in situ* preservation is not possible and excavation and conservation are required, Article 2.6 of the UNESCO 2001 Convention states that "Recovered underwater cultural heritage shall be deposited, conserved and managed in a manner that ensures its long-term preservation".[4] To meet these

---

3   UNESCO 2001, Article 2.5.

4   UNESCO 2001, Article 2.6.

obligations, thorough planning and understanding of the challenges and risks that may occur in the long term are necessary (Fig. 3).

Initial planning considerations

When an underwater archaeological site is disturbed and degraded waterlogged wood is exposed, there is a chain of events and actions to consider for the excavation team. Some very useful guidelines regarding site management and planning of the field work are described in the EU Standard *EN 16873 Guidelines for management of waterlogged wood on terrestrial sites of archaeological significance*.[5] Although the guidelines are written for terrestrial sites and do not include the specifics for marine sites, many of the principles and concerns also apply for marine sites. The guidelines contain advice on important elements of the field work, such as management and protection of sites and finds, recording, labelling, cleaning, lifting, packing, and transportation of the finds. Excellent guidance in the planning process for all involved in underwater excavation projects can also be found in the *Manual for Activities directed at Underwater Cultural Heritage*.[6]

Planning includes the financial planning. Not only for the excavation and field work, but also for the following post-field work and end-use. This is stated as Rule 17 in the *Annex to the UNESCO 2001 Convention*: "Except in cases of emergency, to protect underwater cultural heritage, an adequate funding base shall be assured in advance to complete all stages of the project design, including conservation documentation and curation of recovered artifacts and report preparation, and dissemination".[7] Securing the finances is a huge undertaking which tends

to be underestimated. Another underestimated challenge is securing long-term commitment and clear responsibilities throughout the project period. These issues will be further elaborated in the following.

Field work

From the moment of exposure, waterlogged wood finds are vulnerable to a range of cultural and natural threats. To minimize these threats and prevent damage, several actions in the field must be taken which must include proper management of the site and handling of the finds. These activities should be carried out by professionals, specifically qualified in the management and handling of waterlogged archaeological wood.[8]

When shipwrecks are excavated and salvaged the risks to consider are numerous. In Denmark, the traditional way to excavate and rescue shipwrecks is done by dismantling the (very often) clinker-built structure and remove the individual timbers from the site.[9] In addition to the risks related to diving, heavy equipment, and bad weather, the handling of large and heavy – nevertheless degraded – timbers requires special attention. Approved lifting bars and supports must be able to safely fasten and be adjustable on the seabed as well as for later handling onboard the working ship and on land. Efficient and secure wet/humid packing, stacking, and labelling of timbers in a limited space requires constant dialogue with the divers working under water. In between the heavy timbers, separate solutions for temporary storage and transport must also be prepared for smaller artefacts and fragments. On top of it, shipwreck excavations and salvaging are not frequent events, thus

---

5   European Committee for Standardization 2016.

6   Maarleveld et al. 2013.

7   UNESCO 2001, Annex, Rule 17; Maarleveld et al. 2013, 127.

---

8   European Committee for Standardization 2016, 4.

9   The total ship structure is documented and recorded *in situ* prior to dismantling and lifting.

communication with the press and journalists visiting must be prepared for.

A field work case study: The Kolding Cog excavation

An example of well-planned field work is the excavation of the Kolding Cog (1190 AD), a cog that originally was discovered and partially investigated in 1943. The new excavation project took place in Kolding Fjord early in March 2001 and – very unusually – it was a research project.[10]

The aim of the research was to:
- Record the wreck site applying direct survey mapping
- Study the sediment composition of the burial site
- Study the interactions between the wood and the surrounding environment
- Dismantle the ship and raise the individual timbers
- Bring all ship parts to a specific location for documentation

and finally, to:
- Rebury the ship at the original site on the bottom of the fjord, and
- Monitor the environment

For the environmental study, the concentrations of oxygen, hydrogen sulphide, and pH were measured before excavation. Sediment cores were extracted for further laboratory studies. To determine the chemical and physical condition of the waterlogged wooden timbers, two frames from the wreck were selected for physical, chemical, and microscopic examination.[11]

The Kolding Cog was a well-defined project with a clear purpose and end-use, with the team consisting of diving researchers, archaeologists, a diving conservator and students, gathered on the diving vessel *Henry,* which was equipped with a heavy lifting crane and an open cargo tank for the ship timbers. Once the mapping of timbers was completed, altogether 8 tonnes of wood were to be taken out of the water and some of the pieces weighed up to 450 kg. The exceptional volume and loads required special precautions.

- Solid wooden lifting boards and straps had been padded with rubber foam to prevent imprints in the soft wooden surfaces upon handling under water and when lifting out of the water
- The crane and lifting bars were provided with enough straps to support even the longest planks upon lifting out of the water
- The ship's open cargo tank was cushioned with fibreglass insulation mats that were inserted between each layer of wood ensuring secure stacking of planks and heavy timbers
- Under water, the archaeologists secured a good balance and placement of the lifting straps and supporting boards
- When the wood came close to the ship's side, the wood was rinsed with water and a soft brush before packing for storage on board and transportation
- Before timbers were taken out of the water, the type of timber to expect was communicated to the captain and to the packing and stacking team. Thus, the proper placement and packing could be prepared, and each piece lifted directly to the prepared spot

The precautions saved the excavation team and the timbers from a lot of extra handling and lifting during the excavation. Nevertheless, the next steps in the project such as transportation, documentation, and transfer to temporary storage tanks would re-

---

10   Dokkedal et al. 2001.
11   Study results in Jordan 2003.

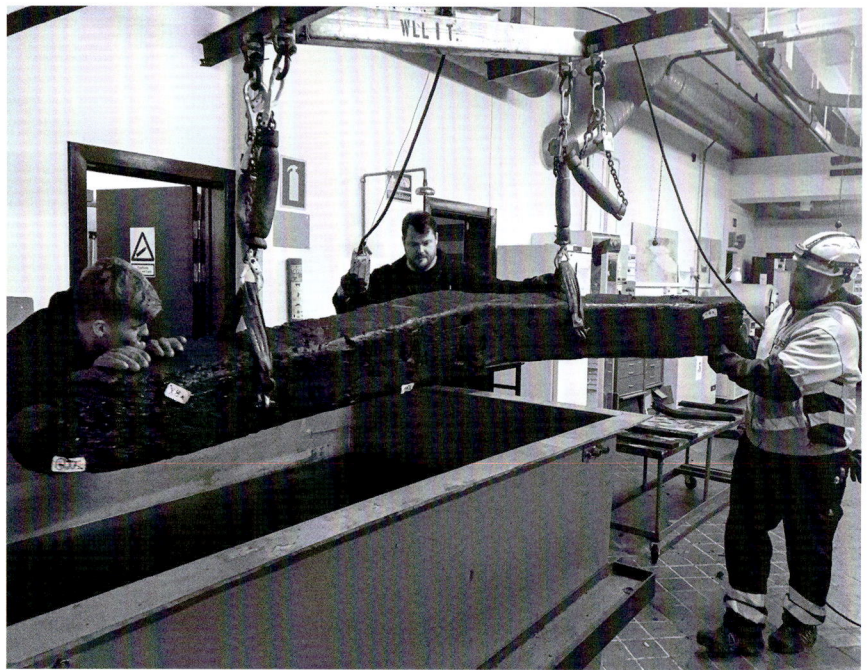

Fig. 4. A timber from the Kolding Cog is placed in a conservation tank in the National Museum's conservation laboratory in Brede, Denmark. Safe lifting without damaging the surface is secured by using the stainless-steel rods with eyebolts (Photo: The National Museum of Denmark).

quire more handling of the heavy timbers. In general, the degree of degradation of the Kolding Cog oak timbers can be compared to the ones shown in Fig. 2, left, with solid cores and degraded surfaces. To avoid damaging imprints from straps on the timbers' surfaces and to make the lifting easier, stainless-steel threaded rods with eyebolts were inserted into the heaviest and most complex timbers. The rods went all the way through the timber – with eyes for lifting hooks at both ends. The seemingly drastic intervention is a gentle one; it is easier to repair a 12 mm hole, than to repair a surface damaged from imprints of straps. The eyebolts also help safe lifting of the timbers. Smaller finds were taken by the divers to the archaeologist and conservator for recording and separate packing.

The Kolding Cog challenge

Until this point, the excavation project followed the original plans. However, the excavation got a lot of attention in the local press, and during the field work, the published story sparked a lot of interest

in the community in and around Kolding. Thus, a demand was made that the cog should not be reburied as planned but be conserved and exhibited in the local museum. Local authorities initiated the fundraising to cover the costs of the preliminary storage of the ship timbers until the full plan was funded and Kolding Cog shares could be purchased for around 14 Euros each. Enough money for temporary storage was raised, and provisional storage tanks were established in nearby Koldinghus (now a museum).

The idea of the locals was to raise further funding for conservation and preparation of the exhibition facilities, but the interest faded, the fundraising stopped, and the timbers sat in Koldinghus in the temporary water-filled storage tanks for 21 years.

As the organisation in charge of the original research project, the National Museum of Denmark had the overall responsibility for the cog. In 2023, the storage facilities in Koldinghus were required for a different purpose, and a relocation of the cog timbers was necessary, so the National Museum was contacted to solve the issue. The solution came from a foundation that wanted to support a new Center for Maritime and Submarine Cultural Heritage at the National Museum. The foundation agreed to cover new documentation with new 3D techniques as well as conservation costs and the cog timbers were transported to the National Museum's conservation laboratory in Brede in October 2023 (Fig. 4). Twenty-three years after the excavation, there seems to be a better future for the Kolding Cog. Here, the wood will be treated according to the conservation protocol that has been applied in the laboratory for decades.

Post-field work

Why conservation?

In fresh wood, the cells and cell walls are intact and can withstand evaporation of water from the wood capillaries. In archaeological wood, the cells walls are degraded and thin. The strength is reduced and owing to the surface tension of the water, the cell walls collapse once the water evaporates. The cell walls become flat, and this collapse cannot be reversed. The aim of conservation of waterlogged archaeological wood is to bring the wood from the wet, unstable chemical and physical condition to a dry and stable one. The challenge in this process is to avoid collapse and to reduce shrinkage while applying a reversible conservation method.[12]

The conservation protocol at the National Museum of Denmark's laboratory for waterlogged wood

In the National Museum's lab, the preferred conservation method is a combination of impregnation with Polyethylene Glycol (PEG), followed by vacuum freeze-drying. PEG was introduced in conservation of waterlogged wood in the early 1960s and has been applied to several major ship-finds, such as *Vasa*, the Skuldelev Viking Ships, the Bremen Cog, and *Mary Rose*. With so many years in use, its long-term properties are well known. Additionally, PEG has several good properties as an impregnation agent.

For example, its water soluble, non-toxic, and can be applied directly to the wood in water tanks. When a high molecular mass PEG (such as PEG2000 or PEG4000) is applied, the treated objects can be stored at generally recommended museum storage and exhibition environments (up to 23° C, RH 45-55%). Once the appropriate equipment is in place, the conservation process is, in theory, straight forward. Although PEG with some difficulties can be removed from the wood after treatment, it is recommended that samples for scientific analyses (i.e. ^{14}C dating or isotope analyses), are taken prior to conservation treatment. As PEG is corrosive to metals, the solution is not always a suitable impregnation agent if the find has a structure combining wood and i.e. bronze or iron. Also, remains of salts inside the wood, such as of sulphur, iron, or calcium, may cause long-term problems with the treated ship timbers (i.e. *Vasa*).[13]

In Denmark, we prefer the use of PEG2000, as this type has suitable chemical and physical properties for the management and control of the impregnation and freeze-drying processes: it's a solid substance at room temperature, it diffuses into the wood within a reasonable time frame, and upon freezing it solidifies at -21° C.[14]

For impregnation, the waterlogged wood is placed in tanks with aqueous PEG2000 solution (concentrations 10% w/w). The impregnation takes place by diffusion and over time, depending on wood volumes, species, and degree of degradation the concentration is increased to 40-45% w/w. The duration of the impregnation can take up to five years for large volumes of oak timber. When the impregnation has reached its end point, the remaining water in the structure is removed by vacuum freeze-drying.

---

12   Basic introduction to the field: Brorson-Christensen 1970; see also Gregory et al. 2012.

13   Hocker 2018.

14   Strætkvern 2024; Jensen & Schnell 2005.

The main purpose of the vacuum freeze-drying process is to avoid the collapse that occurs when water in the wood evaporates uncontrollably. In vacuum freeze-drying, the water and the PEG in the wood capillaries is frozen to a solid substance in a dedicated chamber. At a sufficiently low temperature (-20 to -23° C), vacuum is applied to the chamber. In this atmosphere, ice turns directly to vapor and the vapor is removed from the wood and the chamber to a separate condenser by using a vacuum pump. The PEG remains in wood after drying, shrinkage is reduced, and collapse is avoided.

The method has been successfully applied to several ship-finds, most well-known perhaps is the Roskilde 6 Viking Age longship, where the vacuum freeze-drying process was refined with shaping the timbers in the correct hull shape prior to freezing, enabling assembly of the clinker-built ship after drying.[15] The method produces stable and aesthetically nice timbers and it is also being applied in ship conservation projects outside Denmark, such as for the Sørenga medieval ships in Oslo, Norway, and for several of the 37 shipwrecks from the Yenikapı site in Istanbul.[16]

The treatment method requires a vacuum freeze-drying plant designed to hold long ship timbers, which is not accessible everywhere. Also, vacuum-freeze drying, is a highly energy consuming process and the branch has yet to see equipment driven by solar- or wind power, or other renewable energy sources.

Bringing ship-finds from excavation to an 'appropriate' end-use

While a lot of resources were spent to finalise the conservation of the Roskilde 6 ship and prepare for exhibition and travel, less attention has been given to the remaining ships from the excavation in 1997. The Roskilde 6 ship was one of nine shipwrecks excavated from a construction site in Roskilde Harbour in 1996/97.[17] The enthusiasm when the shipwrecks were discovered was remarkable. All shipwrecks were excavated, documented, and brought to the conservation laboratory, but until today, only one of the nine wrecks, the Roskilde 6 Viking Age ship, has been conserved and made available to the public in exhibitions. Almost five wrecks have been conserved but are not assembled and the ship timbers are placed on shelves in storage. Three wrecks are still in the impregnation tanks, taking up space and blocking the way for other waterlogged finds. If a demand for exhibition of the three wrecks still in impregnation tanks should come up, there is still a chance to shape the timbers prior to freeze-drying and thus enable assembly after drying and mounting in shape for display and public access. No such plans are currently in sight and similar circumstances are the case for one more shipwreck in the wood conservation laboratory. In spite of efforts to bring attention to the potential for exhibiting and telling the stories of the shipwrecks, these finds seem to spark no interest among museum curators or managers.

The obvious reason for the unhappy position of the shipwrecks is that conservation of waterlogged archaeological wood, in particular large structures such as shipwrecks, demands a large number of resources. Moving, lifting, and handling of heavy but degraded timbers requires many hands and often expensive lifting equipment. Storage and conservation require large water tanks and treatment tanks in facilities that are equipped for the purpose. The conservation treatment is costly and may take several years. After conservation treatment, the timber requires considerable storage space or exhibition space. These spaces must be provided with indoor climate control to secure a stable temperature and

---

15   Strætkvern et al. 2016.

124   16   Kocabaş & Özsait-Kocabaş 2023.

17   Gøthche 2006.

avoid damaging fluctuations in the relative humidity. If the end-use is exhibition, costly preparations for drying in shape, mounting, and suitable supports must be included in the process and conservation budget.

Time itself is an additional risk related to such finds. In the long period of temporary storage and impregnation tanks, sometimes 10 to 15 years, the ships are out-of-sight other than to the conservators and other staff tending to them. During this time, the existence and requirements of the finds seem to be forgotten by the archaeologists, museum managers, and other stakeholders, despite efforts to remind them of the cultural heritage hidden in the tanks.

Changes in organisations and ownership also represents a risk to finds requiring long-term funding and commitment. Most professionals change job or institutions several times during their professional careers. Unless post-excavation processes and conservation have been given high priority and sufficient funding, it is not likely that the person responsible for planning and managing a shipwreck project is still around to see (and manage) the end of a project. Part of the management plan should therefore include the secure handing over to a capable successor. To be realistic, it might be difficult to hand over to a successor the enthusiasm and dedication from the beginning of the project, when the shipwreck broke the surface of the water. This is not only the case in Denmark, but similar issues are also recognized where other large finds are being treated under a long timeframe, such as the Yenikapı ships in Türkiye, excavated between 2004 and 2013, where there is still no final exhibition or appropriate storage solutions in place for the exceptional finds.[18]

The finances of state-owned institutions such as the National Museum of Denmark are vulnerable to political changes and priorities. This means that projects being many years under way also tend to suffer from lack of resources. The motivation for politicians or fundraisers to support these types of projects is low. There are not many votes or valuable public relations in finalising projects starting more than 20 years ago, unless there is a really good story to be told.

When projects change hands or take a very long time, the responsibility tends to become unclear, and when action or resources are required, it often becomes the headache of the conservators. This brings me back to the starting point: namely, the planning of the investigation and excavation of shipwreck sites and the cocktail of risks served when shipwrecks are taken out of the water.

A site management decision map, developed by Gregory and Manders in the SASMAP project[19] describes the steps that should be considered for the proper management of underwater cultural sites – from the start until the end-use. The initial steps include the assessment of the significance of a find. The information for considering significance (such as provenance, representative value, uniqueness, completeness, and capacity to inform about the past) must be combined with the threats on the site and potential end-uses, such as *in situ* conservation, reburial, or conservation *ex situ*.

Once it has been decided that a ship is to be removed from its environment and that conservation is the best way to save this cultural heritage for the future, it implies the find has sufficient cultural value to justify this end-use. The decision to raise and conserve a shipwreck should therefore involve stakeholders and managers deciding this end-use, taking on the responsibility for the future of the find. To take on the responsibility means raising funds and securing continued resources to stimulate research and investigate future access and dissemination of the find. As mentioned initially, security of funding to complete the project is crucial. This should be the case also when the timeline is long. Rule 18 of the *Annex of the UNESCO 2001 Conven-*

---

18   Kocabaş & Özsait-Kocabaş 2023.

19   Gregory & Manders 2015, 51-63.3

tion states: "The project design shall demonstrate an ability, such as securing a bond, to fund the project through to completion"[20] and creating a timetable that pays close attention to the above-mentioned risks is crucial.

Although there are rules and guidelines, and despite good intentions, it has proven difficult to avoid uncompleted projects. The main challenge is the proper continued management of the find from beginning until the very end. This involves the allocation of resources including fundraising, clear allocation of responsibilities and ownership, and the ability of the managers to remain dedicated throughout the project and prioritise the completion of the project within a manageable timeframe.

Kristiane Strætkvern
Department of Research, Collections and Conservation
The National Museum of Denmark
kst@natmus.dk

Bibliography

BJÖRDAL, C., J. J. ŁUCEJKO, F. MODUGNO & N. B. PEDERSEN 2021
'Correlation between bacterial decay and chemical changes in waterlogged archaeological wood analysed by light microscopy and Py-GC/MS', *Holzforschung* 75-7, 635-45.

BRORSON-CHRISTENSEN, B. 1970
The Conservation of Waterlogged Wood in the National Museum of Denmark, The National Museum of Denmark, Copenhagen.

DOKKEDAL, L., F. HOCKER & B. JORDAN 2001
Beretning for marinarkæologisk udgravning af Kogge i Kolding fjord. NMU j.nr. 82, Marin nr. 321323. Nationalmuseets Marinarkæologiske Forskningscenter, Roskilde.

EUROPEAN COMMITTEE FOR STANDARDIZATION 2016
EN 16873:2016: Conservation of cultural heritage – Guidelines for the management of waterlogged wood on archaeological terrestrial sites, CEN: the European Committee for Standardisation/TC 346 Conservation of Cultural Heritage/WG9 Waterlogged Archaeological Wood, Brussels.

GREGORY, D., P. JENSEN & K. STRÆTKVERN 2012
'Conservation and in situ preservation of wooden shipwrecks from marine environments', *Journal of Cultural Heritage* 13:3, 139-48.

GREGORY, D. & M. MANDERS (EDS) 2015
Best practices for locating, surveying, assessing, monitoring and preserving underwater archaeological sites, SASMAP Guideline Manual 2, Amersfoort.

GØTHCHE, M. 2006
'The Roskilde Ships' in *Connected to the Sea, Proceedings of the Tenth International Symposium on Boat and Ship Archaeology, ISBSA 10, Roskilde 2003*, L. Blue, F. Hocker & A. Englert (eds), Oxford, 252-8.

HOCKER, E. 2018
Preserving Vasa, London.

JENSEN, P. & U. SCHNELL 2005
'The implications of using low molecular weight PEG for impregnation of waterlogged archaeological wood prior to freeze drying', in *Proceedings of the 9th ICOM group on Wet Organic Archaeological Materials Conference, Copenhagen 2004*, P. Hoffmann, K. Strætkvern, J. Spriggs & D. Gregory (eds), Copenhagen, 279-310.

---

20   UNESCO 2001, Annex, Rule 18; Maarleveld et al. 2013, 136.

JORDAN, B. A. 2003

Analyses of environmental conditions and types of bio-deterioration affecting the preservation of archaeological wood at the Kolding shipwreck site. Unpublished PhD thesis, University of Minnesota, USA.

KOCABAŞ, U. & I. ÖZSAIT-KOCABAŞ 2023

'Comparative Analysis of Lifting from On-Site and Conservation of the Yenikapı Shipwrecks' in *Heritage 2023,* 6, D. Cvikel (ed.), 1871-90.

MAARLEVELD, T. J., U. GUERIN & B. EGGER (EDS) 2013

Manual for Activities directed at Underwater Cultural Heritage, Guidelines to the Annex of the UNESCO 2001 Convention, Paris.

PEDERSEN, N. B. 2015

Microscopic and spectroscopic characterisation of waterlogged archaeological softwood from anoxic environments, Copenhagen.

STRÆTKVERN, K. 2024

'Vacuum Freeze-Drying of Waterlogged Archaeological Wood and Selecting the Impregnation Agent Prior to Drying', in *Actas de la Reunión Internacional de Expertos sobre la extracción y conservación del pecio Mazarrón 2, Proceedings of the International Experts Meeting on the extraction and conservation of the wreck Mazarrón 2,* M. A. García, R. Castillo, C. Belinchón & C. Escribano (eds), Murcia, 303-14.

STRÆTKVERN, K., A. H. PETERSEN, N. POKUP-CIC, I. BOJESEN-KOEFOED, A. MOESGAARD & J. B. JENSEN 2016

'A short story of the conservation of the World's longest Viking Age shipwreck for exhibition and travel', in *Proceedings of the 12th ICOM Group on Wet Organic Archaeological Materials Conference, Istanbul 2013,* T. Grant & C. Cook (eds), Paris, 377-83.

UNESCO 2001

2001 Convention on the Protection of Underwater Cultural Heritage, Paris. Available at: https://www.unesco.org/en/legal-affairs/convention-protection-underwater-cultural-heritage?hub=412, Accessed February, 2025.

Communication

Unlocking the Depths:

Engaging Audiences through Artistic Perspectives in Maritime Archaeology

Andreas Kallmeyer Bloch

Abstract

Maritime archaeology delves into the remnants of human interaction with the sea. This chapter explores the importance of disseminating these findings through various art forms to maintain public interest and support. Focusing on the Danish slave ships Fredericus Quartus *and* Christianus Quintus, *which sank off the coast of Costa Rica in 1710, the article examines how journalists, documentary filmmakers, painters, and writers have brought this story to life. By involving these artists from the outset, the project has ensured widespread public engagement, enhancing the narrative's depth and accessibility. The collaboration includes a journalist writing a detailed book, a documentary filmmaker capturing the excavation process, a painter depicting key moments, and a novelist creating a compelling story. These interdisciplinary efforts demonstrate the potential of combining traditional and innovative methods to communicate archaeological discoveries, fostering a deeper connection between the public and our shared history. The case of the Danish slave ships illustrates how diverse storytelling approaches can enrich our understanding and appreciation of the past, highlighting the crucial role of public dissemination in the field of archaeology.*

Introduction

Maritime archaeology studies human interactions with the sea through shipwrecks, harbours, sailing barriers, fishing systems, and settlements. These archaeological remains are significant for understanding our shared history and identity. However, if archaeological discoveries are only recorded in academic literature, their relevance to the public may diminish. To keep archaeology engaging and significant to a wider audience, it is vital to incorporate various art forms. Public interest is essential for political and societal support; without it, archaeology risks becoming marginalized. This essay explores how artists, journalists, writers, painters, and documentary filmmakers have conveyed the history

of two Danish slave ships, *Fredericus Quartus* and *Christianus Quintus*, which sank in 1710 near Cahuita National Park off the east coast of Costa Rica.

This exploration is based on personal and subjective perspectives, aiming to inspire unique collaborations that blend traditional and innovative dissemination methods. The archaeological site in question is extraordinary, almost like a script for a TV series, though not all investigations yield such evident storytelling opportunities. Nevertheless, every archaeological site holds potential, often revealed by unexpected narrators.

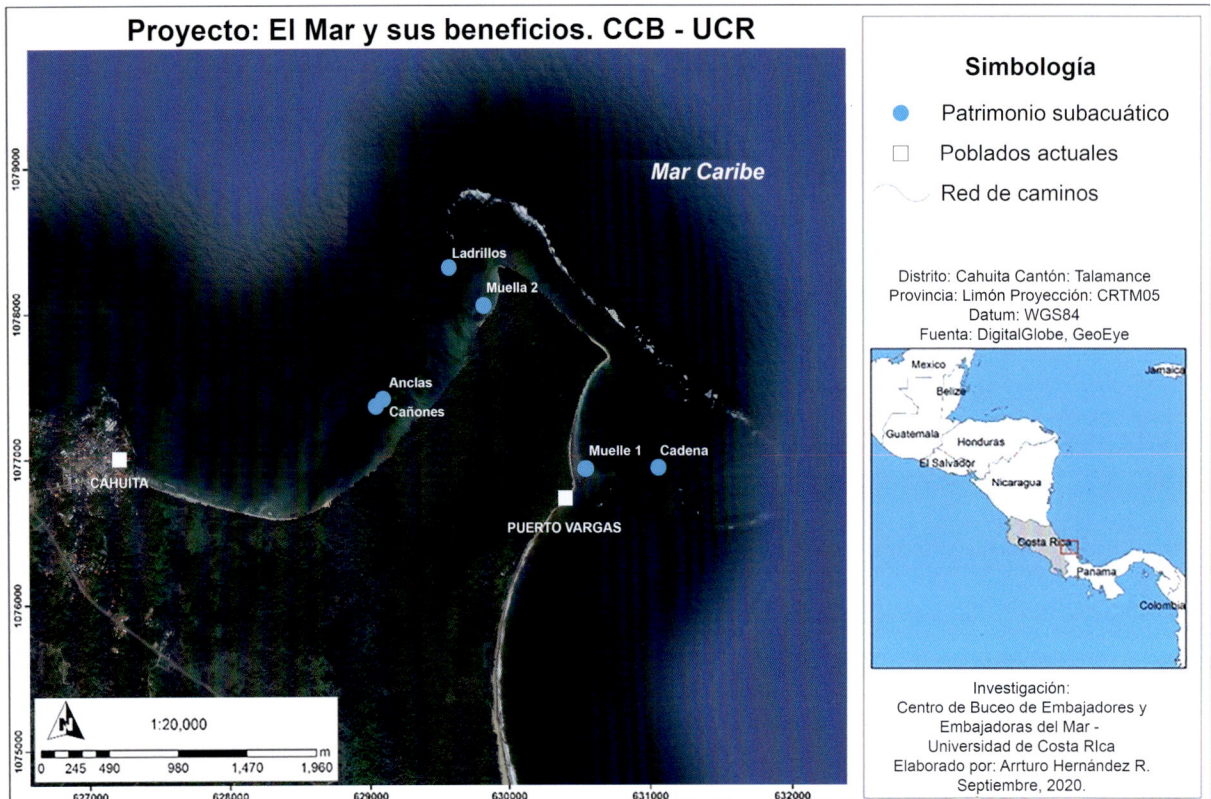

Fig. 1. Map of the area of the wrecks, near Cahuita National Park off the east coast of Costa Rica. *Lardrillos* and *Anclas/Cañones* refer to the two wrecks (Map: based on data from Arturo Hernández).

The story of the two ships

Off the Caribbean coast of Costa Rica lie the remains of two shipwrecks (Fig. 1). Historical records, combined with the wrecks' location and the discovery of numerous yellow bricks, suggest these are the Danish slave ships *Fredericus Quartus* and *Christianus Quintus*, which sank in 1710.[1] This project provided a unique opportunity for archaeological fieldwork, sample analysis, and archival research to confirm their identity.

In late 1708, the two Danish ships departed from Copenhagen, sailing via West Africa to St Thomas in the West Indies. In West Africa, they traded goods for enslaved people, and after months along the coast, the ships were loaded with hundreds of slaves. Shortly after leaving Christiansborg in Ghana (in present-day Accra), a rebellion broke out among the slaves, which was swiftly and harshly suppressed.[2]

By spring 1710, the ships found themselves in the Caribbean, either having sailed too far or been blown off course, ending up about 2,000 km west of their destination, St Thomas. With dwindling supplies, mutiny erupted among the crews. *Fredericus Quartus* was set ablaze, and *Christianus Quintus* had its anchor cut, wrecking in the surf. Written sources indicate the ships sank near the coast, with slaves disembarking beforehand. Some slaves were captured and sold by the Spanish in Costa Rica, but the fate of most remains unknown. Many Danish crew members survived, returning to Denmark or

1 Harris & Richards 2018.

2 Nørregaard 1948, 75.

Norway, where they recounted their ordeal to the royal court, now documented in the Danish National Archives.[3]

In shallow waters off Cahuita National Park in Costa Rica, two shipwrecks were recorded for the first time by an American archaeologist in early 1990s.[4] Their proximity and the abundance of yellow bricks strongly indicated that these were the Danish slave ships. The bricks, likely Flensburg bricks from Flensburg Fjord, required further examination to confirm their origin.

Archaeological investigations and analyses

The National Museum of Denmark and the Viking Ship Museum in Roskilde, Denmark, were invited by a local NGO, *Centro Comunitario de Buceo Embajadores y Embajadoras del Mar* (CCBEE), the Costa Rican Cultural Heritage Authority (*Comisión Arqueológica Nacional* – CAN), and the National Museum of Costa Rica to lead a minor excavation of the wrecks in 2023. The goal was to collect representative samples of bricks and ship timber. The excavation, conducted in September 2023, yielded solid results, and the material has been analysed (Fig. 2).

Professor Kaare Lund Rasmussen from the University of Southern Denmark analysed the chemical composition of the bricks' clay and determine their origin to Egernsund and Iller Strand in Flensborg Fjord. Researchers from the National Museum of Denmark's Department of Environmental Archaeology and Materials Science conducted dendrochronological studies and has dated the timber to 1690-1695 and identified its provenance to the eastern part of the Baltic Sea. Additionally, ten fragments of clay pipes have been dated to the exact

Fig. 2. David Gregory of the National Museum of Denmark during the investigations in 2023 (Photo: Jakob Olling).

same period as the ships departed from Denmark. These analyses confirm the wrecks' identity as the Danish ships.

Preliminary investigations of historical sources and archaeological material were highly convincing.[5] This confidence leading up to the excavation in 2023 allowed early engagement with storytellers, journalists, and artists. Disseminating archaeology can be particularly effective when it follows the research process, not just the final results. Engaging the public in the archaeological process and following the analysis of the material gives a sense of taking part in creating history, not just receiving the results in final conclusions.

---

3   Rigsarkivet (The Danish National Archives), Box 446.
4   Gluckman 1992.

5   Borelli & Harris 2018.

Journalism: Bringing the story to life

Journalists have a unique ability to bring complex historical events to life through their investigative work and storytelling skills. I told the story of these wrecks to the journalist Jakob Olling in 2018, and he was so surprised and fascinated by the story that he took leave from his job and started writing, resulting in a book that provides a detailed and vivid description of the shipwrecks and the people involved both now and then.[6] The book weaves together personal accounts and expert insights, allowing readers to understand the historical and human aspects of the event (Fig. 3). Having a journalist always following all the work leading up to the excavation was a clear advantage for the media coverage. Not only did he write his own book, but he was highly involved in writing press releases and feeding news to the Danish press, before the project in 2023 led to identification of the shipwrecks.

The strength of having a journalist on the sideline was that news about the work could be spread fast though different channels, enabling the public to be part of all new findings. The continuous media coverage gave new sources of information from readers. I was contacted by a descendant of a captain that was on the previous journey with one of the ships, by researchers that had specific areas where they could contribute, and by various people that had a general interest in the story.

The particular challenges that can arise with the journalistic approach include potential mistakes, which can naturally occur due to the fast pace of the work. Journalists are normally not trained historians and do not follow the same scientific methods as we do, but they have communication channels that reach local and national audiences quickly – much faster than we archaeologists do. Errors can occur, and details may turn out to be incorrect.

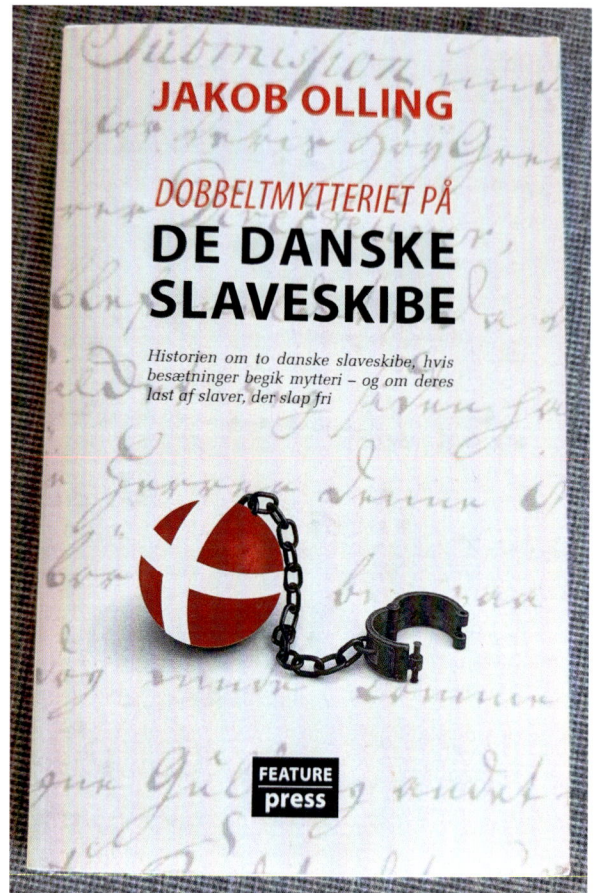

Fig. 3. Journalistic book by Jakob Olling, *Dobbeltmytteriet på de danske slaveskibe* ("Double mutiny on the Danish slave ships"), about the ships and ongoing investigations (Photo: Andreas Kallmeyer Bloch).

However, this is also the strength of journalistic dissemination – it reaches the public quickly and creates a timeliness that scientific articles often cannot achieve. It is very much a matter of the individual archaeologist and project weighing in on whether they are willing to risk these inaccuracies.

Documentary film: Making the story visual

Documentary films have a unique ability to bring history to life through visual and auditory media. The documentary film uses not only images and

6   Olling 2018.

sound to tell the story but also interviews with researchers and people involved, providing insight into the project's significance. Animations showing the ships on route, the rebellion, and the final wrecking have become much more accessible with artificial intelligence and these tools make it possible for filmmakers to visualize the past

A Danish documentary filmmaker also heard about the two wrecks and immediately wanted to film the project from start to finish, which hopefully will result in a documentary depicting the archaeology, history, and all the facets that these two wrecks represent. The filmmaker followed us on the first trip to Costa Rica in 2018, where we met people from the NGO CCBEE, and researchers from the East Carolina University, and we were joined by David Gregory and Louise Sebro from the National Museum of Denmark. It did not cost anything, but it posed an opportunity to document what happened professionally, with good sound and film equipment, and made sure that it could be made into a documentary or as visualizations in museum installations if the theory about the wrecks turned out to be true.

A significant addition to the discussion about documentaries and their role in disseminating maritime archaeology is the documentary *Enslaved*, featuring actor Samuel L. Jackson, CCBEE and the NGO "Diving with a Purpose".[7] *Enslaved* explores the history of the tranatlantic slave trade by following underwater archaeologists searching for slave ships that sank during the transport of enslaved Africans. Although the documentary significantly raises awareness of the slave trade and its consequences, it has also faced criticism for taking certain artistic liberties and not always presenting the full story.

For example, *Enslaved* is criticized for focusing heavily on Jackson's personal journey and experiences, which some believe overshadow the archaeological findings and scientific aspects of the story. Additionally, there is criticism that the documentary sometimes chooses to dramatize events to make them more appealing to viewers, which can lead to a simplification or distortion of historical facts. This underscores the importance of balancing between making the story engaging while preserving its accuracy and complexity.

Denmark's National Broadcasting Channel, DR (*Danmarks Radio*) has also filmed a documentary aimed at finding descendants from the ships and depicting the significance this has for local identity. Through archaeology, written sources, and local narratives, it becomes possible to bring the story into the present and highlight the traces this shipwreck has left. Descendants of both one of the enslaved Africans and one of the Danish captains were found. The programme, *Forsvundne arvinger Special – Mysteriet om slaveskibene* ("The lost heirs special – the mystery of the slave ships"), was broadcast in April 2025, and quickly became one of the most viewed programmes on Danish television.[8]

Being part of documentaries has been the most difficult discipline, because as an archaeologist, you present your face and academic insight to everyone. However, you have no control over the editing process, and words you use can be put in a very different context from what you intended. The filmmaker wants to tell a good story, and sometimes they change history to make it more appealing. It is of course not always the case, however; documentaries should not be seen as factual information, but as a mixture of fiction and fact.

---

7   *Enslaved*, Episode 4, New World Cultures, October 5, 2020 (Canadian Broadcasting Cooperation). Can be visited at: https://www.cbc.ca/documentaries/enslaved/enslaved-episode-4-new-world-cultures-1.5733299, Accessed May, 2025.

8   *Forsvundne arvinger Special – Mysteriet om slaveskibene* on DRTV: https://www.dr.dk/drtv/serie/forsvundne-arvinger-special-_-mysteriet-om-slaveskibene_517621, Accessed May, 2025.

Fig. 4. Painting by Nikolai Fenger Pedersen (Image: Courtesy of Nikolai Fenger Pedersen).

Nevertheless, through multiple documentaries, the story of the two slave ships has been and will be brought to life and made accessible to a wide audience, hopefully contributing to increased interest and understanding of maritime archaeology and our shared history.

Painting: Depicting history through art

Visual art, such as paintings, also plays an essential role in communicating historical events. A colleague from archaeology who also paints joined the project and has created two paintings: one depicting the departure from Copenhagen in 1708 (Fig. 4), and another showing the ships lying in the National Park in Costa Rica (Fig. 5). These paintings offer a visual representation of the ship' journey and their final resting place.[9]

The paintings not only provide an aesthetic experience but also serve as historical documents that can convey complex information in an accessible way. They help viewers visualizing the ships, the situation, and help push the viewers imagination. Through art, we can gain insights into the past that words alone might not provide.

The artist who produced these two paintings, Nikolai Fenger Pedersen, has been meticulous in considering ship types and rigging. As with other participants, there has been no control over what they create; how they interpret the story is entirely up to them. We have invited them because we believe they can add new perspectives.

Unlike journalistic articles and documentaries, paintings have a long lifespan and can live on after articles and documentaries has become outdated. The lifespan of paintings can be endless. I believe this is because it is not only telling the story of the historic event, but it is a fictional representation of the artist's creative soul and goes beyond the facts of the story allowing the beholder to create a connection to the story and its people. It is an open door to the imagination, and not a media where you are told what happened and what it meant. This open door to people's imagination is very similar when

9   In private ownership.

Fig. 5. Painting by Nikolai Fenger Pedersen (Image: Courtesy of Nikolai Fenger Pedersen).

it comes to authors writing fictional works: like the painter, the author takes history, makes it personal, and allows everyone to feel the story. We all know they are not telling the exact truth, but they build a fictional truth around the story – this makes the beholder, and the reader, engage and connect with the story.

Writing: Novels and academic works

Academic books and articles play a crucial role in disseminating archaeological findings. A series of articles and reports have been published by the staff at East Carolina University, contributing to the academic understanding of the wrecks and the historical context of the ships.[10] These articles provide a detailed analysis of the archaeological findings and historical sources, helping other researchers understand the significance of the wrecks.

Academic articles will be produced by the Danish team when the analysis of the excavated material has been concluded; however, the people that will read these articles are partly the same as those who will read this article. And we do not need to tell other archaeologists or historians that our work is important; we also need to tell this to a broad audience.

A novel is currently being written by Danish author Merlin P. Mann about the two Danish ships. This novel will combine factual information with a (hopefully) compelling narrative, offering readers a more immersive experience. By blending history with fiction, the novel will engage readers on an emotional level, helping them to connect with the past. The same author has already included the two wrecks' final day in a novel for younger children, dramatizing the mutiny and disseminating history in fiction (Fig. 6).

The author says:

Fiction as such is merely a tool in order to make history and archaeology seem relevant to children and adults. I'm fascinated by archaeological findings, but

---

10   Harris & Richards 2018; Borelli & Harris 2018 includes other articles, reports, and books.

137

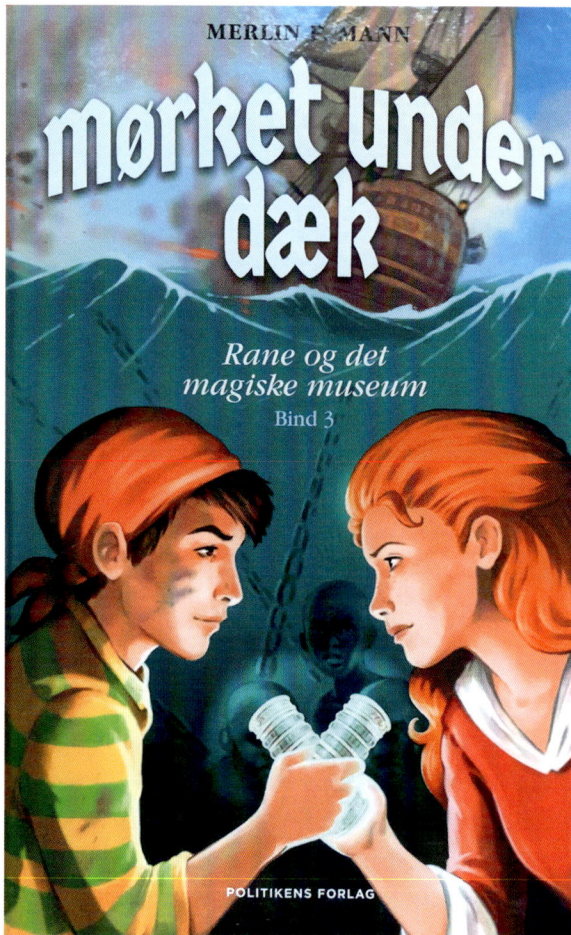

Fig. 6. Cover of Merlin P. Mann's book, *Mørket under dæk – Rane og det magiske museum* ("Darkness below decks – Rane and the magic museum") (Image: Courtesy of Merlin P. Mann).

about history, but we also need people to be able to understand that every piece of history, and every piece of archaeology is part of a framing, and is part of story, and that you as a human being need to interact with the story in order to understand, and in order to understand yourself as a human being.[11]

The process of writing articles and books about archaeological projects can be time-consuming but it is essential for creating a lasting record of the findings. By publishing both academic and popular works, archaeologists can reach a wide audience, from scholars to general readers. Not just today, but also for generations to come.

Challenges and benefits of engaging with multiple art forms

Engaging various art forms and media in disseminating archaeology has its challenges and benefits. One challenge is ensuring accuracy and maintaining the scientific integrity of the findings. Different art forms have different ways of presenting information, and it can be challenging to balance engaging storytelling with factual accuracy. Collaboration between artists, storytellers, and archaeologists is crucial to ensure that the story remains true to the evidence while being accessible and engaging to the public. It is essential to maintain open communication and collaboration to mitigate these risks.

However, the benefits of engaging with various art forms, I feel, far outweigh the challenges. By involving journalists, filmmakers, painters, and writers, we can reach a broader audience and make archaeology more accessible and engaging. Each art form brings a unique perspective and can highlight different aspects of the story, enriching our understanding of the past.

if you want to pass this fascination on to others, you need to use tools that they can relate to. The artefact itself is not important, but who has interacted with this artefact. Because it is the people of the past, I think that it is important for us as human beings today to relate to. We are not just singular individuals at one point in time, but that we are connected. The closest we can come to a universal truth or some sort of objectivity is by touching and being a part of a network of as many other people and as many other facts as humanly possible, and we do that by telling each other stories and we have always done that. Basically, I would say that we need people to have a curiosity

---

11   Quote from the author Merlin P. Mann during a filmed personal conversation in 2024. Translation, author.

Through the involvement of various artists, the story of *Fredericus Quartus* and *Christianus Quintus* has been brought to life in multiple ways. Journalists have provided detailed accounts, filmmakers have created visual narratives, painters have depicted historical scenes, and writers have woven factual information into compelling stories. Together, these efforts have made the story of these two Danish slave ships more accessible and engaging, ensuring that the history they represent is not forgotten.

Conclusion

Archaeology offers a window into our past, revealing stories of human interaction with the sea that are both fascinating and significant. However, to ensure that these stories reach a broader audience, it is essential to involve various art forms and media in the dissemination process. By engaging journalists, filmmakers, painters, and writers, we can create a multi-faceted narrative that brings historical events to life in ways that academic reports alone cannot achieve.

The case of *Fredericus Quartus* and *Christianus Quintus* demonstrates the potential for interdisciplinary collaboration in disseminating archaeological findings. Through the efforts of various artists and media, the story of these Danish slave ships will be told in engaging and accessible ways, reaching a wide audience and preserving the history they represent for future generations.

As emphasized earlier, opening our field to both semi-factual and fictional storytellers can transform how we present our findings. Engaging the public in archaeology helps them understand that archaeological stories connect us across time and borders, keeping the discipline relevant and vital for understanding ourselves. By fostering this connection, we ensure the continued support and appreciation of archaeology, securing its place in our collective consciousness.

"If history were taught in the form of stories, it would never be forgotten" – Rudyard Kipling, *The Collected Works*.

Andreas Kallmeyer Bloch
The Viking Ship Museum, Roskilde, Denmark / Njord – Center for Maritime and Underwater Cultural Heritage, National Museum of Denmark
Andreas.Kallmeyer.Bloch@natmus.dk

Bibliography

BORELLI, J. & L. HARRIS 2016
'Bricks as Ballast: An Archaeological Investigation of a Shipwreck Site in Cahuita National Park, Costa Rica', in *2016 Advisory Council on Underwater Archaeology Proceedings*, P. Johnston (ed.), Washington, DC, 8-16.

GLUCKMAN, S. 1992
'Preliminary Investigation of a Shipwreck, Pumpata Cahuita National Park, Costa Rica', in *Maritime Archaeology: A Reader of Substantive and Theoretical Contributions*, L. E. Babits & H. Van Tilberg (eds), New York, 453-69.

HARRIS, L. & N. RICHARDS 2018
'Preliminary Investigations of Two Shipwreck Sites in Cahuita National Park, Costa Rica', *The International Journal of Nautical Archaeology* 47:2, 405-18.

NØRREGAARD, G. 1948
'Forliset ved Nicaragua', *Aarbog 1948, Handels og Søfartsmuseet på Kronborg*, Helsingør, 69-98.

OLLING, J. 2018
Dobbeltmytteriet på de danske slaveskibe, Featurepress e-book (on-demand).

139

The Antikythera Mechanism in Comix:

Communicating Maritime Archaeology through a Multimodal Narrative Medium

Alexandros Tourtas

Abstract

Sharing archaeology with the public is nowadays an acknowledged scientific aspect of our job. Not only because it is socially ethical, but also because it helps us evaluate our perspective and develop our scientific process. However, this is no easy feat. One must find the right equilibrium between scientific accuracy and simplification, avoid manipulation, and promote inquiry and further engagement in order to increase the level of interactivity between archaeology and the public. Since the 1980s and the emergence of "New Museology", cultural communication experts have developed many theories and methodologies concerning the various media that can be used in the creation of attractive narratives with scientific content. The Antikythera Mechanism in Comix graphic novel was shaped in this framework. It tells the story of a unique artefact that was found in a 1st-century BC shipwreck in southwestern Greece, but at the same time it provides information about maritime archaeology and other scientific data concerning either the artefact itself or the scientific research that was developed around it. In this paper we use the book – along with other similar publications – as an example of the ability of graphic novels to transfer archaeological knowledge in an engaging yet scientifically based manner.

It has been called a landmark in the history of engineering, a one-of-a-kind piece of machinery, an astronomical and mathematical wonder, a navigation device, an astrological map, an education instrument, an eclipse predictor, the world's first computer, a fake, a time machine, a piece of alien technology, among other things. For more than a century people have been intrigued by its unique features and postulated theories about the place and the people who made it, the way it worked, its significance in the development of ancient technology and the way its discovery changed our view on the level of sophistication science and engineering had reached in antiquity. If nothing else, the Antikythera Mechanism is a really interesting archaeological find (Fig. 1).

However, when it comes down to explaining all that to someone who has not been sucked down the rabbit hole of archaeological interpretation, things get tricky. The extended scientific bibliography[1] is undeniably not reaching the wider public both due to its complicated structure and its specialized terminology.[2] Hence, although there is an interesting cluster of information to be communicated, the lack of effective means of communication condemns it to be circulated mostly among scientists. This, of course, leaves space to people outside the scope of

---

1   For a list, see Anastasakis 2013; Edmunds 2014; Lin & Yan 2016; Nicolaidis & Skordoulis 2016; Tourtas et al. 2016; David 2017; Jones 2017.

2   Meadows 1998, 54.

141

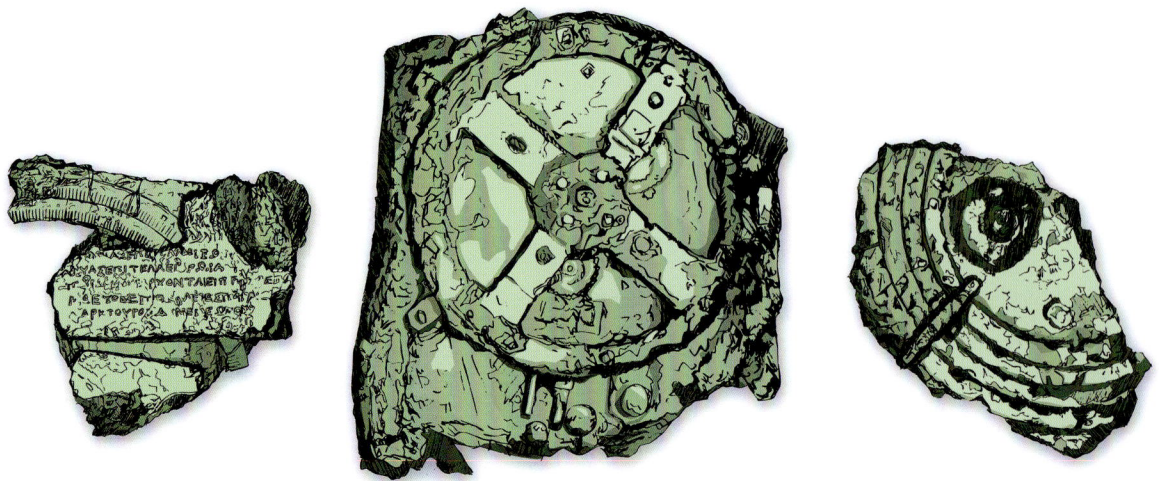

Fig. 1. The three largest fragments (A, B and C) of the Antikythera Mechanism (Tourtas 2023, 24).

science to fabricate narratives that have no scientific background and produce misguided views and delusive cognitive landscapes of the ancient world.

Admittedly, this is a wider problem that has to do with the development of an interaction scheme between scientists and the wider public and is not limited to a single archaeological find.[3] Especially in humanities and among the people who study the past, the production of coherent scientifically based narratives is a challenging endeavour in a world full of post-modern fluid 'truths' and interpretations.[4] Nonetheless, 'challenging' does not only mean difficult and problematic; rather it can also mean fascinating and full of potential. The concept of "narrative turn" that was formed within the whirlpool of post-modernity actually identifies narrative as the way to understand not only history but also politics, natural sciences, and other kinds of knowledge, as well as cognitive science.[5] In this perspective, when it comes

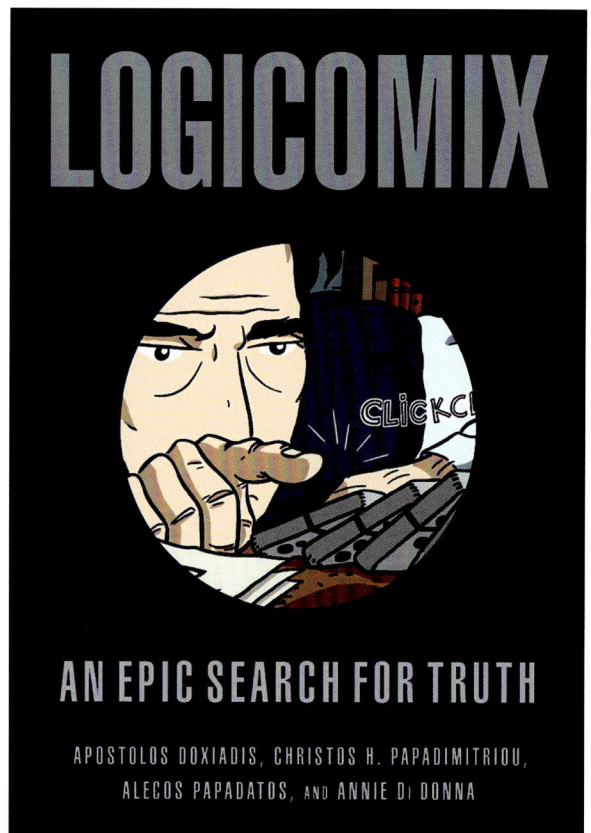

Figure 2. A very successful example of communicating mathematical and philosophical concepts through the graphic novel format is LOGICOMIX *LOGICOMIX* by Apostolos Doxiadis and Christos Papadimitriou (2009).

---

3   Meadows 1998; Weigold 2001; Thomas et al. 2015; National Academies: Sciences, Engineering, Medicine 2017.

4   Laneri 2002; Watkins 2006; Harding 2007; Holtorf 2007.

5   Raine 2013; Puckett 2016, 120; Χουρμουζιάδη 2022, 28-9.

to essential scientific and ethical guidelines it makes no difference whether the medium is an esteemed peer-reviewed academic journal or a podcast, a book or a movie/documentary, etc. In each case, the scientist needs to figure out the optimal way to communicate with other people providing a scientifically documented narrative. Of course, the target group changes, hence the communicative choices may differ, however, the basic principle remains the same. This way, the importance of communication is not ranked as 'more' or 'less' significant, 'more' or 'less' serious. The use of alternative media and forms of communication becomes a vital part of the scientific procedure that builds an interaction between the scientific community and society beyond the stereotypical and in many cases incomprehensible wording of scientific publications (Fig. 2).

Antiquity especially, or archaeology as a discipline that manages the past, have been the subject of numerous narratives in literature, theatre, music, and cinema compositions. From Homer's *Iliad* to Steven Pressfield's *Gates of Fire* (1998), from Shakespeare's *The tragedy of Julius Caesar* (1599) to Mankiewicz's *Cleopatra* (1963) with Richard Burton and Liz Taylor, and from Gluck's *Orfeo ed Euridice* (1762) to Steven Spielberg's and James Mangold's *Indiana Jones* (Spielberg 1981; 1984; 1989; 2008; Mangold 2023), there is an ongoing list of cultural products that use the past as fertile ground to spawn a good story. Likewise, archaeological museums are filled with either obvious and consciously designed or – more frequently – vague and basic conceptual exhibition narratives. Oral histories and traditional narratives carry the flame of unofficial historical knowledge through overlapping generations. And then, there is comic art and graphic novels.[6]

In this plethora of narrative tools that engage with the past there are many examples where either comic art in general or graphic novels in particular have been used in various contexts.[7] Comic art features, for example, characters in single frames or short strips, text balloons, pop art typography and comic art paintings of various landscapes, which have been used to enhance existing narratives in different forms, such as popular science texts,[8] pieces of literature, or museum exhibitions[9] providing a more entertaining aspect to the already-set scenery. The power of visualization makes the subject of those narratives more accessible and entertaining. Graphic novels, on the other hand, provide their own narrative. And this is indeed a powerful tool. The basic features of a graphic novel such as temporality, character development, and the building of a story-world that can fluctuate easily between reality and fiction, can be used successfully in the effort of conveying scientific information in an entertaining yet scientifically accurate way. Moreover, in comparison to other dramatization media such as literature, theatre, or cinema, one can argue that on the painted surface of the comic strip (seen in a socially textured sort of way),[10] even if the image strives for naturalistic depiction of material realities, the 'creator' is always present. In other words, the threat of total immersion into a virtual world that tricks the mind to lose all critical skills and accept it as 'real' and consequently forget the existential role of interpretation in the creation of images of the past, is minimized by the medium itself.

We can generally identify two major types of graphic novels that source the past in their narrative. The first one is more common and comprises graphic novels that use antiquity as the background for the development of the story. *Asterix* (1959-2023)

6   Eisner 1985; Aldama 2010; Sabin 2013; Stein & Thon 2013; Borkent 2017; Bramlett et al. 2017; Mikkonen 2017; Linek & Huff 2018; Hatfield & Beaty 2020; Barletta & Lo Manto 2022; McCloud 2022, 109-29.

7   Barletta & Lo Manto 2022; Kamash et al. 2022.
8   Velasco 2012.
9   Picone 2014.
10   Gibson-Ingold 2007, 4-9.

Figure 4. Hugo Pratt's Corto Maltese graphic novels have been highly praised for the aesthetically pleasing and accurate way that historic scenography has been incorporated in the narrative (Pratt 2017).

by René Goscinny and Albert Uderzo is a wonderful example (Fig. 3). The creators of the series wanted to produce an entertaining piece of narrative art, and they used historical and archaeological knowledge as inspiration within the framework of historical fiction. However, they did not commit to any scientific guidelines and produced a narrative that includes lots of anachronisms, imaginary situations, and paraphrasing in order to create a humoristic effect. Fair enough, this choice does not devalue the importance of the artistic product. It just signifies the lack of scientific motivation behind the creation of these graphic novels.[11] Likewise, Frank Miller's *300*,[12] that eventually led to a film adaptation by Zack Sny-

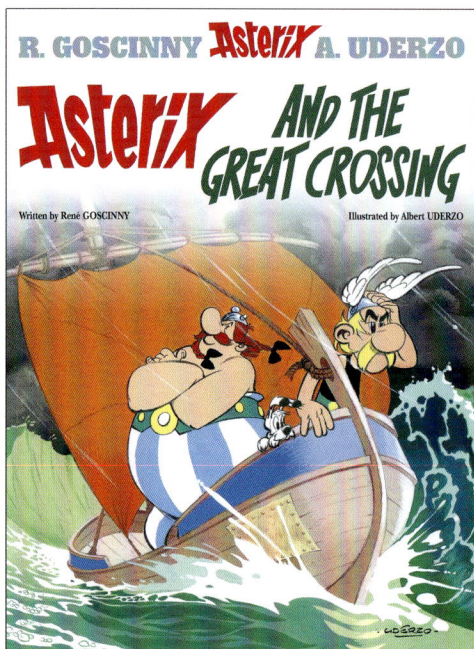

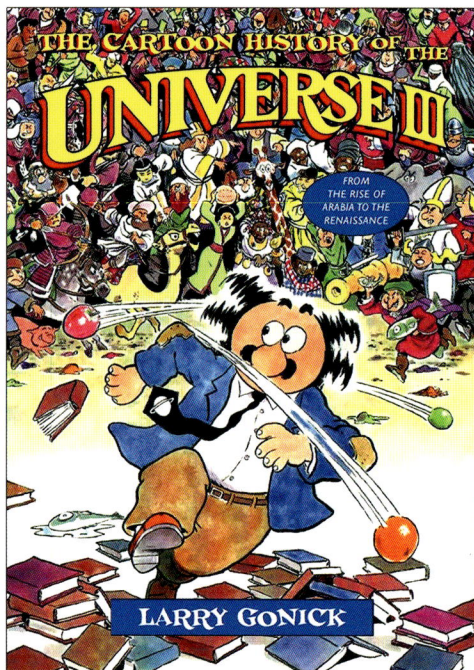

Figure 3. Maritime themes are included in "Asterix" *Asterix* (Goscinny & Uderzo 1982) and The Cartoon History of the Universe III (Gonick, 1990). Although Uderzo draws based on archaeological data, the story has nothing to do with actual historic events. Larry Gonick, on the other hand, presents a history-based narrative even if he is also interested in the humoristic aspect of his frames.

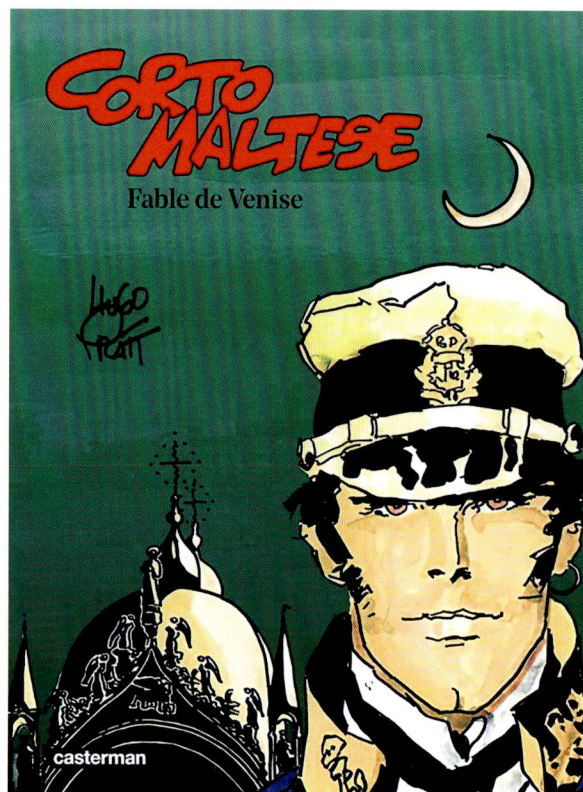

---

11   Kalita 2014; Shmeleva et al. 2019; Breslin 2022.

12   Miller & Varley 1998.

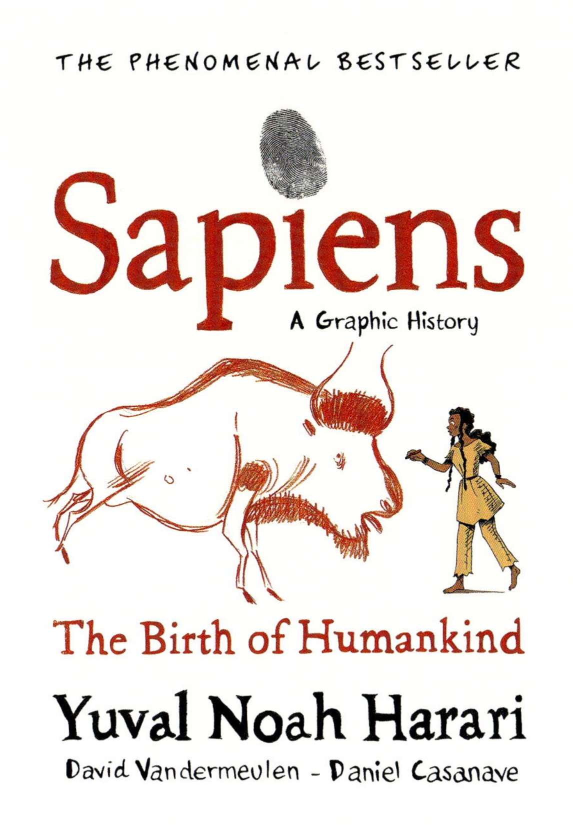

Figure 5. The conceptualization of non-human characters can be used successfully in graphic novels to narrate 'agency'. In Sapiens: A Graphic Novel (Harari et al. 2020), the creators present pivotal moments of human development in a simple, funny yet simultaneously full of visual and textual semantics way.

Figure 6. In "Archaeology: The comic" Archaeology: The Comic by J.H Loubser (2003) describes archaeological procedures in an educative way.

der (2006), was largely accepted by audiences as a masterpiece in comic art but was never considered to be a historical approach on the events of the Persian War. There are hundreds, if not thousands, of similarly constructed graphic novels like Hugo Pratt's *Corto Maltese* (1967-1989) (Fig. 4), Hergé's *Tin Tin* (1929-1976), or *Lucky Luke* (1946-present) by Morris and Goscinny, just to name a few of the most successful series. And of course, there is always the *Classics Illustrated* series (1941-1969) that trans-mediates classical literature from Sophocles' *Antigone* to Victor Hugo's *Les Misérables* into graphic novels.

On the other hand, the second category comprises graphic novels that have been created right from the start aiming at providing scientific information in an amusing way. Of course, within this list there are different sub-types depending on the subject and the level of scientific orientation. We can find graphic novels that present general cultural development narratives like Larry Gonick's *The Cartoon History of the Universe* (1978-2009) (Fig. 3) or Juval Harari's *Sapiens: A Graphic History* (Fig. 5),[13] or more focused ones like Jaques Martin's *Les voyages d'Alix* (1996-2013) and Johanes H. N. Loubser's, *Archaeology: The Comic* (2003) that discuss either spe-

---

13   Harari et al. 2020; 2021; 2024.

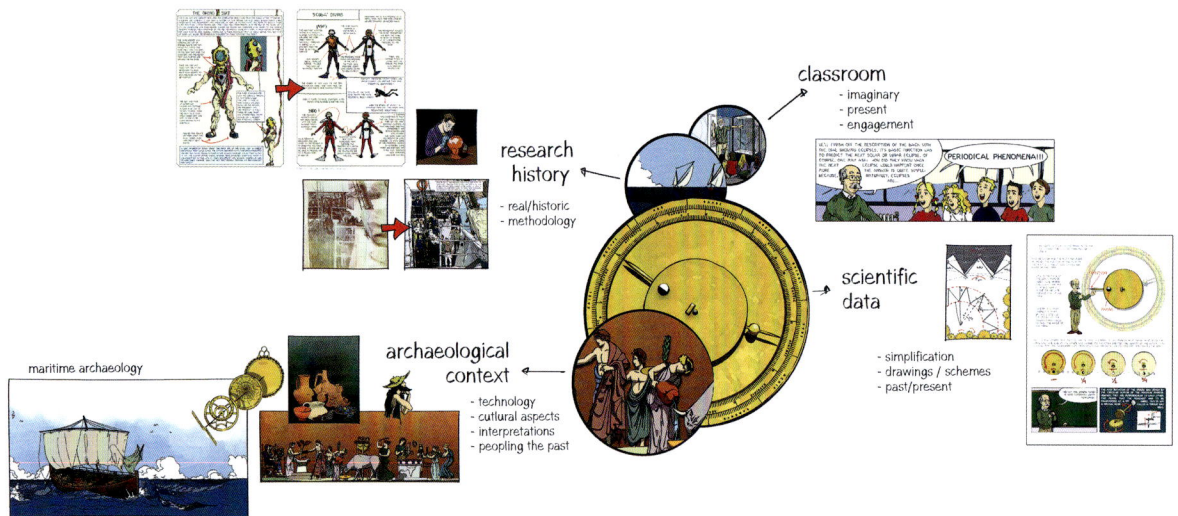

Fig. 7. The content of the graphic novel *The Antikythera Mechanism in Comix* was built around/on four axes/levels (Author).

cific periods and subjects or archaeological practices (Fig. 6). This second type of graphic novels falls into the category of "serious comics",[14] a combination of art and science that strives to narrate scientific facts and thoughts in an educating yet entertaining way, hence falling under the term "edutainment".[15] John Swogger[16] proposes that the graphic novel form can be used even in academic publications postulating facts and interpretations putting all the stereotypical forms aside and levelling the field of scientific communication. Although this last option will be hard to bend into the rigid academic publication scheme, there is no doubt that graphic novels have already become part of the wider archaeological communication network.

That is the basic concept on which *The Antikythera Mechanism in Comix* graphic novel was created.[17] The Antikythera Mechanism engages not only archaeology but also astronomy, mathematics,

physics, engineering, and other disciplines in the stage of its construction and use in antiquity, as well as in the effort of understanding it as an archaeological find by modern-day scientists. The multifaceted nature of the artefact combined with the fact that its research and interpretation history spans more than a century, provide a challenge to anyone who would like to communicate this information with the public. There have been so far various successful attempts that have confronted this challenge in the form of books like Joe Marchant's *Decoding the Heavens: A 2,000-Year-old Computer and the Century Long Search to Discover Its Secrets* (2009) and Alexander Jones' *A Portable Cosmos: Revealing the Antikythera Mechanism, Scientific Wonder of the Ancient World*,[18] magazine articles[19] as well as documentaries like the BBC's *The Two Thousand Year Old Computer* (2014) that have of course been met with their pseudoscience counterparts, for example, the recent *Indiana Jones and the Dial of Destiny* film (Mangold 2023). However, this seems to be the first time that a graphic novel has been dedicated to this

---

14   Linek & Huff 2018.

15   Aksakal 2015.

16   Swogger 2022.

17   Tourtas 2023. For more information about the Antikythera Mechanism in a comix graphic novel: https://www.antimech-comic.com/, Accessed May, 2025.

18   Marchant 2009; Jones 2017.

19   Efstathiou & Efstathiou 2018.

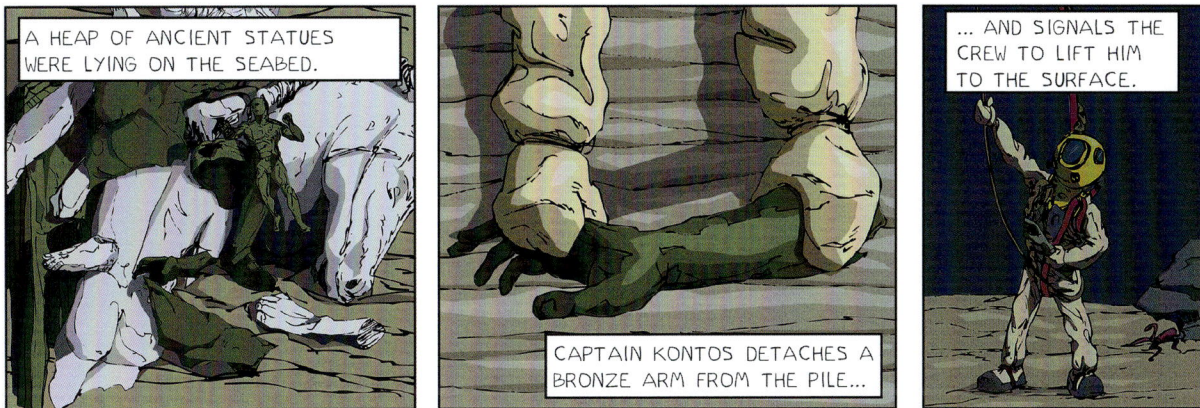

Fig. 8. The story about the discovery of the shipwreck in the 1900s was the most narrative part of the original data (Tourtas 2023, 18).

unique artefact. The closest thing I managed to spot are Serafini's *Le Mystère de l'Atlantide* (1993) in the series *Les Aventures de L'Equipe Cousteau en Bandes Dessinées* that narrates the 1976 research expedition on the Antikythera shipwreck. Hence, creating one sounded like a great idea.

This is, however, where the challenges arise. Just to mention the major ones: decisions needed to be made not only on theoretical matters like the "simplification factor" since the vast amount of information – in its raw scientific form – and its complexity was counterproductive, the level of scientific "accuracy/authenticity", given the fact that there is a great deal of interpretation involved in the archaeological process, but also on practical matters like the text to image ratio, the aesthetics of the design, the page layout, etc. Stating that this is a scientifically oriented art project means that all the above choices, even the practical ones, had to be justified.

The process started by breaking down the information into manageable chunks and then finding the best way to explain them in a coherent story. So, to begin, there is the core knowledge about the Mechanism's form and function, the history of its discovery and the research that has been done on it since the beginning of the 20th century, and of course their relevant contexts. The history of research is probably the most factual and well documented part of this information, and thus the most stable.[20] The story about the discovery of the Mechanism in the 1900s, although not very well documented and seemingly a bit romanticized, seems to be close enough to the original.[21] Likewise, the quantitative data about the form of the Mechanism (size, composition, etc.) combined with the most probable or commonly accepted interpretations about the function of its various parts, seem safe enough to handle.[22] All the above have been researched and published in specialized scientific publications.

However, these are not enough to yield a narrative on their own. People need context in order to understand scientific data, in this case interpretations about the past, either in the form of contemporary examples or through the creation of comprehensible environments. Thus, the information about the Mechanism was enriched by references to wider contexts (e.g. history of astronomy, theory and methodology of maritime archaeology, religion and sports in antiquity, time-keeping practices) or embedded to short stories that take place in the past within the basic narrative of the book. The final sci-

---

20   Bitsakis 2012; Anastasakis 2013; Jones 2017.
21   Tourtas et al. 2016.
22   Bitsakis 2012; Kaltsas et al. 2012; Edmunds 2014; Lin & Yan 2016; Jones 2017; Freeth et al. 2021.

147

Fig. 9. The depiction of historical figures and events were based on archival data (Tourtas 2023, 85).

entific content was then aligned to three narrative axes (scientific data, research history, and archaeological context) that have an intertwined development throughout the book. There was then the need to build a core narrative axis that would keep the whole thing together and that would carry the story forward (Figs. 7-8). A classroom seemed to be the right environment for a Q&A type of communication like the one I was trying to build with this book. The actors, a professor and some young students, reflect in a way the experts and the public, and the discussion between them, was driven by the most probable questions one can have about the Mechanism. The narrative progresses smoothly without a predetermined sequence. In other words, the storyboard was created resembling a spontaneous oral presentation with its disruptions, interventions and twists, so as to break the monotonous scientific presentation paradigm.

Subsequently, the four narrative axes/levels required their own aesthetic choices. Prior to that however, some basic principles about the overall illustration style needed to be set. A key factor was the reader's age. By necessity, the book is addressed to teenagers and adults, rather than younger children.[23] Due to the complexity of the matter at hand, the difficult choice was either to simplify the content

at the cost of omitting important details and concepts, or to create an explanatory and educational work for a more mature readership. However, the final outcome with its colourful palette and smooth lines is friendly to younger audiences, even if they will probably need an older person to help them out when the underlying concepts are more complex. The aesthetic differences among the four narrative levels are subtle, aiming at a sub-conscious differentiation. The classroom is an imaginary world that holds present day events. The students in it are depicted in a more abstract cartoonish way since they are imaginary characters, and the classroom has generic characteristics. The only exception is the professor who is based on an actual person. Like all the historic figures and places or events that are depicted in the research history part, he and other characters were drawn closer to reality based on photographs and other archival data that were found through research. Some of the frames are reproductions of photographic snapshots, while others were based on narrations of the actual events (Fig. 9). The "rule of thumb" is: closer to naturalism in form means closer to reality in concept. Beyond providing historical information, this level also tries to convey basic aspects of scientific research methodology concerning the disciplines that were involved in the study of the Mechanism. Nevertheless, the most challenging task was to describe the actual data and the inter-

23   Sabin 2013.

Fig. 10. Explaining the importance of solar and lunar calendar use through the concept of ancient maritime trade (Tourtas 2023, 46).

THE DIVING SUIT

THE DIVING SUIT WAS ALREADY BEING USED FOR UNDERWATER OPERATIONS FROM THE MIDDLE OF THE 19TH CENTURY IN EUROPE AND AMERICA. IT WAS ONLY A MATTER OF TIME BEFORE THE BOLD GREEK SPONGE DIVERS WOULD INCORPORATE THIS TECHNOLOGY INTO THEIR LINE OF WORK. UP TO THIS POINT, THE DEPTH TO WHICH A DIVER COULD REACH WAS LIMITED TO HOW LONG THEY COULD HOLD THEIR BREATH. WITH THE HELP OF THE DIVING SUIT, STAYING UNDERWATER WAS CONSIDERABLY LONGER AND EASIER AND THEREFORE A BIG BOOST TO THE SPONGE INDUSTRY. HOWEVER, THE ADVANTAGES OF THIS NEW TECHNOLOGY CAME AT A COST. A GREAT NUMBER OF DIVERS MET THEIR FATE OR WERE SEVERELY INJURED DUE TO THEIR PROLONGED STAY AT GREAT DEPTHS. THIS NEW TYPE OF INJURY WAS NAMED 'DECOMPRESSION SICKNESS' OR MORE COMMONLY 'THE BENDS'.

THE DIVING HELMET WAS CONSTRUCTED OUT OF BRONZE ALLOYS AND COMPRISED TWO PARTS: THE BASE THAT WAS ATTACHED TO THE BODY SUIT OVER THE SHOULDERS AND THE HELMET THAT WAS MOUNTED AND SECURED ON THE BASE.

SINCE THE SUIT WAS FILLED WITH AIR, IT WAS NECESSARY TO WEAR HEAVY LEAD WEIGHTS TO HOLD THE DIVER ON THE SEA BOTTOM.

THE SUIT WAS MADE OF WATERTIGHT CANVAS AND STITCHED IN SUCH A WAY SO AS TO NOT TO LEAK. GIVEN THE FACT THAT MOST CREWS OWNED ONLY ONE SUIT, IT HAD TO BE LARGE ENOUGH TO FIT EVERYBODY.

THE DIVER COMMUNICATED WITH THE SURFACE THROUGH A THIN ROPE CALLED 'THE LINE'. A CODE OF LINE SIGNALS WAS USED BASED ON THE NUMBER, THE FREQUENCY AND THE INTENSITY OF PULLS. THREE OR MORE SHORT AND INTENSE PULLS MEANT DANGER AND A REQUEST FOR IMMEDIATE ASCENT.

BESIDES THE WEIGHTS ON THEIR CHEST AND BACK, DIVERS ALSO WORE HEAVY LEAD BOOTS.

A VERY INTERESTING STORY ABOUT THE FIRST USE OF THE DIVING SUIT IN GREECE REPORTEDLY TOOK PLACE IN 1863. THE SYMIAN MERCHANT FOTIS MASTORIDIS PRESENTED THE NEW SUIT TO HIS FELLOW SYMIANS, ASKING THEM TO TRY IT OUT IN THE HARBOUR. THE SYMIAN SPONGE DIVERS, HOWEVER, WERE EXTREMELY SCEPTICAL ABOUT IT AND RELUCTANT TO DIVE WITH IT. THEN, NESTORIDIS' WIFE, EUGENIA, STEPPED UP AND, TO EVERYONE'S SURPRISE, USED THE SUIT SUCCESSFULLY, PROVING ITS FUNCTIONALITY AND SAFETY.

SCUBA* DIVING

BREATHING AIR IS NOW PROVIDED BY A METAL TANK THAT THE DIVER CARRIES AROUND STRAPPED ON HIS/HER BACK.

1950's

THE BUOYANCY CONTROL DEVICE IS ACTUALLY A BLADDER THAT FILLS WITH AIR WHEN THE DIVER NEEDS POSITIVE BUOYANCY. MOREOVER, IT SERVES AS A LIFE-VEST WHEN THE DIVER IS ON THE SURFACE.

THE DIVER ALWAYS CARRIES A WATCH AND A DEPTH GAUGE.

THE 'REGULATOR' ADJUSTS THE HIGHLY PRESSURISED AIR FROM THE TANK IN ORDER TO PROVIDE IT AT A BREATHABLE PRESSURE TO THE DIVER.

LEAD WEIGHTS SERVE - SAME AS BEFORE - TO HELP THE DIVER GET NEGATIVELY BUOYANT.

THE PRESSURE GAUGE SHOWS THE PRESSURE OF THE AIR IN THE TANK. LESS PRESSURE MEANS LESS VOLUME OF AIR TO BREATH FROM.

THERE ARE VARIOUS TYPES OF DIVING SUITS TO PROVIDE THE DIVER WITH THERMAL PROTECTION.

THE DIVERS DO NOT WALK ON THE SEA BOTTOM ANY MORE - THEY SWIM. THUS, THE HEAVY LEAD BOOTS WERE SWAPPED FOR FINS.

WHEN LIFT OVERCOMES GRAVITY DIVERS ARE DRAWN TOWARDS THE SURFACE. THEY HAVE POSITIVE BUOYANCY.

WHEN IT COMES TO BASIC EQUIPMENT, A FEW THINGS HAVE CHANGED SINCE THE 1950s.

STAYING AT THE SAME LEVEL MEANS THEY HAVE NEUTRAL BUOYANCY.

WHEN THE EFFECT OF GRAVITY IS STRONGER THAN LIFT, THE DIVERS HAVE NEGATIVE BUOYANCY.

2000 +

THE BUOYANCY CONTROL DEVICE HAS BEEN MERGED WITH THE TANK HARNESS INTO A COMPACT DIVING JACKET.

AN ALTERNATIVE BREATHING END WAS ADDED TO THE REGULATOR IN ORDER FOR THE DIVER TO HAVE A SPARE AND TO BE ABLE TO PROVIDE AIR TO A FELLOW DIVER, IF NEED BE.

NOWADAYS, DIVERS WEAR DIVING COMPUTERS THAT COMBINE THE FUNCTION OF A WATCH AND A DEPTH GAUGE AND CALCULATE THE SAFETY LIMITS DURING THE DIVE.

A COMMON MISCONCEPTION IS THAT THE DIVE TANK CONTAINS PURE OXYGEN. WHAT NORMALLY HAPPENS IS THAT THE DIVER BREATHS ATMOSPHERIC AIR (80% NITROGEN AND 20% OXYGEN). THE SAME THING WE ALL BREATH ON LAND. HOWEVER, TO AVOID SOME OF THE PROBLEMS CAUSED BY NITROGEN, SOME DIVERS USE ENRICHED AIR MIXES THAT CONTAIN LESS NITROGEN AND MORE OXYGEN.

* SELF-CONTAINED UNDERWATER BREATHING APPARATUS

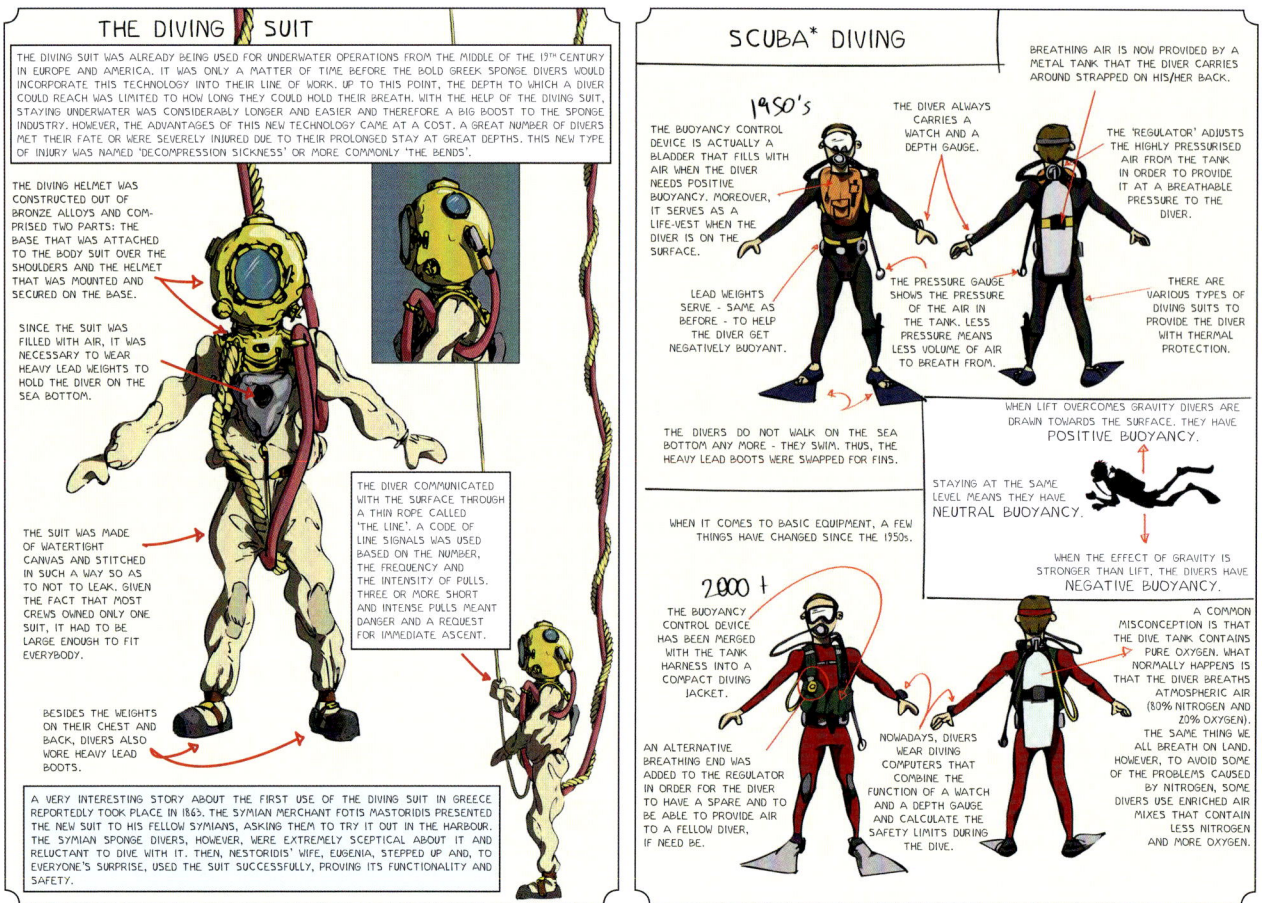

Fig. 11. Complementary pages/boxes provide extra information within the narrative (Tourtas 2023, 17, 65).

pretation concerning the form and function of the device. Sketches and explanatory schemes were used extensively to that end in order to reduce the text to a minimum. Lastly, the presentation of the archaeological context was a combination of interpretative concepts and imaginary characters and situations with the use of drawings that depict actual artefacts and sites or are inspired by them.

There are more things to say about the way the book was built, like the page layout, the additional information in the annexes, the typography, etc. – but let us focus here more on its maritime archaeological aspect. On that front, the first question to be asked probably is whether the Mechanism is or is not a maritime archaeological artefact. Many would shout "of course", since it was found on a shipwreck,

however, there is also the option of arguing that since it was not built as a navigational instrument, it had no place onboard the ship or in any other maritime context aside from being part of a luxurious cargo. This is evident in the way the Mechanism is exhibited in the National Archaeological Museum in Athens. It has its own pedestal in the centre of a room, among other bronze objects and there is no reference to its maritime context. However, a temporary exhibition that was organized by the same museum in 2012 gathered all the artefacts from the Antikythera shipwreck in one place and presented the site as one maritime archaeological ensemble.[24] In other words, the Mechanism, as any other find,

24   Christopoulou et al. 2012; Kaltsas et al. 2012.

Albert Rehm (1871-1949) was a German classical philologist. He travelled in Italy, Greece and Asia Minor, taking part in various excavation projects and studying Greek culture. He worked as a professor at the Ludwig Maximilian University of Munich, where he was appointed the position of rector. He was also a member of the Bavarian Academy of Sciences and Humanities.

Chemist **Othon Roussopoulos** (1856-1922) (son of archaeology professor Athanasios Roussopoulos) was born in the Kastoria region of Northern Greece. He got his degree in Athens and then continued his postgraduate studies in Germany. He translated many important chemistry books and wrote a couple of educational books himself, bringing chemistry closer to the general public. Moreover, he contributed immensely to the establishment of new terminology. Roussopoulos was a pioneer in archaeological conservation, both in terms of lab work and scientific documentation.

The shiny artefacts we see in display cases in museum exhibitions are more often than not found in the dirt of an excavation trench, broken and twisted, either eroded or with layers of deposits. The science of **archaeological conservation** has radically advanced over the past few decades both in theory and practice. Using methodological tools for several natural sciences (physics, chemistry, geology etc.) and following basic rules for restoration and reconstruction, conservators are valuable collaborators for archaeologists and other scientists studying the past.

Marcus Tullius Cicero (106-43 BCE) was a Roman politician, orator, lawyer and philosopher. He came from a rich aristocratic family and is considered to be one of the most prominent writers of the Roman world. He produced impressive literary works which are still studied today. Concerning our story, we should say that it is due to Cicero's work that we know details about the interest Roman aristocracy showed in Greek works of art (he personally kept correspondence with various traders of artwork in Greece, assigning them the task of collecting artefacts for him to decorate his villas) and he is our primary source of the existence of planetaria (he explicitly refers to one made by Poseidonius in one of his texts).

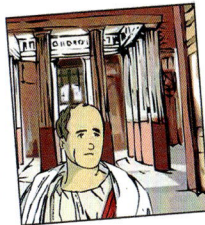

77

me, it's a symbol of technological innovation, ... is a set of mechanical gears. There are thos... ...teracting trinket from the past. Some even ...ery least, an object suitable for imaginative ...e fact that it has captured public attention. ...nd what it could do. Certainly, the most ...y is the Antikythera Mechanism?" This is ...here and by whom it was designed and ...e than a century since it was discovered ...n purpose of this book is to answer this ...students or lofty rocket scientists. To ...rnative medium, the graphic narrative ...ed by the places and actors involved ...and the functions it performed. The ...ifically accurate, narrative about the

The format of this book was something that was decided on right from the start: "Something between Asterix and LOGICOMIX," I once explained enthusiastically to a (rather patient) friend. Of course, during development, a bit of Bill Watterson, a spoon of Carl Barks, half a portion of Morris, a pinch of Hugo Pratt, reflections of the Cousteau adventures by Serafini and many other inspiring ingredients from countless other books I have buried my nose in since I was a kid came into the mix. The narrative progressed smoothly and although I had a list of specific features that needed to be said there was no predetermined sequence. In other words, the storyboard was created resembling a spontaneous oral presentation with its disruptions, interventions and twists.

84

Fig. 12. At the end of the book the reader can find additional information about the 'actors', as well as about the creation of the book (Tourtas 2023, 77, 84).

becomes potentially part of many narratives, one of which is based on its maritime context. This narrative thread in its turn provides the 'storyteller' with the opportunity to expand the plot into subsidiary themes that surround its "life on the sea", in order to clarify or enhance the scientific information. Following the development of diving technology, for example, the reader learns about the development of underwater archaeological research and the way underwater sites have been approached from the beginning of the 20th century until today. This information comes in the way of specially assigned pages, references in the text, and of course images that have been designed with care to detail providing non-verbal information. All the expeditions that excavated the shipwreck are included in the narrative, from the sponge divers to Cousteau's team and the modern expeditions by the Greek Department (Ephorate) of Underwater Antiquities. In each of them one can find the state-of-the-art technology that was used and the contemporary methodologies that were followed. And of course, there is information about the Antikythera shipwreck and its finds, the dating of the artefacts, the theories about the size of the ship, its route, and the rest of the cargo. There are also references to nautical features like ancient ships' sailing capabilities, maritime networks, the way astrolabes worked, and in the notes sector at the end of the book there is more information about sponge diving, the bends, transport amphorae, nautical studies, and archaeological conservation of maritime finds, etc. (Figs. 10-12).

All things considered, the graphic novel form proves to be an effective two-dimensional medium in our effort to communicate complex scientific concepts to a wider audience through an interesting and scientifically based narrative. Its multimodality though, allows us to move even beyond the flat surface of a printed book. The digital form of webcomics for example that has been developed in the past few years seems to be an interesting alternative that transforms the graphic novel to a more interactive

online platform. Furthermore, modern technology can detach its content from the physical space and create either completely digital or hybrid reality story-worlds within which the readers/users immerse or even become part of the narrative. Likewise, innovative exhibition designers looking for crossovers between narrative tools turn to graphic novels as a new approach to present the past in non-traditional museum narratives. Let us see what the future holds.

Alexandros Tourtas
The University of Aegean, Greece
alextourtas@gmail.com

Bibliography

AKSAKAL, N. 2015
'Theoretical View to The Approach of The Edutainment', *Procedia – Social and Behavioral Sciences* 186, 1232-9.

ALDAMA, F. L. 2010
'Characters in Comic Books', in *Characters in Fictional Worlds: Understanding Imaginary Beings in Literature, Film, and Other Media,* J. Eder, F. Jannidis & R. Schneider (eds), Berlin, 318-28.

ANASTASAKIS, M. 2013
The Antikythera Mechanism: historical review, current understanding and educational potential, Unpublished Master's Thesis, University of Crete, Greece.

BARLETTA, E. & A. LO MANTO 2022
'Archaeology and Comics', *Ex Novo: Journal of Archaeology* 7:December, 95-107.

BITSAKIS, Y. 2012
'The Antikythera Mechanism', in *The Antikythera Shipwreck – The technology of the ship, the cargo, the Mechanism,* A. Christopoulou, A. Gadolou & P. Bouyia (eds), Athens, 94-107.

BORKENT, M. 2017
'Mediated characters: Multimodal viewpoint construction in comics', *Cognitive Linguistics* 28:3, 539-63.

BRAMLETT, F., R. T. COOK & A. MESKIN (EDS) 2017
The Routledge Companion to Comics, New York.

BRESLIN, J. 2022
'Astérix and the Historical Interpretation', *Medium. com*. Available at: https://medium.com/@johnbreslin/astérix-and-the-historical-interpretation-60eb285155a, Accessed May, 2025.

CHRISTOPOULOU, A., A. GADOLOU & P. BOUYIA (EDS) 2012
The Antikythera Shipwreck – The technology of the ship, the cargo, the Mechanism, Athens.

DAVID, N. 2017
'The Antikythera mechanism: Its dating and place in the history of technology', *Journal of Mediterranean Archaeology* 30:1, 85-104.

DOXIADIS, A. & C. PAPADIMITRIOU 2009
Logicomix: An Epic Search for Truth, New York, Berlin, London.

EDMUNDS, M. G. 2014
'The Antikythera mechanism and the mechanical universe', *Contemporary Physics* 55:4, 263-85.

EFSTATHIOU, K. & M. EFSTATHIOU 2018
'Celestial Gearbox', *Mechanical Engineering* 09:140, 31-5.

EISNER, W. 1985
Comics and Sequential Art, Tamarac, FL, USA.

FREETH, T., D. HIGGON, A. DACANALIS, L. MACDONALD, M. GEORGAKOPOULOU & A. WOJCIK 2021
'A Model of the Cosmos in the ancient Greek Antikythera Mechanism', *Scientific Reports* 11:1, 1-15.

GIBSON-INGOLD, T. 2007
'Materials against materiality', *Archaeological Dialogues* 14:1, 1-16.

GLUCK, C. W. 1762
Orfeo ed Euridice (Vienna version), Kassel.

GONICK, L. 1990
The Cartoon History of the Universe, Volumes 1-7, New York.

GOSCINNY, R. & A. UDERZO 1982
Asterix and the Black Gold, London.

HARARI, Y. N., D. VANDERMEULEN & D. CASANAVE 2020
Sapiens: A Graphic History, Vol.1: *The birth of Humankind*, New York.

HARARI, Y. N., D. VANDERMEULEN & D. CASANAVE 2021
Sapiens: A Graphic History, Vol. 2: *The Pillars of Civilization*, New York.

HARARI, Y. N., D. VANDERMEULEN & D. CASANAVE 2024
Sapiens: A Graphic History, Vol. 3: *The Masters of History*, New York.

HARDING, A. 2007
'Communication in archaeology', *European Journal of Archaeology* 10:2-3, 119-33.
https://doi.org/10.1177/1461957108095980

HATFIELD, C. & B. BEATY (EDS) 2020
Comic Studies: a Guidebook, New Brunswick, NJ, USA.

153

HOLTORF, C. 2007
'Can you hear me at the back? Archaeology, communication and society', *European Journal of Archaeology* 10:2-3, 149-65.
https://doi.org/10.1177/1461957108095982

JONES, A. 2017
A portable cosmos: revealing the Antikythera Mechanism, scientific wonder of the ancient world, New York.

KALITA, J. 2014
'Historicizing Asterix and Obelix: A case of Graphic Literature', *International Journal of English Language, Literature and Humanities* II:VII, 142-50.

KALTSAS, N., E. VLACHOGIANNI & P. BOUYIA (EDS) 2012
The Antikythera Shipwreck. The ship, the treasures, the Mechanism, Athens.

KAMASH, Z., K. SOAR & L. VAN BROECK (EDS) 2022
Comics and Archaeology, London.

LANERI, N. 2002
'Crossing boundaries: Some thoughts about communication in archaeology', *Archaeological Dialogues* 9:2, 90-7.

LIN, J. L. & H. S. YAN 2016
Decoding the mechanisms of Antikythera astronomical device, Berlin.

LINEK, S. B. & M. HUFF 2018
'Serious comics: a new approach for science communication and learning', in *Proceedings of the 12th International Technology, Education and Development Conference (INTED 2018), 5th-7th March, 2018, Valencia, Spain*, 388390.

LOUBSER, J. H. N. 2003
Archaeology: The Comic, Walnut Creek, CA, USA.

MANGOLD, J. 2023
Indiana Jones and the Dial of Destiny, Walt Disney Pictures, Lucasfilm Ltd.

MANKIEWICZ, J. L. 1963
Cleopatra. Twentieth Century Studios.

MARCHANT, J. 2009
Decoding the Heavens. A 2,000-Year-Old Computer-And the Century-Long Search to Discover Its Secrets, Boston.

MCCLOUD, S. 2022
Making Comics. Storytelling secrets of comics, manga and graphic novels, New York.

MEADOWS, A. J. 1998
Communicating research, Leeds.

MIKKONEN, K. 2017
The narratology of comic art, New York.

MILLER, F. & L. VARLEY 1998
300, Milwaukie, OR, USA.

NATIONAL ACADEMIES: SCIENCES, ENGINEERING, MEDICINE 2017
Communicating Science Effectively: A Research Agenda, Washington, DC. Available at: https://nap.nationalacademies.org/catalog/23674/communicating-science-effectively-a-research-agenda, Accessed May, 2025.

NICOLAIDIS, E. & C. SKORDOULIS (EDS) 2016
'The Inscriptions of the Antikythera Mechanism', *Almagest* 7:1, 315.

PICONE, M. D. 2014
'Comic Art in Museums and Museums in Comic Art', *European Comic Art* 6:2, 40-68.

PRATT, H. 2017
Corto Maltese, Fable of Venice, London.

PRESSFIELD, S. 1998
Gates of Fire: an Epic Novel of the Battle of Thermopylae, New York.

PUCKETT, K. 2016
Narrative Theory. A critical introduction, Cambridge, New York.

RAINE, S. 2013
'The Narrative Turn: Interdisciplinary Methods and Perspectives', *Student Anthropologist* 3:3, 64-80.

SABIN, R. 2013
Adult Comics, Oxford.

SERAFINI, D. 1993
Le Mystère de l'Atlantide, France.

SHMELEVA, L. M., G. E. VLADIMIROVNA, A. M. MAMUTDINOVA & D. V. SHMELEV 2019
'The comics about Asterix as a way of representing modernity', *Opción*: Revista de Ciencias Humanas y Sociales 22, 819-31.

SNYDER, Z. 2006
300. Legendary Pictures, Virtual Studios, Atmosphere Pictures.

SPIELBERG, S. 1981
Raiders of the Lost Ark. Lucasfilm Ltd.

SPIELBERG, S. 1984
Indiana Jones and the Temple of Doom. Lucasfilm Ltd.

SPIELBERG, S. 1989
Indiana Jones and the Last Crusade. Lucasfilm Ltd.

SPIELBERG, S. 2008
Indiana Jones and the Kingdom of the Crystal Skull. Lucasfilm Ltd.

STEIN, D. & J. N. THON (EDS) 2013
From Comic Strips to Graphic Novels: Contributions to the Theory and History of Graphic Narrative, Berlin, Boston.

SWOGGER, J. G. 2022
'They Do Things Differently There": Articulating the Unfamiliar Past in Community Heritage Comics', in *Comics and Archaeology*, Z. Kamash, K. Soar & L. Van Broeck (eds), London, 155-71.

THOMAS, J. E., T. A. SAXBY, A. B. JONES, T. J. B. CARRUTHERS, E. G. ABAL & W. C. DENNISON 2015
'Communicating Science Effectively – A Practical Handbook for Integrating Visual Elements', *Water Intelligence Online* 6, 9781780402208.

TOURTAS, A. 2023
The Antikythera Mechanism in Comix, Thessaloniki. Available at: https://www.antimech-comic.com/, Accessed May, 2025.

TOURTAS, A., T. THEODOULOU, D. KOURKOUMELIS, B. FOLEY & J. H. SEIRADAKIS 2016
'Data and interpretations on the discovery of the Antikythera Mechanism. Notes for the future', *Stoa of Sciences-Scientific Review* 1:B, 38-63.

VELASCO, J. 2012
'Death of Ötzi the Iceman: A graphic novel in National Geographic', *National Infographic*. Available at: https://juanvelascoblog.wordpress.com/2012/11/19/death-of-otzi-the-iceman-a-graphic-novel-in-national-geographic/, Accessed May, 2025.

WATKINS, J. E. 2006
'Communicating archaeology. Words to the wise', *Journal of Social Archaeology* 6:1, 100-18.

WEIGOLD, M. F. 2001
'Communicating Science', *Science Communication* 23:2, 164-93.

ΧΟΥΡΜΟΥΖΙΑΔΗ, Α. 2022
Εισαγωγή στον Εκθεσιακό Σχεδιασμό Κάλλιπος, on-line Open Academic Editions.
Available at: https://repository.kallipos.gr/handle/11419/8555, Accessed May, 2025.

The New Strandingsmuseum St George:

Concepts Behind the New Museum in Thorsminde

Anders Jensen

Abstract

Strandingsmuseum St George reopened in 2017 after a major expansion with new architecture and new exhibitions. Initially it was established in 1992 to exhibit the objects from the National Museum of Denmark's excavation of the wreck of the English ship-of-the-line, HMS St George, which ran aground on the Danish west coast in 1811 during the Napoleonic Wars. The museum later expanded its dissemination to include the cultural history of wrecked ships on the Danish west coast in general, including their influence on the local population.

The museum is site specific, located by the North Sea in the small harbour and tourist town of Thorsminde, close to the place where HMS St George was wrecked. The museum won the Stilletto Prize for community participation and engagement in 2019.

HMS St George's dimensions are integrated in the new architecture, where, for example, the number of floors corresponds to the ship's decks. The building's distinctive landmark is the high tower, which forms one large display case that stretches up through all the museum's floors. This display case contains the 11.5 m-long rudder from HMS St George. The five new exhibition rooms are built as independent scenarios, each with its own theme, with HMS St George's stranding and the objects from this wreck as the central narrative. In each exhibition space, lighting design, sounds, smells, animations and interactions are part of the communication as strong elements that appeal to both the senses and curiosity. The engaging design means that everyone, regardless of age and background, is enlightened, touched, and enriched by the stories.

Introduction[1]

Strandingsmuseum St George reopened in 2017 after a major expansion, with new architecture and a new exhibition. The museum takes its name after the English ship-of-the-line, HMS *St George*, which stranded on the west coast of Jutland, Denmark, on December 24, 1811, during the so-called "Great Christmas Gale of 1811".

Another English ship-of-the-line, HMS *Defence*, stranded a bit further north on that same day. On the following days, *St George* lost almost her entire crew with only 11 surviving the cold, strong current along the west coast of Jutland. Only six sailors from *Defence* survived. Both Denmark and England perceived this event as a complete disaster. In total, more than 1,300 people from the two ships drowned.[2]

---

[1] The editors would like to thank Curator Christopher Jacob Ries for his assistance with the publication of this chapter.

[2] The exact number of drowned is impossible to state, but estimates vary from around 1,300 to more than 1,400; see Cloves 1997, 498; Jepsen 2017, 167.

Figure 1. The First Rescue Station in Thorsminde (Public domain from https://www.jernkysten.dk/Default.aspx?ID=1274&itemId=Fortaelling:62, Accessed July 2025).

Originally established in 1992, the first museum opened to exhibit the objects from the wreck of *St George* after the first series of excavations. Strandingsmuseum St George is one of three museums under the umbrella of the Cultural History Museums in Holstebro. The museum is located in Thorsminde on the narrow isthmus between Nissum Fjord and the North Sea.

Site specific

The location of the museum is specific to the site of the strandings of *St George* and *Defence* and, to a lesser extent, to the other stories we tell. The small village of Thorsminde is located right between the sites where the ships stranded, c. 2 km south and north, respectively, on the outermost sandbar.

The west coast of Jutland was referred to as the "Iron Coast". This nickname dates back to at least 1866 as used in *Den danske lods* (The Danish Pilot): "This coast [from Skagen to Blaavands Huk] is an iron coast, with no harbour or shelter; therefore, it is to be avoided by shipping, whenever the wind does not blow from land."[3] For centuries, seafarers

feared this coast because the currents were difficult to predict and ships could easily go off course in stormy weather. There were no bays or harbours in which to seek refuge, and if a ship ran aground, it was broken apart in short time.[4] In 1882, the Regional Lifeboat Institution, *Det Nørrejyske Redningsvæsen*, established a rescue station in Thorsminde (Fig. 1).[5] Today the rescue station functions as the local church, but the village still has a search-and-rescue station manned by the local people.

The rudder

In 2003, 11 years after the opening of the old museum, a large rudder was discovered at Rødsand Banks south of the island of Lolland, Denmark. *St George* had originally lost this rudder during a storm on November 15, 1811, when it was *en route* from the Baltic Sea to England.

The rudder is central to the story we tell in the new museum (Fig. 2). It was the loss of this rudder that indirectly caused the shipwrecks off Thorsminde later that same year. This was also the perception

---

3   Søkortarkivet 1866, 387 (translation by the author).

4   Grandjean 1947, 112.

5   Eisenreich 1927, 305.

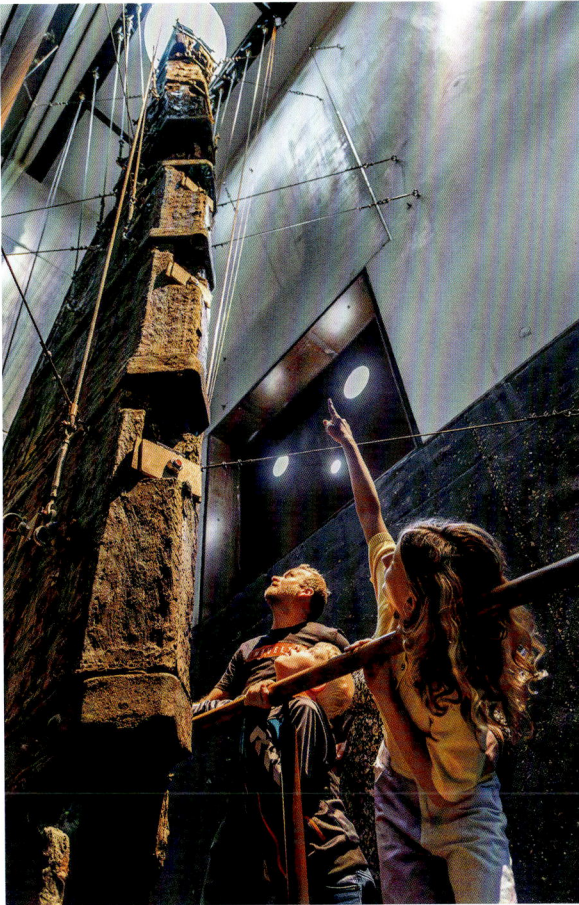

Figure 2. The rudder (Photo: Sebastian Mirz).

Figure 3. Isometric view of the rudder (Image: Strandingsmuseum St George).

The original rudder that was lost is also the main reason for the restoration of the museum. This rudder, currently weighing 5 tonnes and with a length of 11.5 m, and the story behind it, was so impressive that a large private Danish foundation, together with the museum's municipality, Holstebro, invested in the complete transformation of the museum.

of Vice-Admiral Saumarez, British commander of the Baltic Fleet at the time, who considered the first collision between *St George* and a merchantman vessel on November 15 to be the key to the later disaster.[6] This was due both to the delay the collision had caused, and the fact that *St George*'s Pakenham substitute rudder[7] apparently was not able function in the harsh weather conditions.[8]

---

6   Durey 2007, 80.

7   Pakenham 1793.

8   On *Defence*, Captain Atkins was not willing to abandon his commanding officer, Rear-Admiral Robert Carthew Reynolds, on *St George*, so *Defence* suffered the same fate. This decision by Atkins, to stay with his commanding officer, regardless of the risk, was considered the correct and honourable thing to do at the time. Jepsen 2017, 197.

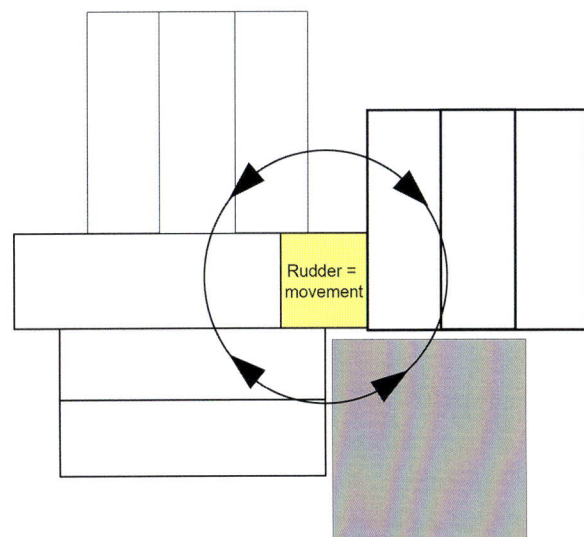

Figure 4. Central placement of rudder = movement (Image: Strandingsmuseum St George).

159

Figure 5. The museum: a shipwreck in a rough sea (Photo: Sebastian Mirz).

Architecture

Due to considerations regarding its preservation, the best and safest way to present the rudder was by suspending it vertically from wires. This required a tower (Fig. 3). The museum had to be built in a way that this tower and the building would both fit into the small village of Thorsminde and develop into a distinctive landmark for the city. The architects behind the new building, the Spanish-Danish couple Frank Maali and Gemma Lalanda, accomplished this by keeping the structure simple, but with an inherent strength to support the dramatic stories. The rudder has a central placement in the museum and is an active object. It forms one large display case that stretches up and down through all the museum's major floors, functioning as a reference point to the guests when they move through the different galleries (Figs. 4-5). Together the different elements of the new and old buildings look like a shipwreck in a rough sea.

Integrating objects

Some of the timbers from *St George* have been integrated as furniture or otherwise as part of the exhibition. These timbers are not objects but instead function as benches in areas where longer spans of attention are required. Some of the timbers function as flooring on two bridges (Fig. 6).

The reason for this was that we do not have the means to conserve all the different ship timbers we have in storage. In fact, we do not even have enough storage space for them. Before we could integrate them into the building, however, we first had to exclude the objects from the museum's collection.

Theoretical background

The theoretical starting point of the new museum is in Anders Bloksgaard's analysis on the history of

Figure 6. Ship timber as flooring (Photo: Anders Jensen).

Stranding

Bloksgaard's analysis and research of stranding events deals with the causes, extent, nature, and technological innovation.[11] The dangerous conditions and the weather of the North Sea and the west coast of Denmark is explained in Gallery One of the museum. This gallery functions as an introduction to the North Sea. It presents the basic navigational tools available in the 19th century. It explains the dangers of the weather and of the coast, and it explains how to best mitigate danger during a stranding.

The story of one particular stranding, that of *St George*, is presented through an animation in Gallery Two. We present objects from the ship, organised in the general area where they were excavated on the orlop deck. For example, the tools and equipment of the surgeon John Cleland are in the display case located in the area where the surgeon's cockpit was on the orlop deck.

strandings in Denmark from 1800 to 2000.[9] This work deals with the strandings, the management of them, the developments they led to on the coast, and the culture that arose around these developments, including crime, greed, helpfulness, compassion, and self-sacrifice. Bloksgaard defines the history of a stranding as consisting of three elements: stranding, rescue, and salvage.[10]

Rescue

Rescue operations became much more effective with the passage of a law concerning the rescue service on Danish coasts from 1852. The few search-and-rescue stations that remain today are of course far more effective.[12] The events and procedure during a stranding, including rescue operations, is told by animation in Gallery Three, which also has installations about this theme. What happens afterwards to the stranded seamen, both the living and the dead, is also explained in Gallery Three.

---

9   Bloksgaard 2003; see also Clemmesen 2005 on the same topic but focused on just the west coast of Jutland specifically from 1800 to 1920.

10   To set the scene, Bloksgaard begins with discussing the topographical, legal and cultural frameworks to analyse how these influences, what he terms as the three main elements, mentioned above. Bloksgaard 2003, 55.

---

11   Bloksgaard 2003, 82.

12   Bloksgaard 2003, 121. When the Danish Maritime Safety Administration was established in 1973, the Rescue Service was placed under its auspices. Today it is maintained by the Navy.

Figure 7. Locals giving a lecture at the museum (Photo: Anders Jensen).

Salvage

Salvage is described with a focus on the analysis of the variety and the development of the structure of the different companies and organizations involved.[13] Salvage on the beach and subsequent auctioning of salvaged goods is presented in an animation in Gallery Three. The importance of salvage is also described here. Underwater salvage and the development of diving equipment for these activities are presented in Gallery Four. Small local salvage and diving companies are also featured here, as is the rise of the larger players of this industry.

Cultural Meetings

Mads Kinch Clemmensen presents another view on the topic of strandings. He focuses primarily on the strandings as a cultural phenomenon. A stranded ship, he argues, was primarily a piece of foreign daily life that became exposed to the local population. This encounter then, had a number of consequences for all parties.[14]

This view of strandings as primarily a cultural meeting represents a big part of the exhibition in Gallery Three. The stranding of *St George* in 1811 was also a very deadly cultural meeting. In Gallery

Two, we try to present the foreign daily life onboard the ship to the audience of today.

Engagement with the local community

Another important part of the new museum is the engagement with the local community (Fig. 7). The local community in Thorsminde has contributed a lot to the individual stories we tell. They have also donated many objects to the museum. Many members of the museum's group of supporters are also very engaged volunteers and tour guides at the museum.

Strandingsmuseum St George is a tribute to the culture of a special region; it strives to give the local community pride in their history and community and to help create and support the identity of this area. One of the purposes of the engagement is the empowerment of the area. In 2019, the museum won the prestigious European Museum of the Year Award in the Stilletto Prize category. This is an award for the museum's co-creation with the surrounding, local community.

Communication

It was important to appeal to a broad target audience. There are many tourists in the area. Many local schools visit every year, and through outreach, the

---

13   Bloksgaard 2003, 152.
14   Clemmesen 2005, 70.

Gallery	Text	Category	Type	Length	Author
Gallery Two	THE LAST VOYAGE	Gallery introduction	Wall text	Max. 100 words	Helle Sigh
Gallery Two	HMS *St George* & HMS *Defence*	Map legend	Wall text	Max. 20 words	Helle Sigh
Gallery Two	The Broad Arrow about the mark of the Royal Navy	Star Story	Text sign hanging on pole	Max. 50 words	Anders M. Jensen
Gallery Two	The Naval Surgeon	Introduction to display case	Text on glass display case	Max. 20 words	Helle Sigh
Gallery Two	John Cleland about the naval surgeon	Star Story	Text sign hanging on pole	Max. 50 words	Helle Sigh
Gallery Two	Many Buttons, Many Men	Museum label	Horizontal sloping stand	Max. 20 words	Jens Aarup Jensen
Gallery Four	DRAWN TOWARDS THE DEEP	Gallery introduction	Wall text	Max. 100 words	Christopher Jacob Ries
Gallery Four	Creatures of the Deep	Artist presentation	Wall text	Max. 100 words	Christopher Jacob Ries
Gallery Four	Machinobiota abyssalis	Artwork title	Text on base of artwork	Max. 20	Joel Illerhag
Gallery Four	Darwin to Steenstrup July 28, 1881	Quote	Horizontal sloping stand	Max. 20 words	Charles Darwin

Table 1: A selection of different kinds of texts. The length given are for the Danish texts. The different texts and quotes also appear in English and German translations, and usually these are a bit longer, with the German translation generally being the longest. Joel Illerhag is one of the four artists presented as part of the exhibition in Gallery Four (https://joelillerhag.com/, Accessed May, 2025).

museum has become a stop on the routes of many tour busses. These consist mostly of visitors of an older demographic.

The Ekarv Method

Because of the very broad target audience, the museum seeks to present its stories in a way that will appeal to everyone, regardless of age. The basic premise is that a parent should be able to read the texts to their child. Studies have shown that when they visit a museum, most guests do not read the longer texts

in an exhibition, and some not even the shorter museum labels.[15]

When creating the texts for the new museum, the work of the Swedish author Margareta Ekarv was a big inspiration. Her method of text writing was developed for adults with reading difficulties, but the method has been used in many museums.[16] In our museum, there are many sounds and moving images and the light is dim, which makes reading more difficult for everyone. Where present, technical words are described in layman's terms. Given the subject

15 Gazi 2018, 14.
16 Ekarv et al. 1991.

matter, it is impossible to avoid technical nautical terms, but maybe this is for the best.[17] Our temporary exhibition in Gallery Five has an accompanying pamphlet that explains various technical terms related to ship building, but this is an exception, and these explanations are very short.

There are certain things we try to keep in mind when we write the different texts:

- Be specific about the topic
- Avoid complex sentences
- Avoid long lists of adjectives
- Place the subject before the verb
- Use the verb in the active form
- Explain difficult terms – e.g. nautical terms
- Avoid abbreviations
- Divide the text into shorter sections

No guideline is strictly enforced, but they are good to keep in mind. Newer texts should aim to follow the format established and not deviate too much. In line with the approach taken by the staff at the Royal Naval Museum in Portsmouth, England, we view the Ekarv Method more as an underlying philosophy than a strict series of steps to follow.[18]

Even though individual texts are often short, there are more than 40 full pages of text in the exhibition, so if you read everything, it will take some time. The aim was that you should be able to experience, and read, everything in the museum in c. 2 hours. Many guests spend more time than this, but we tell visitors who arrive an hour or less before closing time that it is possible to experience the museum, but you will have to hurry.

Figure 8. Star Stories in front of a display case (Photo: Sebastian Mirz).

Sections

There is a clear hierarchy in the length of the different kinds of texts used in the museum (Table 1).

Gallery Introductions – 100 words

Since there are five galleries, there are also five introductions. These texts are all wall texts and written in a very large font size, so it should be clear to the visitor that they present the gallery's main theme.

Star Stories – max. 50 words

Star Stories are by far the most numerous of the different kinds of texts in the museum, but there is a strict limit on their number. To prevent bloat in the general amount of text in the museum, when we write a new Star Story, an old Star Story has to be removed (Fig. 8). The Star Stories mostly hang

---

17 Gazi 2018, 2-4.
18 Davies 2000, 60.

Figure 9. Surgical instruments on display; no labels (Photo: Anders Jensen).

on short poles in front of a display case or one of the larger objects. In Gallery Three, most of them are nested in the table in front of the display cases. Star Story formats enable tactility because the visitor has to grab and handle the Star Stories in order to read them. This format also stresses the point: that reading a certain story is voluntary.

We try to engage the guest with some of our Star Stories. To give just one example: next to the fourth anchor in Gallery Two is the Star Story about the Royal Navy's Broad Arrow mark – what it means, why it was used, etc. This text also encourages the visitor to be on the lookout for the mark on other objects. There are many of these in Gallery Three, and now the visitor is prepared to recognise this mark on them.

Museum labels – max. 20 words

The museum labels are featured mostly inside the display cases, but some are on walls or the glass of a display case, as an introduction to the theme. They are primarily on horizontal sloping stands, though the museum labels that introduce the seven main display cases in Gallery Two are printed on the glass of these (e.g. "The Naval Surgeon"). The two museum labels that describe the rudder and its discovery are likewise on the glass in front of the object. We try to minimize the use of museum labels, since they can be hard to read for the visitors due to their small size.

Quotations – max. 20 words

Some of the museum labels include quotes. The introduction to the display case "The Naval Surgeon", which presents the objects belonging to *St George*'s surgeon, quotes the British Vice-Admiral Horatio Nelson as saying: "The great thing in all military service is health".[19] The name of the quoted person is given, but neither the context nor date of the quote is given (Fig. 9).

In other instances, the quote constitutes the entire text. An example of this is a quotation from a letter from 1881 from Charles Darwin to Japetus Steenstrup.[20] Here, both the quoted person, the date and the recipient is given underneath the quote.

Other texts

There are two types of texts that do not fit in any of these categories. One is the descriptions in the map legend of "The Last Voyage" in Gallery Two. Another is the artwork titles in Gallery Four. With five to ten words, these are all very short.

You only remember one story!

The basic premise of the exhibition is that you only really remember one story from each visit to a museum. When designing the new exhibition, there was a special focus on the thoughts and feelings with which the guest could leave the museum.

Focus on "The Last Voyage"

There is no explanation of the context of "The Last Voyage". That context being, of course, the Napoleonic Wars in general, why and how it involved Denmark, the Gunboat War, etc. On a large map of "The Last Voyage", there is only a single mention in the map legend that Danish privateers attacked the

ships of the English convoy. This is the only hint at the context of the Napoleonic Wars. Nevertheless, we hope the guests are inspired to learn more about this on their own. Our shop has books on many different topics touched upon in the exhibition if people are interested.

Main message

When our guests leave, the main thing we hope they have learned is that the west coast of Denmark is a very dangerous place; even very large warships are not safe from nature. We hope this message inspires and stimulates reflection in the guests. Maybe they will think about what this danger meant, not only to the seamen but also for the local community, the next time they visit the beach. Ideally, they will also reflect on the impact the sea has had on the culture of the people who live here.

Anders Jensen
Formerly at Strandingsmuseum St George
Thorsminde, Denmark
andersvejle75@gmail.com

Bibliography

BLOKSGAARD, A. 2003
Dansk Strandingshistorie; Den enes død – den andens brød; En definition og analyse af dansk strandingshistorie ca. 1800 – 2000. Master's thesis, University of Copenhagen, Denmark.

BROWN, K. 2015
The Seasick Admiral, Nelson and the Health of the Navy, Barnsley.

BROWNE, G. L. 1851
The Life of the right honourable Horatio Lord Viscount Nelson, London.

---

19 Laughton 1886, 339, for the entire letter to Dr Moseley (March 11, 1804); and Browne 1851, 140, for the context and discussion of the letter; also Brown 2015 for a broader context of health in the navy.

20 To Japetus Steenstrup July 28, 1881: https://www.darwinproject.ac.uk/letter/?docId=letters/DCP-LETT-13254.xml, Accessed May 2025.

CLEMMESEN, M. K. 2005
Hvor hver lever kristelig og nærer sig ved vrag? Strand-ingshistorie og kystkultur på Vestkysten ca. 1800 – 1920, Speciale ved Historisk Afdeling, Institut for Historie og Områdestudier, Aarhus.

CLOVES, W. L. 1997
The Royal Navy: A history from the earliest times to 1900, Vol. 5, London.

DAVIES, M. 2000
'Ekarv text method in practice', *Museum Practice: Inter-pretation* 13, 59-61.

DUREY, M. 2007
'"A Perfect Hurricane": naval disaster off Jutland, 1811', *The Journal of the Scottish Society for Northern Studies* 40, 71-81.

EISENREICH, C. P. 1927
Det Nørrejydske Redningsvæsen; Dets tilblivelse, organi-sation og historie, Copenhagen.

EKARV, M., E. OLOFSSON & B. ED 1991
Smaka på orden, En bok om att skriva utställningstexter, Stockholm.

GAZI, A. 2018
'Writing text for museums of technology the case of the Industrial Gas Museum in Athens', *Museum Manage-ment and Curatorship* 33:2, 1-22.

GRANDJEAN, L. E. 1947
Skibbruddets Saga, Høst & Søns Forlag, Copenhagen.

JEPSEN, P. U. 2017
Den Sidste Rejse, Historien om linjeskibene HMS St. George og HMS Defence og deres tid til de forliste på Jyl-lands vestkyst den 24. December 1811, Holstebro.

LAUGHTON, J. K. 1886
Letters and Despatches of Horation, Viscount Nelson, K.B. Duke of Bronte, Vice-admiral of the White Squad-ron, London.

PAKENHAM, E. M. 1793
Captain Pakenham's Invention of a Substitute for a lost Rudder, and to prevent its being lost. Also a method of restoring the masts of ships, when wounded, or otherwise injured, London.

SØKORTARKIVET 1866
Den danske lods: Beskrivelse over di danske farvande (3rd edition), Copenhagen.

Contemporary Approaches to Traditional Wooden Boatbuilding:

The Case of the Museum of Aegean Boatbuilding and Maritime Crafts (MNNTA) in Samos, Greece

Eleni Stefanou

Abstract

What is the role of a contemporary maritime museum in displaying, safeguarding, and communicating the knowledge, experiences, techniques, and oral traditions of the people associated with traditional wooden boatbuilding? This paper aims to approach the above through the case study of the municipal Museum of Aegean Boatbuilding and Maritime Crafts (MNNTA), which will open to the public in 2025 in the village of Heraio on the Greek island of Samos. This paper discusses how a maritime museum as an institution can encourage the potential socioeconomic impact of traditional wooden boatbuilding on modern coastal and island societies, as well as the threats that traditional wooden boatbuilding is currently facing in Greec. This is mainly the excessive subsidy by the EU and the Greek State of the destruction of old fishing caiques in the context of control and renewal of the Greek fishing fleet, which has led to a tremendous loss of intangible and tangible cultural heritage elements relating to wooden boatbuilding.

Introduction

As a maritime archaeologist I felt early on that maritime archaeology extends well beyond the seabed, is not limited only to the act of underwater excavation and conservation, and relates to issues of heritage representation, cultural practices, narratives and identity discourses outside the water and especially in maritime museums. One of the most intriguing topics of the maritime past is traditional wooden boatbuilding as intangible heritage and as a set of techniques that has been orally and empirically transmitted for centuries. This chapter discusses how this complex set of knowledge and practices is approached, researched, exhibited, and represented within the museum practices developed at the Museum of Aegean Boatbuilding and Maritime Crafts (MNNTA), which will open to the public in 2025 in the village of Heraio on the Greek island of

Fig. 1. The Museum of Aegean Boatbuilding and Maritime Crafts, Heraio, Samos, Greece (Photo: Kostas Damianidis).

Samos in the eastern Aegean Sea. It is a project of the Municipality of Eastern Samos funded by the Operational Programme "Competitiveness, Entrepreneurship and Innovation 2014-2020" of the Ministry of Development. Both its museological and its museographical studies have been approved by the Ministry of Culture and Sports (Fig. 1).[1]

To begin with, why is maritime heritage important and relevant nowadays? Greece has long considered itself as a maritime nation with an important and long-lasting maritime tradition, a claim that becomes apparent through various manifestations of state bodies and institutions, the national curriculum in education, and of course the national maritime historiography, as well as the maritime museum narratives.[2]

However, there is a significant paradox between the hegemonic rhetoric concerning the Greek maritime past and the state policies applied for its preservation. Greece's portrayal in official discourses as a powerful maritime nation from time immemorial, contradicts the actual lack of systematic care for the maritime past, limited preservation, and state promotion of maritime heritage, which lacks funding.[3] Even though for the past decades the Greek State is promoting tourism as the sole resource of income for island and coastal communities,[4] at the same time it is diminishing and devaluing traditional crafts and lifeways including maritime heritage. Moreover, the construction of images of Greek maritime heritage in national historiography and maritime museum displays is based on a limited array of elements, namely specific historical personalities, naval military triumphs or tragedies, and certain historical events, which are perceived as important for the national narrative.[5] Most initiatives focus on glorifying

and event-based approaches to the maritime past, even though maritime historiography in Greece has long shifted its focus from the study of the navy and sea-borne conflict to a more inclusive study of "…all aspects of the interaction between mankind and the sea".[6] Hence, among maritime historians in Greece there has been a growth of interest towards socioeconomic aspects of the maritime past,[7] such as maritime economies[8] (e.g. fishing, coastal trade, maritime labour,[9] shipping,[10] and shipbuilding[11]), as well as ethnographic and sociological studies of seafarers,[12] or gender-specific studies by maritime historians.[13]

Nevertheless, most of the Greek maritime museums have only recently started to adopt and reflect on the aforementioned historiographic approaches, as they are largely established as places were navalism is praised through antiquarian and hero-worshipping approaches to the maritime past,[14] much like the trends of traditional maritime historiography. As a counter-argument, maritime museums may well follow the path of contemporary and critical maritime historiography in order to explore and display "all experiences of mankind related to its use of the sea",[15] such as fishing, naval technology, piracy, development of port cities, coastal trade, and the organisation of merchant marines, technological innovations of seafaring people and maritime communities, traditional shipbuilding, and so on.

In this vein, the MNNTA is the only maritime museum in Greece fully dedicated to the rescue,

---

1   Damianidis 2023, 121-6.
2   Stefanou 2008; 2009; 2011.
3   Damianidis 2023, 121-6.
4   Kizos 2007; Tsartas 2003.
5   Damianidis 2023, 121-6.

6   Broeze 1987, 36; Broeze 1995, xix.
7   Harlaftis & Vassallo 2004.
8   Harlaftis 2020.
9   Delis et al. 2022.
10   Harlaftis 2015.
11   Damianidis 1998; Delis 2015.
12   Papadopoulou 2019; Tsimouris 2021; Velentza 2024.
13   Kizos 2007; Tsartas 2003; see also Davies 2012, 3.
14   Broeze 1987, 36.
15   Harlaftis & Vassallo 2004.

ΤΑ ΧΝΑΡΙΑ ΤΗΣ ΣΑΛΑΣ
THE MOULDS OF THE LOFTING FLOOR

Τα χνάρια είναι αντίγραφα των γραμμών της σάλας και χρησιμοποιούν για να τις μεταφέρουν πάνω στα ξύλα που θα κοπούν. Τα παλαιότερα χνάρια αποτελούσαν το «αρχείο» από προηγούμενες χρήσεις της σάλας. Φυλάγοντας στο ναυπηγείο ή στον χώρο της σάλας θα μπορούσαν να επαναχρησιμοποιηθούν ή να προσαρμοστούν για τη σχεδίαση ενός νέου σκάφους.

The moulds represent copies of the lines drawn on the lofting floor (sala) and are used to transfer those lines onto the timbers that will be cut. The older moulds served as a record of the previous uses of the lofting floor. They were kept at the boatyard or in the lofting space and could be re-used or adapted for the construction of a new boat.

Ξύλινα χνάρια για το πλωριό ποδόσταμα τρεχαντηριού.
Wooden moulds for the stem-piece of trehantiri (2f.)

Δουλεύοντας στη σάλα του ναυπηγείου του αδελφού Κοντού στο Καρλόβασι, Σάμος, 1985, Εικ. Αλ. Δαμιανίδης.
Working on the lofting floor of the Kontos brothers' boatyard at Karlovasi, Samos, 1985

Ξύλα στο Πέραμα Αττικής, τη δεκαετία του 1950.
Lofting floor at Perama, Attica in the 1950s.

Χνάρια της σάλας στο ναυπηγείο των Μαράτων, Σάμος, 1985.
Moulds of the lofting floor at the Maratos boatyard, Samos, 1985.

Fig. 2. The museum's informative panel on the "Moulds of the Lofting Floor" (Copyright: MNNTA, Graphic Design poyptychon.gr).

research, and display of all aspects of wooden shipbuilding and maritime crafts of the Aegean.

The MNNTA is inextricably linked with Samos and its communities as a geographical location and as a cultural landscape. Samos is an island with a long boatbuilding tradition and active traditional shipyards, thanks to its mountainous terrain and the wealth of pine trees (*Pinus brutia* and *Pinus nigra*), which ensure the availability and aptness of shipbuilding timber. As asserted by Damianidis,[16] throughout the 20th century most traditional shipyards in Greece ordered timber from Samos as, due to its high content of pine resin, it was considered the most appropriate for constructing durable caiques

(*καΐκια / kaikia*),[17] suitable for the Aegean Sea's weather conditions.

Thus, the museum's main aim is to preserve, safeguard, research, present, and communicate to the public both the tangible and the intangible aspects of wooden shipbuilding as maritime heritage (Fig. 2).

According to the National Inventory of Intangible Cultural Heritage of Greece, "wooden boatbuilding is the handicraft construction of a vessel through the use of natural timber" and all its related stages, from "conception and design to construction, equipment, decoration, and its relevant cultural practices and mentalities".[18] Wooden boatbuilding was inscribed

16 Damianidis 2014; see also Damianidis & Zivas 1986, 74.

17 Post-medieval traditional wooden fishing boats in the Aegean Sea, Ionian Sea and Bosporus.

18 https://ayla.culture.gr/catalogue/xylonaypigiki/, Accessed May, 2025. Translation by author.

on the National Inventory in 2013 and is considered as:

> …a living traditional craft that has been practiced in Greece for centuries. It possesses unique technical, typological and cultural characteristics, some of which can be traced in the Middle Ages and the Byzantine Empire. The craft's transmission from one generation to the next is accomplished through empirical apprenticeship, which entails younger people learning the craft by working side by side with a master craftsman.[19]

Traditional Wooden Boatbuilding at the MNNTA

As a contemporary maritime museum, the MNNTA faces the challenge of talking about a traditional maritime craft in a non-traditional, modern, and inviting way. Therefore, the MNNTA moves beyond the traditional object-oriented museological schemes and adopts visitor-centred approaches as modes of multimodal museum-visitor communication:[20] the public is called to delve into both the material culture and the intangible aspects of wooden boatbuilding through mixed media and different materials that frame the objects, such as texts, photographs, sounds, audiovisual, and animated content, hands-on activities, etc. According to Bünz:

> …museum exhibitions are narratives that are organized in the room. They consist of spatiality, materials, colours, sound, light, images, artefacts and props. They are a four-dimensional storyscape and meanings are created when visitors perceive and experience the

room and all the materials in it, both through their senses and by being and moving in the room.[21]

Thus, in the MNNTA the visitor is encouraged to associate the principal expressions of wooden shipbuilding, predominantly the caiques themselves and the shipbuilders' tools, with aspects such as:

1. **Traditional craftsmanship** that places shipbuilding among the most complex traditional practices drawing from broad and diverse fields of knowledge and techniques, closely associated with the technical developments of each period as well as the raw materials available.

2. **Oral traditions and expressions** relating (a) to the techniques and knowledge applied to wooden shipbuilding, which are even nowadays transmitted from one generation to the next mainly through oral tradition and apprenticeship, and (b) the vernacular terminology used during all phases of construction, repair, conservation, and even the mere description of a ship.

3. **Social practices**, rituals and festive events enacted in the process of shipbuilding, including traditions and beliefs, so that the craft is to be fortunate, wholesome, and seaworthy.

4. **Knowledge and practice about nature and the universe** relating to the experience for the acquisition of the most suitable timber for shipbuilding, the wood cutting, the resin content of the wood, the manipulation of its fibres and its proper drying after the cutting. Moreover, each vessel and its construction techniques are inextricably associated with the environment in which it will sail. That is the reason for wooden boats being so different in typology, form and construction, differences that mainly stem from the craftsmen's knowledge of local conditions, such as the environment, raw materials, regional diversifications in the use of the boat, etc.

---

19   https://ayla.culture.gr/catalogue/xylonaypigiki/, Accessed May, 2025. Translation by author.

20   Kress 2010.

21   Bünz 2022, 5.

The museum is designed to operate through a network of educational and research activities, attempting to reflect on the museum definition by the International Council of Museums (ICOM):

> A museum is a not-for-profit, permanent institution in the service of society that researches, collects, conserves, interprets and exhibits tangible and intangible heritage. Open to the public, accessible and inclusive, museums foster diversity and sustainability. They operate and communicate ethically, professionally and with the participation of communities, offering varied experiences for education, enjoyment, reflection, and knowledge sharing.[22]

In this vein, as a non-profit institution, the MNNTA researches, collects, conserves, interprets, and exhibits key aspects of maritime craftsmanship explored through ethnographic studies in the boatyards and ports of the Aegean and through archaeological research on Aegean shipwrecks. The museological design aims to interpret the material remains and the intangible elements of boatbuilding tradition, focusing on the individuals behind the techniques and on the empirically transmitted knowledge. The technical maritime culture of the Aegean is also displayed, including its continuity since antiquity and the ruptures and changes it underwent until modern times.

The permanent exhibition has a large collection of tangible and intangible elements relating to traditional shipbuilding. An impressive part of this collection is the 10 traditional boats/caiques, which have been salvaged from different places of the Aegean by the Municipality of Eastern Samos, and once conserved, they will be exhibited at the museum premises (Fig. 3).

Additionally, more than 200 shipbuilding tools form part of the museum's collection, along with

Fig. 3. The caique *Minavra*, type *perama*, in the courtyard of the MNNTA. Built in 1968 on Lesbos by the shipwrights Yannis Moutzourellis and Grigoris Grigoriou. *Minavra* was reconstructed by the shipwright Yannis Kontaras and his associates, and it was donated to the MNNTA by Stathis Potamitis, Ian Miller, and Don Matthews (Photo: Eleni Stefanou).

many ship's drawings, ship models and moulds will be on display. Other categories of exhibits are the fittings of the vessels, nautical instruments, logs and notarial documents, business records, and other material evidence from shipyards and naval enterprises of the Aegean (Figs. 4 & 5).

The museum's collection, however, is not only limited to the material culture of wooden shipbuilding, as it also documents, safeguards, and communicates to the public evidence of the intangible cultural heritage, such as recorded or videotaped oral testimonies of craftsmen and sailors, archival photographs, and film or video footage documenting shipbuilding and maritime activities in the

---

22 https://icom.museum/en/resources/standards-guidelines/museum-definition/, Accessed May 2025.

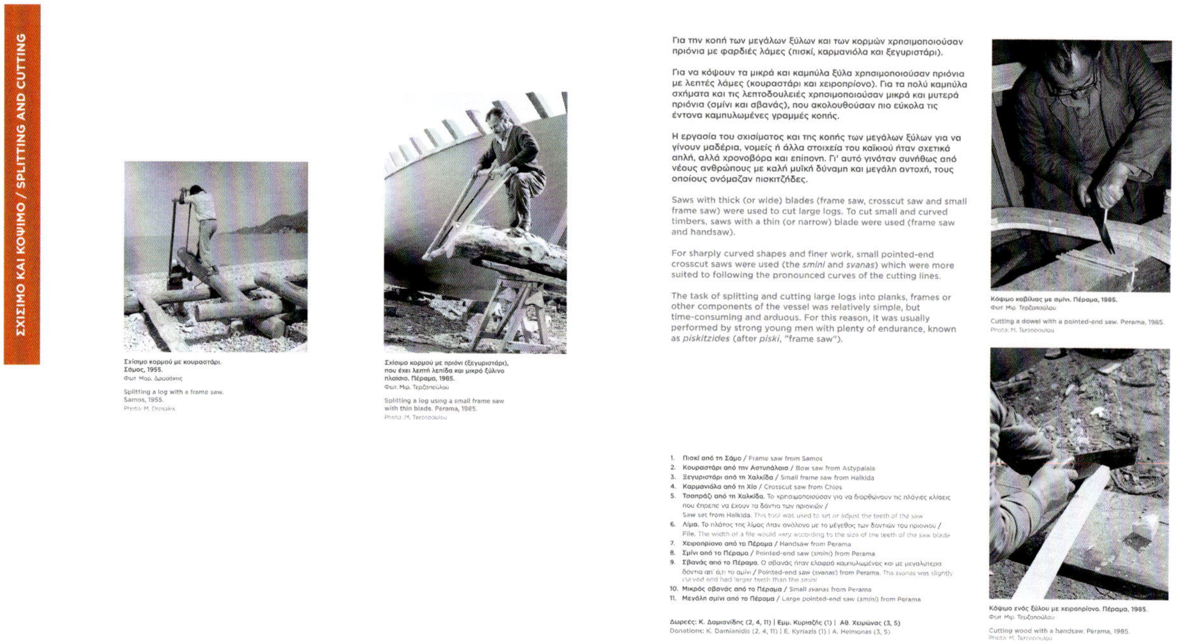

Fig. 4. The museum's informative panel on "Splitting and Cutting" tools (Copyright: MNNTA, Graphic Design poyptychon.gr).

Aegean mainly from the second half of the 20th century.

In this context, the Archive of Oral Testimonies has been established in the museum's library. It will be accessible to academic researchers, and it includes data obtained nationwide from 1984 until today. The interviews are personal testimonies about the life, employment, techniques, professions, customs, and social practices of the people of the sea, namely boatbuilders, craftsmen, fishermen, sailors, etc. The number of interviews included today in the Archive of Oral Testimonies exceeds beyond 200 and it is constantly being enriched as new research is being carried out. Also in the museum's library, researchers will be granted access to the museum's Photographic Archive, the Archive of Drawings, and the Video Archive. As a result of the close collaboration between the museum and the University of the Aegean, the Laboratory of Mathematical Modelling will operate at the museum premises as part of the Department of Mathematics.

Moreover, the Open Conservation Laboratory is a fully equipped space of 125 m² where conservation of exhibits and various technical applications will take place. Visitors will be able to watch the work process, to use or make traditional tools, participate in the design phases of a wooden boat, or try other work related to shipbuilding, thus gaining knowledge on woodworking.

Lastly, also at the museum's premises, the certified apprenticeship school on traditional shipbuilding will begin to operate in 2025. It is a two-year programme followed by one year of apprenticeship in shipyards of the Aegean and at the museum, especially regarding the conservation of the permanent exhibition's wooden boats. It is a programme of the Ministry of Culture, carried out by the University of the Aegean (School of Science, Department of Mathematics), and subsidized since 2021 by the Directorate of Modern Cultural and Intangible Cultural Heritage (DINEPOK) and the Special Research Funds Account (ELKE) of the University of the Ae-

ΤΑ ΕΡΓΑΛΕΙΑ ΤΩΝ ΞΥΛΟΝΑΥΠΗΓΩΝ
THE SHIPWRIGHTS' TOOLS

Οι ξυλοναυπηγοί χρησιμοποιούσαν πολλά χειροκίνητα εργαλεία για την κατασκευή των καϊκιών, τα οποία ήταν συχνά αυτοσχέδια ή ειδικές κατασκευές, προσαρμοσμένες στις ναυπηγικές εργασίες. Τα περισσότερα από αυτά, τα χρησιμοποιούσαν σε όλες σχεδόν τις φάσεις ναυπήγησης ενός καϊκιού.

Τα εργαλεία των ξυλοναυπηγών παρουσιάζονται στην έκθεση σε επτά ομάδες που αντιστοιχούν σε διαφορετικές ενότητες εργασιών.

When building a vessel, shipwrights would use a large number of hand tools, which were often improvised or purpose-made, adapted to the needs of particular boatbuilding tasks. Most were used in nearly all stages of building a vessel.

The tools of the shipwrights are presented in the exhibition in seven groups which correspond to the different categories of tasks.

Fig. 5. The museum's informative panel on "The Shipwrights Tools" (Copyright: MNNTA, Graphic Design poyptychon.gr).

Fig. 6. Participatory activity between the museum's commissioned artists, Marianna Aslani and Emmanouil Stergiou, and members of the local community for the construction of the museum's lofting floor, which is an exact copy of the lofting floor at the shipyard of the Mavrikos Brothers on Syros (Photo: Kostas Damianidis).

gean. The Center for Lifelong Learning (KEDIVIM) of the University of the Aegean will be responsible for administrative and operational issues, as well as for the certification of its graduates. The managing body is the Municipality of Eastern Samos. So far, the curriculum along with the four bilingual manuals for teachers and students are ready.

Of course, the museum is not destined only for academic researchers. Providing first-hand experiences to the broad public and to different sub-groups is one of the museum's main aims. Therefore, its permanent exhibition is addressed to a wide range of people, from tourists, locals, senior residents, and school groups to experts and researchers. The museum aims to become a place of cultural education and entertainment for the Aegean communities, as well as a chosen destination amongst the tourist routes. Therefore, emphasis is placed on education through the design of educational programmes for different public groups. In the specially-designed education room and multi-purpose room, there will be programmes for school students throughout the year and for independent groups of children during the summer months. Also, summer courses are planned that will last from one week to one month, focusing on specific techniques of wooden boatbuilding, such as the design on the lofting floor called "sala", the construction of ship models, or the traditional caulking of a boat.

Part of the public outreach and awareness actions is the Association of the Friends of the MNNTA.

175

The Association was established in 2017 and has as its statutory purpose the moral and material support of the museum and its various actions around boatbuilding and the Aegean maritime heritage, as well as the promotion of Samos as a centre of boatbuilding tradition (Fig. 6).

The Friends' Association aims at:
1. Connecting the museum with the local community
2. Promoting caiques as monuments of maritime cultural heritage of the Aegean, sensitizing both the wider public and social actors about their value, the need to save them, and the necessity to develop a long-term, sustainable maritime heritage management policy
3. Nurturing young people's interest about Aegean maritime heritage through educational activities, guided tours, cruising of traditional vessels, and more
4. Supporting research, educational, exhibition, cultural and publishing activities of the MNNTA

In this vein, the Friends' Association created the online platform http://woodenboats.gr[23] to promote awareness regarding the rapidly-changing cultural landscape of the Aegean coastal areas, as traditional boats of artisanal fishing are disappearing, shipyards are closing, plastic boats are taking over, and fishermen are leaving their profession. It is anticipated that the above actions demonstrate a very systematic attempt to care for the heritage of Aegean wooden shipbuilding on a cultural, educational, and institutional basis, especially to counteract the threats that wooden boatbuilding has been facing for the last 30 years.

Epilogue

The traditional shipbuilding profession is in rapid decline since the last decades of the 20th century due to several core problems that shipbuilders are facing:[24]
1. Promotion of tourism that changes the local economies
2. Reduced fleet of traditional wooden boats
3. No official governmental protection or support to shipbuilders and artisanal fishermen
4. Aggressive competition by the plastic and fibreglass boat market
5. Unfair competition against big fishing trawlers
6. Reduced manpower and lack of skilled workers trained in traditional boatbuilding
7. Government subsidies for the regulation of the fishing fleet, which demands that the fishermen give away their licences and their wooden boats for destruction[25]

As stated by the Traditional Boats Association of Greece[26] more than 13,000 traditional wooden caiques have been destroyed in the last 25 years (Fig. 7). Velentza asserts that:

> Artisanal fishermen with traditional wooden boats are frequently targeted by the government and offered substantial monetary funds, higher than the worth of their boat, in exchange of their fishing licence and the destruction of their vessel. … Even though the EU Commission for Environment Oceans and Fisheries … has explained … that there is no legal obligation for the Greek authorities to demand the physical

---

23 See also http://woodenboats.gr/en/home-en/, Accessed May 2025.

24 Velentza 2024, 130-1.

25 The European regulation of the Maritime and Fisheries Fund (2014-2020) includes the subsidies for the destruction of fishing boats (see: https://eur-lex.europa.eu/legal-content/EL/TXT/?uri=LEGISSUM:0202_1, Accessed May, 2025).

26 https://www.traditionalboats.gr/el, Accessed May, 2025.

Fig. 7. The caique *Analipsis* during its subsidized destruction in 2018 (Photo: Georgia Papadimitriou, source: https://woodenboats.gr/en/fishing-boats-destruction/national-and-european-funding-of-the-destruction-of-shipping-boats/, Accessed July, 2025).

dismantling of any vessel to implement the relevant legislation and reduce the impact of fisheries.[27]

The MNNTA as a contemporary institution strives not only to tell its public the stories of the maritime past but also the story of the early 21st century, that of the loss of the maritime traditions and expressions of Greece that are being obliterated under the responsibility of the Greek State and the EU. Within the principles of museum activism[28] it acts against the destruction of fishing boats, which is done with state and European subsidies and results in the devaluing of the creations of traditional boatbuilding.[29] The MNNTA advocates that it is unacceptable for Greece to have registered the craft of wooden boatbuilding in the National Inventory of Intangible Cultural Heritage of Greece and at the same time to keep subsidizing its destruction.

It is amidst this complex situation that the Museum of the Aegean Boatbuilding and Maritime Crafts, along with the Association of the Friends of the MNNTA, aspire to act at a level of prevention,

safeguarding, dissemination of knowledge, and local engagement, as is the sociopolitical role of any contemporary museum that actively involves itself in pertinent matters beyond the limits of its premises.

Eleni Stefanou
The Heritage Management Organization / University of Bologna, Italy
stefanoueleni@gmail.com

Bibliography

BROEZE, F. 1987
'Maritime museums: an historian's reflections on their purposes, objectives, and methods', in L. M. Akveld (ed.), *6th International Congress of Maritime Museums Proceedings*, Amsterdam, Rotterdam, 36.

BROEZE, F. 1995
'Maritime history at the crossroads: a critical review of recent historiography', in *Research in maritime history No. 9, Maritime history at the crossroads: a critical review of recent historiography*, F. Broeze (ed.), St. John's, Canada, ix-xxii.

---

27   Velentza 2024, 130-1
28   Janes & Sandell 2019.
29   Damianidis 2023, 2-3.

BÜNZ, A. 2022
Museum, Place, Architecture and Narrative: Nordic Maritime Museums' Portrayals of Shipping, Seafarers and Maritime Communities (Museums and Collections 15), New York, Oxford.

DAMIANIDIS, K. 1998
Elliniki Paradosiaki Nafpigiki, Athens.

DAMIANIDIS, K. 2014
'To Samiotiko pefko kai i paradosiaki ylotomia sti Samo', in *To Samiotiko Pefko kai i Paradosiaki Ylotomia sti Samo,* V. Dimitriadis & C. Landros (eds), Samos, 29-40.

DAMIANIDIS, K. 2023
'Mouseio Nafpigikon kai Naftikon Tehnon tou Aegaiou: H Proetoimasia enos Mouseiou – Ergastiriou gia tin Paradosiaki Xylonafpigiki sta Hronia tis Oikonomikis Krisis', in *Ayli Politistiki Klironomia se Kairous Oikonomikis Krisis: Entaxi stin Agora kai Anthektikotita,* P. Karampampas (ed.), Athens, 121-6.

DAMIANIDIS, K. & A. ZIVAS, 1986
To Trehantiri stin Elliniki Nafpigiki Tehni, Athens.

DAVIES, S. 2012
'Maritime Museums: Who Needs Them', *NSC Working Paper Series* 11, 1-46.

DELIS, A. 2015
'Modern Greece's first industry? The shipbuilding center of sailing merchant marine of Syros, 1830-70', *European Review of Economic History, European Historical Economics Society* 19:3, 255-74.

DELIS, A., J. IBARZ, A. SYDORENKO & M. BARBANO, 2022
Mediterranean Seafarers in Transition. Maritime Labour, Communities, Shipping and the Challenge of Industrialization 1850s-1920s (Brill's Studies in Maritime History, Volume 11), Leiden.

HARLAFTIS, G. 2015
A History of Greek-Owned Shipping (Maritime History), London.

HARLAFTIS, G. 2020
'Maritime history: A new version of the old version and the true history of the sea', *International Journal of Maritime History* 32:2, 383-402.

HARLAFTIS, G. & C. VASSALLO (EDS) 2004
New Directions in Mediterranean Maritime History (Research in Maritime History), Liverpool.

JANES, R. R. & R. SANDELL 2019
'Posterity has arrived: the necessary emergence of Museum Activism', in *Museum Activism*, R. R. Janes & R. Sandell (eds), London, 1-18.

KIZOS, T. 2007
'Island lifestyles in the Aegean Islands, Greece: Heaven in summer, hell in winter?', in *Seasonal landscapes,* H. Palang, H. Soovӓli & A. Printsmann (eds), Berlin, 127-49.

KRESS, G. 2010
Multimodality: A Social Semiotic Approach to Contemporary Communication, London.

PAPADOPOULOU, C. (ED.) 2019
The Culture of Ships and Maritime Narratives, London.

STEFANOU, E. 2008
Aspects of Identity and Nationhood: Commemorating, Representing and Replicating the Greek Maritime Past, Unpublished PhD Thesis, Southampton University, England.

STEFANOU, E. 2009
'Anaparastaseis tou Parelthontos sta Nautika Mouseia tis Elladas kai tou Exoterikou', *Museology – International Scientific Electronic Journal* 5, 49-62.

STEFANOU, E. 2011
'The materiality of death: human relics and the 'resurrection' of the Greek maritime past in museum spaces', *International Journal of Heritage Studies* 18:4, 385-99.

TSARTAS, P. 2003
'Tourism development in Greek insular and coastal areas: Sociocultural changes and crucial policy issues', *Journal of Sustainable Tourism* 11:2-3, 116-32.

TSIMOURIS, G. 2021
Emeis oi naftikoi, barkarismenoi kai xebarkoi, Athens.

VELENTZA, K. 2024
'Traditional Shipbuilding on the Island of Samos, Greece: Recording the Tangible and Intangible Data', *International Journal of Nautical Archaeology* 54:1, 129-54.